WHY PEOPLE STAY

Why People Stay is the result of a doctoral study that revealed participants' sense of commitment (to the organization, to the team, to the mission, or to something else). This was in spite of numerous experiences of antisocial workplace behavior, or AWB, reported by each participant. Yet they all stayed in their workplace. Why? And what does this suggest about employee engagement, in toxic workplaces or work groups?

This book explores these questions, and more, and sounds an alarm to executives and culture monitors that the root cause of your human capital losses is that your people do not feel seen, safe, and valued and you can change that. It looks at organizational commitment and organizational engagement in an environment where it can be difficult to remain authentically committed in the presence of AWB. The participants in this study were queried as to just why they stayed under such conditions. The aim of this book is to share their surprising results.

This positive book about negative experiences is essential reading for executives, HR and organizational development professionals, as well as students at both postgraduate and undergraduate levels.

Angela N. Spranger is an engaging facilitator, college lecturer, corporate trainer, and human resources professional. She is principal consultant with StepOne Consulting, LLC, consulting on compliance, performance management, and professional development concerns such as strengths-building, diversity, and mentoring. Her specialty is engaging with individuals and small groups on a deep level and coaching them toward attaining their own stretch goals.

WHY PEOPLE STAY

Helping Your Employees Feel Seen, Safe, and Valued

Angela N. Spranger

Routledge
Taylor & Francis Group

LONDON AND NEW YORK

First published 2019
by Routledge
2 Park Square, Milton Park, Abingdon, Oxon OX14 4RN

and by Routledge
711 Third Avenue, New York, NY 10017

Routledge is an imprint of the Taylor & Francis Group, an informa business

© 2019 Angela N. Spranger

The right of Angela N. Spranger to be identified as author of this work has been asserted by her in accordance with sections 77 and 78 of the Copyright, Designs and Patents Act 1988.

Trademark notice: Product or corporate names may be trademarks or registered trademarks, and are used only for identification and explanation without intent to infringe.

British Library Cataloguing-in-Publication Data
A catalogue record for this book is available from the British Library

Library of Congress Cataloging-in-Publication Data
Names: Spranger, Angela N., author.
Title: Why people stay: helping your employees feel seen, safe, and valued / Angela N Spranger.
Description: 1 Edition. | New York: Routledge, 2018. |
Includes bibliographical references and index. |
Identifiers: LCCN 2018011987 (print) | LCCN 2018020701 (ebook) |
ISBN 9781315455495 (eBook) | ISBN 9781138210301 (hardback: alk. paper) |
ISBN 9781138210318 (pbk.: alk. paper) | ISBN 9781315455495 (ebk)
Subjects: LCSH: Work environment. | Organizational commitment. |
Corporate culture. | Employee motivation.
Classification: LCC HD7261 (ebook) |
LCC HD7261 .S687 2018 (print) | DDC 658.3/14—dc23
LC record available at https://lccn.loc.gov/2018011987

ISBN: 978-1-138-21030-1 (hbk)
ISBN: 978-1-138-21031-8 (pbk)
ISBN: 978-1-3154-5549-5 (ebk)

Typeset in Bembo
by codeMantra
Printed and bound by CPI Group (UK) Ltd, Croydon, CR0 4YY

I dedicate this book to the memory of my mother, Donna M. DeLowell, with deepest gratitude to my wonderful husband Keith Spranger. Without the two of them, and the support and guidance of so many others, this project would never have happened.

CONTENTS

ILLUSTRATIONS

Figures

Tables

PART I

Introduction

Welcome to *Why People Stay*. This is a business book aimed at executives, organizational leaders, and HR professionals... a book that can also be used in educational settings. That said, I'd like to make the business case for investigating why people stay in organizations. I had to lay out this case in order to gain approval to do the underlying study, and I am prepared to make this case for corporate clients at any time.

First, it's been said that **the best leaders are the best readers** – I believe I first heard this from management and leadership guru Marshall Goldsmith in a webinar sometime around 2009, but a quick internet search shows that President Harry S. Truman said it first, and leadership authors and creators of The Leadership Challenge®, Jim Kouzes and Barry Posner, said it too. It's not a new concept: we need to read.

So here is the business case for why it's important that we engage in this dialogue about why people stay. Usually, a business case would provide "the why, what, how and who" (Mallory, 2016) needed to make a Go/No-Go decision on whether to accept a project proposal. Here I've made the case for investing in your own professional development, with the potential result of increasing your influence over your workplace culture.

To improve your leadership skills, to get more out of your team's performance and productivity, you have to invest an hour a day in reading and reflecting on how you are leading, managing, and influencing others. In this book I am inviting you to read (knowing that for some, reading is a pleasure; for others, a trial) and consider, and perhaps make a change in, the way you lead and influence others. Implicitly we are changed as we read and consider new and different ideas, but I am explicitly stating that this book will challenge you to consider the culture of your organization, to look closely and intentionally at the conditions that encourage employee commitment and engagement, and to critically analyze the degree to which you are fostering those conditions as a leader.

> Read. Consider. Make small changes.

"Integrity has no need of rules."
– Albert Camus, French philosopher (Roberts, 2016)

WHO: Who is this book written for?

You should read this book if you are responsible for influencing the behavior of other people, through whom you work to achieve shared goals and objectives – or what you believe are shared goals and objectives. This means you, if you are a supervisor, team leader, coordinator, manager, director, executive, or entrepreneur. That's not a cop-out to say that everyone should read this book. It's only relevant for you if you are an influencer. If you are seeking to develop, ratify, and accomplish shared goals through the labor of other people in concert with your own efforts, this book is for you. Welcome.

> *This is only relevant for you if you are an influencer.*

WHAT: What is this, just another book about leadership?

It's **not** just another book about leadership. It's a guidebook for getting to the positive outcome by going through the difficult and challenging experiences and picking out the lessons to be learned from each.

> *This is a guidebook for getting to the positive outcome by going through the difficult and challenging experiences and picking out the lessons to be learned from each.*

In this book, I'm sharing with you the experiences of a sample of individuals and what those experiences mean, according to established theory. We'll make the theory-into-practice connection so that you can make incremental changes, or significant ones, to deepen the organizational commitment and engagement (I'll differentiate between the two) in your organization. Imagine your organizational culture and climate to be radio dials on your organizational dashboard, built into your Balanced ScoreCard layout. (See insert for a description of the Balanced ScoreCard, if you're not already using it.)

> The Balanced ScoreCard (BSC) approach is a system or toolset that facilitates intentional, strategy-focused dialogue within an organization. It is a highly visible means of measuring what matters (you've heard that, right? You measure what matters. If you don't measure it, it doesn't matter.). Kaplan and Norton (Kaplan & Norton, 2007) designed the BSC to connect mission (the what and who of your organization), vision (the why and how), and values (our rails, or parameters) with functional strategies and links those to the daily tactical tasks and processes.

The BSC, simplified, allows organizations to identify and assess performance to goals. Specifically, those would be Financial goals, Customer goals, Process goals, and People goals (or Learning and Growth goals). The goals may be viewed as "perspectives" for strategic planning purposes, and you can consult with the executives of each area to ensure that the Perspective (Financial, Customer, Learning and Growth, or Internal Processes) aligns with the overall mission, vision, and values of the organization. All of these are aspirational; for example, Kaplan and Norton suggested that a company's Financial perspective asks, "in order for us to succeed financially, how should we appear to our shareholders?" How do we show up to the people or other organizations we want to buy from us? The Internal Business Process perspective asks, "to satisfy our shareholders and customers, what business processes must we excel at?" Under the Customer perspective, we should be asking, "to achieve our vision, how should we appear to our customers?" That is, what do they need from us, in order to feel comfortable buying our product or service? And, finally, the Learning and Growth or People perspective asks, "to achieve our vision, how will we sustain our ability to change and improve?" These are huge, vague questions that require some detailed strategic planning of objectives, design of initiatives to achieve those objectives, definition of metrics and measures, and targets that are both low-hanging fruit for easy celebration and confidence-building, as well as challenging and aspirational for significant development, growth, and organizational evolution.

The Financial and Customer perspectives have goals and metrics that indicate what the organization gets, what we receive, as the fruit of our efforts. The People (L & G) perspective and the Internal Process perspective both indicate what we do, what we offer, to our target market. After identifying the objectives under each area, and the means or metrics by which success is measured for each objective, of course you want to set targets for those objectives, and design initiatives to help achieve them.

Remember, these are the "radio dials" that you can manipulate through minimal but significant investments in your organization's culture. Those incremental changes can yield significant long-term benefits, the kind that the 10×'ers, companies that outperformed their markets by TEN TIMES over the review period in Collins and Hansen's *Great by Choice*, reaped.

WHY: Why do I need to read this book; what's different about it?

Why take up this challenge? Aren't things going along well enough? Why bother to focus in on why people stay in workplaces... as long as they're there, right? Warm bodies, mildly engaged, get the work done... right? Wrong! The proposal on the table is whether or not to devote some of your time to reading a book (this book) about why people stay in organizations. The book includes ideas for how to ensure that the people in *your* organization feel seen, safe, and valued, so that they'll stay and contribute their best. That would be a positive outcome, wouldn't it? But to get there, you need to read the book.

This book is unique. The study on which it is based was unique. And while small in scale, it is huge in significance. You see, there's been no other qualitative research in which the study participants are actually just *asked* why they've chosen to stay, despite having experienced behaviors that can be called "antisocial." We'll get into *antisocial workplace behaviors*, and explain what they are and why they happen. But you'll also get a peek into the mindset of employees who power through (or endure) those instances and choose to stay and contribute to the workplace. And at its root, it's still a business book. So we're exploring social psychology and communication, leadership and management, and ethics… in the business context.

HOW: How should we go about achieving this "positive outcome"? How is this book going to help?

Each chapter will end with "key points" that you can flip to right from the start, or just pick up along the way. These key points will provide you with the takeaways from the chapter so that you can identify how strongly you identify with that chapter's issues and literally "take away" the results of the research or the concepts from the literature, and apply them to your specific workplace. This book is designed not only to share theoretical research material, or the results of the initial study, but also – and more importantly – to give you practical tools to add to your leadership toolkit. Additionally, at the end of the book there are resources listed to support any change initiatives you launch as a result of reading this book. The last few chapters will address the Exit Interview, Intentional Mentoring Programs, and Stay Interviews. Each of these is defined and their value described in those chapters. Even if you're already doing all of these, as institutionalized and cultural components in your organization, you're still guaranteed a positive outcome as a result of just reading the narratives shared in this book and understanding the different types of organizational commitment, what they sound like, how to feed them, or seeing how certain cultural artifacts can starve them.

Structure of the book

At the beginning of each section or chapter, there will be an Executive Summary. At the end of each chapter there will be a review of the key points / takeaways / action steps and recommendations in the chapter. There are also insightful quotes from sources and business leaders throughout.

Part I of this book is this introduction, in which I laid out the "business case" for even reading about *Why People Stay*. Here I explained the personal and professional assumptions that underlie the study on which this book is based. Please don't accept the simple, snap response to the idea of asking *Why People Stay* – "because they need money!" It's deeper than that, and worth your consideration.

Part II: The Concept is broken down into General Concepts and Practical Application sections, to quickly provide you with the WIIFM – what's in it for me, or "Why should I read this?" You may be wondering why you were given, or encouraged to buy, a copy of *Why People Stay: Helping Your Employees Feel Seen, Safe, and Valued.* Actually, the vision setters and culture monitors of any organization should quickly grasp the value of such a book – you want to retain the knowledge capital in your existing employee base, and to prevent the turnover of valuable employees who become disillusioned and leave the company because of how they are treated by peers or superiors. This turnover phenomenon leads to reduced psychological safety (why people leave – they feel unsafe), and creates a climate of fear and low motivation (why people disengage – they feel undervalued). Possibly the worst consequence happens when people feel invisible – they may miss opportunities to learn from mistakes, withhold suggestions, and behave in counterproductive ways. This section covers the general concepts of antisocial workplace behavior (AWB), organizational commitment, and organizational engagement – and their practical applications in any company.

Part III provides the details of the Theoretical Background and Rationale for the Study. Built from a cross-disciplinary body of knowledge including management, leadership, communication, and industrial and organizational psychology, the study allowed participants to make sense of why they do what they do, why they commit and engage in organizations and groups, and (most importantly) why they tolerate, or constrain, or ignore, uncivil behavior from their superiors, subordinates, or peers in the workplace. The section ends with a discussion of the Related Constructs, offering a history of research and definition of terms.

Part IV offers some Composite Themes – the takeaways from the study and the supporting research. In Part IV, we'll make sense of what we've seen, and then identify the next steps for executives and HR professionals to take if you identify familiar issues from your own workplace culture reflected here… or if you want to prevent them.

> "There are no second chances for those who violate the ethical code."
> – *Robert Slater, author (Roberts, 2016)*

Welcome… let's get started.

PART II

The concept – executive summary

"You will get all you want in life if you help enough other people get what they want."

– *Zig Ziglar, motivational speaker (Roberts, 2016)*

"Why should I read this?" asks the busy executive or HR manager, wondering why he or she has been handed or sent a copy of *Why People Stay: Helping Your Employees Feel Seen, Safe, and Valued*. Actually, the vision setters and culture monitors of any organization will quickly grasp the value of such a book – they want to retain the knowledge capital that resides in their existing employee base, and they want to prevent the turnover of valuable employees who become disillusioned and leave the company because of how they are treated by peers or superiors. The simple truth is that when employees don't feel that you see them, that they are safe with you (you care for them), and that you value them, their organizational commitment changes and their engagement drops.

> Employees need to feel seen, safe, and valued.

This turnover phenomenon leads to reduced psychological safety (why people leave – they feel unsafe), and creates a climate of fear and low motivation (they feel undervalued). Possibly the worst consequence happens when people feel invisible – they may miss opportunities to learn from mistakes, withhold suggestions, and behave in counterproductive ways. Chapter 1 covers the general concepts of antisocial workplace behavior (AWB), organizational commitment, and organizational engagement – and their practical applications in any company.

1

GENERAL CONCEPTS AND PRACTICAL APPLICATION (WIIFM?)

You may recognize the "WIIFM?" in the chapter title as the abbreviation for "What's In It For Me?" In this chapter we'll be discussing the practical application of this subject matter. Prior to 1990, there were only around 200 academic articles published on the topic of "bad behavior in the workplace" (O'Leary-Kelly, Duffy, & Griffin, 2000). Between 1990 and 2000, that number jumped to over 750 articles. The concept of workplace incivility, and its many variants, had become a thing of significant theoretical interest. Full disclosure, and this still makes me chuckle at my own naiveté: as I started working on a paper for a class I was taking in 2006, I thought I had coined the phrases "workplace incivility" and "bad behavior in the workplace." When I initiated my research for the literature review I was stunned at the amount of literature that already existed… how could it be that work, and working, could be such an unpleasant experience and so many people would just endure the ugliness they reported?

Yet the research and writing on the oppressive and painful perceptions of work went back decades; in 1994, Matthew Fox authored a book called *The Reinvention of Work*. Harmless enough, right? Yet he titled the opening chapter in his book "The Pain of Work: Work as Nothingness and Lamentation." Wow. Fox quoted several highly respected sources in the opening segments of each chapter, including Studs Terkel and Diane Fassel. The latter said, "Everywhere I go it seems people are killing themselves with work, busyness, rushing, caring, and rescuing. Work addiction is a modern epidemic and it is sweeping our land" (Fassel, quoted in Fox, 1994, p. 26). Fox himself attempted to demonstrate the demanding, frustrating, heart-wrenching nature of work. He cites feminist perspectives on work, and the nature of women's influence in the workplace, and men's movements and work, specifically emphasizing the idea that focusing on others reduces the time and energy men have available to focus on selfish concerns and slights that might lead to violence toward self and others. Specifically,

Fox says that "male violence is invariably directed initially toward the self and is then reenacted toward partners, children, and others" (Fox, 1994, p. 30). Provocative! And… beyond our reach, here. But his challenge to fulfill both the obligation to end abusive behavior toward self and others, balanced with the obligation to care for others and improve our communities, should be taken seriously regardless of gender. Fox explains that:

> [a]t work we may be forced to interact with persons whose company we do not enjoy and with whose values we do not agree. Work can be a place of irritation and of misunderstanding, of competition and of frenzy. It can rob us of our spirit and oppress our souls.
>
> *(Fox, 1994, p. 32)*

What a bleak outlook! But he does go on to move through the clouds toward the light, if you will, stating that "Bringing something new and worthwhile into the world is always difficult" (p. 32).

Further back, in 1974, Studs Terkel had offered a powerful testimony of the agony of working:

> Work, by its very nature, [is] about violence – the spirit as well as to the body. It is about ulcers as well as accidents, about shouting matches as well as fist-fights, about nervous breakdowns as well as kicking the dog around. It is, above all (or beneath all), about daily humiliations. To survive the day is triumph enough for the walking wounded among the great many of us.
>
> *(Terkel, 1974, p. xi)*

So while it might have been a surprise to me, these concepts were definitely not new. In my own career, after more corporate experience and more academic research, I found a single overarching construct, or theme, that described behaviors that harm the organization and/or its employees: antisocial workplace behavior (AWB). This construct includes several subsets of behaviors easily recognizable to anyone who has ever worked in a toxic work environment: theft, sabotage, verbal abuse, psychological abuse (also called "hazing"), lying, withholding effort, refusing to cooperate, assault, sexual harassment, workplace incivility (a combined theme including rudeness, discourtesy, and disrespect), bullying, and abusive supervision. This book, and the study that inspired it, addresses them all. But the reason I use the overarching construct of antisocial workplace behavior, or AWB, is that it addresses behaviors specifically deviant from the organization's cultural norms.

The answer to "Why do people stay?" rests in the investment organizations make in their people's personal *and* professional development.

In the consulting work I do, I often get to speak to client groups and professional associations about personal marketing and networking, and to offer encouraging words to individual employees. Let me explain: it is a significant intangible asset when your organization offers workshops that do not directly relate to the employees' ability to do their current job, but that allow them to do some careful introspection, team development and collaborating with others, and/or some personal brand development. Participants always, without fail, express to me their gratitude that their employers "let" them do "something like this." They leave my workshops with new insights about themselves. They take away substantive tools to facilitate how they work and interrelate. But, most importantly, they leave with a deeper appreciation for the employer that paid to arrange for someone to come and do this work with them. They feel seen, and valued, when their employer makes such an investment.

Seen, safe, and valued

In my experience, associates need – humans need – to hear that they are valued, in word and deed. In one workshop I literally take the time to say aloud and post on screen, "You are a valuable product. No one can do what you do like you do." Employers and professional associations that have had me come and talk about personal marketing, networking, and branding have allowed me to encourage members to be courageous about the choices they make as individuals, and the messages they convey to leaders and associates, as well as to their clients or targets (would-be clients). At the end of this section, I will provide the "reading list" of books I strongly recommend in these personal development workshops. In one of them, *The Courageous Follower*, my friend Ira Chaleff describes different types of working styles.

I have long admired this book and Ira's spirit, because it *gives permission*. I have tremendous respect for people of influence who use their power to uplift, encourage, and make room for others. In this work, Chaleff creates a two-by-two matrix of working styles, based on the individual's level of support for leadership (high – low) and the individual's personal level of challenging behavior. If they have a low level of challenging behavior and their support for leadership is low, they may be a **Resource** member of the team. They will be present and available, but not inclined to take initiative or give extra energy. They represent an extra pair of hands, and may bring a very specific skillset, but they are uncommitted. They may report low to median levels of employee engagement. This is because their primary interests lie elsewhere, so they execute the minimum requirements on the job and avoid the attention of authority figures. This may sound negative at first, but these individuals may have small children, or may be pursuing a degree in their own time, or they may be caring for elderly or handicapped relatives. In other words, they contribute, and still deserve to be seen and made to feel safe and valued in the workplace.

Chaleff's second working type is the **Implementer**, who has low challenging behavior (is not particularly aggressive, perhaps sometimes assertive) and a high degree of support for leadership. In one workshop where I introduced these types to executive and middle management at a large manufacturing company, leaders indicated that if they had a team of ten, they would want eight to be Implementers. These are the people who are dependable, energetically supporting the leader and the team, and who advocate for and defend the group's initiatives. They are competent and compliant, respectful of authority, and on-board with the leader's perspectives. (One can see why they were so highly prized by my workshop attendees.) One good thing that leaders can do for followers of this type is to encourage them to speak their own opinions and not fall into the trap of solely seeking to please and support the leader; leaders do need to be challenged to ensure that their positions are well considered and logical.

This is why the leaders in my session knew that they needed one **Partner** on their team. That might be all that the leader could handle, but they knew that it was good to have this kind of high-initiative, purpose-driven individual on the team. The Partner focuses on the mission of the organization and the team, holding the team and the leader accountable to their agreed-upon values. They will confront even sensitive issues when needed, agitate and advocate for the needs and goals of the team, and help keep the group focused on its strengths. The Partner views himself as a peer with authority figures, and while he complements the leader's perspective, he may be somewhat... challenging to supervise. Here's an example:

To: Dave (Manager)

From: Paul (team member, Partner type)

Re: Idea pitch meeting with CEO!

I bet that got your attention Dave! Good morning … just thought I should let you know, I rode up in the elevator this morning with Stan (CEO) and we chatted about the good work our team is doing. Stan got so interested that he invited me to come to share more of our initiatives with him over coffee/tea at the Starbucks near his office this afternoon; he says it will be his down-time after a series of meetings and he's looking forward to it. I thought I should let you know, and ask if there is anything specific you want me to mention (or not mention)?

Best,

Paul

Since this fictitious email is based on a real situation, I find myself chuckling uncontrollably as I type it. The managers in my workshops have all responded very strongly to that scenario. Usually they have a negative response, because it makes them uncomfortable and nervous to have a subordinate chatting to, and meeting with, their executive bosses. Sometimes, they have a positive response, because they can appreciate having an advocate for their team who has captured the ear of top leadership. Generally, they understand that a Partner can be a huge benefit to the team, but it feels uncomfortable to have someone with so much personal power, barely under control. One Director even described this kind of person as a "thoroughbred racehorse." This kind of employee requires clarity and specific direction, and a lot of trust and confidence on the leader's part. Still, he deserves to be seen, acknowledged, and made to feel safe in bringing his "whole self" to work (as Neal Chalofsky would say), and valued as a contributor to the team.

Finally, there is the **Individualist**, that member of the team who shows low support for leadership and high challenging behavior. This person may feel less valued on the team sometimes because her contribution is a little less obvious. The Individualist is confrontational and forthright, self-assured and independent, and is the person who serves as the fact-checker, who challenges the leader's every idea and suggestion. The Individualist brings a dose of reality to each meeting. A few ways to lead and manage an Individualist include challenging them not to self-marginalize, try to keep them engaged, and respect their expertise.

I suggest that leaders should work to understand and accept employees at their level of professional capacity. Each person has reasons for why they invest their energy as they do; still, we as managers can honor the level of energy and psychological investment that each employee brings to the team.

Organizational culture

Let's ease into this, and talk about culture for a moment. Every team, company, or other organization has a culture. *Culture* is different from *climate*. Climate has to do with the mood, energy, and feeling at a particular point in time. An organization's culture is comprised of three components: artifacts, shared values, and shared assumptions (McShane & Von Glinow, 2009). Artifacts are those things about your organization that you can see and observe, like the physical structures and decorations, the rituals and ceremonies you follow, the layout of the office, and the way you talk in your group. Language is a huge part of culture – are you a formal or informal culture? How about "blue" or profane language? The language we use is a building block for the rituals and ceremonies of your organization – how is the phone answered, and is it answered by a receptionist or secretary first, or does it ring right to your desk? What happens when you close a deal, gain a new client or member, achieve a milestone, or survive a failure or loss? All of that has meaning and communicates a message about your company or organization. Finally, the artifacts include the stories and legends you and your colleagues tell each other, and your clients, customers, or members. They are the cocktail stories, the dinner presentations, the recognition tales… "I remember the time we were faced with a layoff, and Joe here found a way to restructure the… saving twelve jobs and …" or "I heard that in X division, the *Vice President* put on a hardhat and came down into the production area, crawling around with the crew to find out what the real deal was that his directors and managers couldn't tell him, and it was the workers, the hourly folks, who got him to understand… and he made changes…" Legends, stories, narratives that frame who we are. These are all artifacts, the first level of organizational culture and the only level that is visible and can be observed.

The second level of organizational culture, as we dig deeper, is comprised of shared values. These are the conscious beliefs that we may discuss, or learn through experience, about what is good or bad, right and wrong. Congruence between our personal values and our organizational values is important, but some incongruence can be supported if it leads to productive discourse and diversity of thought. Too much, and you tend to have people complaining about and working against the company's values. What are your company's values? Do you know them? Do you agree with them? If you didn't, would you still work there? What would you do, could you voice that disagreement? Values are a touchy, touchy subject. In my workshops and classes, I spend a great deal of time on individual values; here, I'll provide some references and takeaways for you if you choose to do some of what I call "values surfacing" for yourself and your team.

The third, and deepest, level of organizational culture is the shared assumptions within a group. These are taken for granted, or assumed. That makes them mysterious, hard to convey, and often hard to identify. They are perceptions, often unconscious, and they shape our worldview (paradigm) of the organization and its environment. They structure our mental models, ways of being and thinking. Scary stuff, right? Sometimes, yes. They're invisible, and they're the first thing that can torpedo a career if you ignore them. Our shared assumptions around what it means to be a believer, in a church organization, or what it means to be professional, in a corporate setting; what it means to be a "good leader." These are the mental models that can stop a high potential junior manager's career in its tracks, or propel her beyond her wildest expectations.

In your organization, you may have spoken or unspoken norms of behavior that allow socializing only at certain times of the day, dictate supportive behaviors within and across teams, prohibit use of foul language, or manifest what's called a "strong work ethic." Deliberately violating, or deviating from, these norms and behaving in ways that are destructive to the psychological or physical health of other people in the organization, or to the stability and safety of the organization itself, would constitute AWB.

Management and leadership

Management and Leadership are different but complementary and equally necessary behavior sets. Both can be taught and learned, particularly the leadership competencies of emotional intelligence. People stay when their superiors see them, acknowledge their needs, make them feel safe, and value them.

Organizations, rather, the people who lead the organization, have a responsibility to create intentional professional development programs that address tactical management concerns as well as strategic leadership skills and behaviors. For the purposes of this book, let us please accept that while there are differences between management behavior and leadership behavior, an effective manager should be able to lead, and an effective leader should be able to manage.

We must choose our position on leadership and management, because even after 40 years, there is still the perception that leadership and management are significantly different, as in, at the internal or trait level. Psychoanalyst and Harvard professor Abraham Zaleznik wrote in a highly provocative 1977 article that leaders tend to be "twice-born personalities, people who feel separate from their environment" (p. 8). Managers, he wrote, fully engage in the organization and "see themselves as conservators and regulators" of the existing order of things, and this perpetuation of established institutional structures and rules fortifies the manager's sense of duty and identity. The leader, according to Zaleznik, is attracted to and motivated by change, rather than the maintenance of the current state. The manager must persuade and mediate, coordinating and balancing opposing views in times of conflict, while leaders provoke and challenge, deliberately offering new ideas and solutions to old problems and strategizing over open issues. Zaleznik suggested that "what it takes to develop managers may *inhibit* developing leaders" (Zaleznik, 1992, p. 3), emphasis mine. He was saying that the tactical skills necessary for effective management and maintenance of order and existing structure were directly opposed to the strategic, provocative thinking, and risk-taking behavior required for effective leadership toward a challenging new goal. His position has influenced many other theorists and authors over the years.

Contemporary thought leaders like Seth Godin suggest that leaders embrace failure, accept ambiguity, and help others grow "in quantum ways," while managers have no such directives beyond facilitating and maintaining existing systems. John Maxwell suggested that (perhaps oversimplifying) "leadership is influence" in his book *The 21 Irrefutable Laws of Leadership*, and its accompanying speeches and online posts. His description of leadership starts with character, moves on to relationships, and then knowledge, intuition, experience, past successes, and ability. Similarly, I teach an acronym for a model of leadership competencies – which is trait-based: a leader IS LIKED, because a leader shows Integrity, Self-Confidence, Leadership Motivation, Intelligence, Knowledge of the Business, Emotional Intelligence, and

Drive. Challenges to a model like this, of course, are that it is by no means universal and that it lists a set of personality traits rather than a set of teachable behaviors. This implies that leadership is intrinsic, that we are born with it, and not that it is something that can be encouraged and trained in an organizational context.

Again, I prefer to think that we can improve retention and engagement by focusing on what we invest in employees. When we invest in their personal and professional leadership development, we are saying that we believe leadership is a set of behaviors that can be encouraged and developed. While traits like integrity/character, intuition, and drive may not be teachable, emotional intelligence certainly is. This is why I prefer to think of leadership as a set of behaviors – I have hope that we can positively influence the atmosphere, climate, and culture of our organizations by how we think of leadership, how we treat people as if they are whole and complete and can only add to their repertoire of effective management tools. People stay when they know you value them and their potential.

Dan Goleman's model of emotional intelligence involves five specific components: self-awareness, self-regulation, motivation, empathy, and social skill. One has to possess the motivation "to work for reasons that go beyond money or status" (Goleman, 1998, p. 4), and the participants in my study certainly did. Perhaps the individuals in your organization demonstrate significant motivation as well. Unfortunately, I have observed lower self-awareness than one might expect and, as a result, almost nonexistent self-management, among working adults. Self-awareness is that internal indicator, not "overly critical nor unrealistically hopeful" (Goleman, 1998, p. 4), of how you feel and how to protect yourself. When I teach this material, I ask students to repeat and write down the statement "I am feeling a feeling. And that's ok. Now, what is that feeling? It's still ok." It is giving oneself permission to feel, emotionally, as a result of some external stimulus. Goleman says that a person with high self-awareness will recognize that "tight deadlines bring out the worst in him [so he] plans his time carefully and gets his work done well in advance" (p. 1). Or, if his colleague knows that she is pressure-prompted and does her best work under a deadline, she may give herself permission to start work closer to the deadline, but block off the time needed to get it done. Self-awareness means having surfaced one's own values and knowing one's own strengths, and it leads to, or manifests as, the ability to assess one's own performance candidly.

Goleman's second level of emotional intelligence is self-regulation, or self-management. It's the ability that one has to control one's own impulses, internal states, and resources. So, pursuing the previous examples, that fellow (let's call him Tim) who does his work in advance has freed up his energy to move on to the next project, and prepare for it in advance. And when faced with a new demand, say, for a quick-turnaround project because he's the only person on the team who has any bandwidth, Tim may experience feelings of frustration that others don't work the way he does. Because he has high self-regulation, he will acknowledge the feeling at least internally and consider if he has to react to the feeling externally. If so, he will moderate the reaction. The person who has low self-regulation is prone to snap at others, yell, whine, and overreact. As Goleman described, people who can control themselves and behave reasonably can engender feelings of trust and fairness in their colleagues.

Now, the woman on the same team who is pressure-prompted but still has high emotional intelligence may say in the staff meeting, "I hear you boss, we've got another project in the pipeline, due next week, and that's great. Now, I'm on lockdown all day today so that I can get project X done, but I can get with Tim to help him start thinking it through on Wednesday. I don't want him to feel like he's got no support on this."

Tim's colleague and teammate just displayed social awareness, or empathy. She recognizes that Tim may have some thoughts and feelings around this project situation, and she knows her work style is not the same as his. Easily recognized, empathy is the kind of behavior that demonstrates thoughtfulness toward others. Managers and leaders of all kinds need to consider the impact of their communications on subordinates and colleagues. Moreover, in our increasingly multigenerational and multicultural workplaces, managers who display empathy across the boundaries of age, race, gender, culture, and social position will be the managers who retain the greatest diversity of talent, whose groups develop the deepest team cohesion, and whose employees display the greatest innovation. People stay, especially people who are culturally or otherwise heterogeneous, when they feel safe and when they perceive that their contributions lead to synergy; people stay when they see that the whole is greater than the parts, and that their part is important.

It takes social skill, as Goleman termed it, to navigate this concept most effectively, though. For a manager to know that the diverse team he must lead requires a specific balance of task orientation and relationship management, that manager must strive toward and demonstrate this social skill, or relationship management, the highest level of emotional intelligence. Very few people get to this level of communication and leadership proficiency. These people have a wide social circle, or several varying social circles. They interact freely with many different kinds of people. They remain positive and encourage other people, even while seeing situations clearly and understanding their own dominant and lesser strengths. Employees will want to continue working with the manager who shows relationship management, because it never makes them feel manipulated. They know that the manager cares about and influences the feelings of her team. So people stay because they appreciate the way the manager leads, looks out for them, and shows respect and consideration for everyone on the team.

Emotional intelligence is a set of competencies. Through intentional leadership development, mentoring, and coaching, EI can be improved, increased, and more effectively deployed.

The work of management

We need to rethink the work of management. Operating from a new mental model about what managers do should help managers to feel seen, safe, and valued enough to facilitate career growth and development for their associates.

Almost 50 years ago, management professor Henry Mintzberg published an article in the *Harvard Business Review* addressing the myths around leadership and management, and HBR republished that article in 1990 (Mintzberg, 1990). The republishing was necessary because (and I can attest to this) business schools at both the undergraduate and graduate levels were and are still teaching that management involves, as Fayol suggested in 1916, planning, organizing, leading (coordinating), and controlling the work of others. Mintzberg argued that these vague, overgeneralized categories failed to explain clearly what managers really do. With all due respect to Fayol, Mintzberg offered four myths about the "Plan-Organize-Lead-Control" functions of management that are still prevalent in some workplaces. Let's take a quick look at them.

First, Mintzberg identified through an extensive review of the literature that the perception of management is that a manager is a reflective, systematic planner. But the truth is, managers often work in fits and starts, but at an "unrelenting pace." They are action-oriented doers and reluctant to engage in reflective work, despite powerful evidence from research (see work on experiential learning by Kolb and others). That evidence indicates that we learn best only upon reflection, and can refine our processes and improve individual and team performance only after taking time to think about and revise our methods of approaching organizational work. Unfortunately, managers in most organizational contexts just do not have, or take, the time to do this kind of reflection, and the organizations in which they work do not require or even encourage this kind of reflection.

Second, Mintzberg stated the perception that managers have no regular duties to perform. Instead, the folklore about a "manager" title, and I find this to be true in the undergraduate business students I teach, is that the job involves planning, delegating, even orchestrating the work of others, and then perhaps addressing problems on occasion. The truth here, though, according to real-world research, is a much colder, more stark view of management (and, I would have a very hard time citing research that was solely based on undergraduates' guesses in the university psychology lab, sorry). In fact, management means doing daily rituals and periodic ceremonies, upholding the traditions of the team and organization. Rituals might include management by walking around, entering and validating employees' daily time entry, ensuring that the office manager has replenished the office supplies, and that the receptionist has someone to cover for lunches. It means checking in on each employee and facilitating staff meetings as well as representing the team at meetings with internal and external customers and suppliers. Ceremonies range from the occasional hosting of top executives as they tour a facility, to the more frequent monthly recognition meetings, birthday and other celebration parties, retirement sendoffs, new contract signing celebrations, new business acquisition lunches, and employee-of-the-month designations. Then there are the negotiations, and the processing of soft information like the daily news from industry and other sources that indicate an open-loop processing cycle, that allow the organization and its teams to grow and prosper from the incorporation of new, external data.

All of this is in addition to the routine activities of contributing to the productivity of the team, because the research has shown that many organizations expect the manager to remain an individual contributor, carrying a share of the actual production output of the team while coordinating the work of others. Managers engage in these routine activities because their companies operate in a "one-deep" position. Anecdotally, I was told this was the philosophy at my last employer, as in, "no, we can't allow you to create training for backfilling key positions, because we can't spare anyone to learn the positions as backups. You know we're one-deep."

In addressing the final routine task of management, securing soft information to share with subordinates, Mintzberg hints at the manager's role in accessing and managing the company grapevine. Researchers have identified three levels of organizational communications: the informal grapevine, formal organizational communication patterns, and opinion-leader level communication. Mintzberg's suggestion that managers gather soft external data to share with their teams falls under informal grapevine communication, although to lower-level employees, a manager may be an opinion leader as well.

The value of the grapevine

The grapevine is that informal communication network that flows in a chain, often a cluster chain, formation. It is the "major informal communication medium in an organization" (Crampton, Hodge, & Mishra, 1998, p. 569). During the American Civil War, soldiers identified the telegraph lines strung from tree to tree as a sort of "grapevine," which often distorted messages, hence the association between the grapevine and inaccurate message conveyance (Crampton, Hodge, & Mishra, 1998; Karathanos & Auriemmo, 1999). Keith Davis first wrote about the grapevine in a 1975 *Management Review* article, suggesting that it could not be controlled, but that it could definitely be influenced (Davis, 1975). The grapevine is more flexible than any formal communication chain system, and can be visualized as a single-strand chain, a gossip chain, a probability chain, or a cluster chain. The cluster chain best fits the example Mintzberg gave of managers acquiring soft external information based on their status and role (from the *Harvard Business Review* subscription provided by their company, or from their membership in a local professional association, or from a meeting with company executives). The grapevine still carries information rapidly, even more so due to contemporary technologies like Twitter, LinkedIn, Facebook, Glassdoor, and other online tools. Managers can use these to steer the ways employees communicate informally about what will affect their teams directly, or what jobs they are interested in (how many analysts is our company hiring to accommodate this next acquisition?). Additionally, managers can provide data on what associates most want to know about (what is our company's stand on the collapse of our supplier's factory in a third world country?). The immediacy of the data and its timing definitely affect the spread of information via the grapevine.

The grapevine is often beneficial and can help improve organizational effectiveness, reduce anxiety, help make sense of limited information, and identify pending problems based on external data review and the impact those data have on the organization and the team. Regarding sensemaking, as Weick stated, organizations are sensemaking systems that create and recreate conceptions of themselves, and they do this through the ongoing intake of information that affects how individuals and teams see themselves and interrelate (Pugh & Hickson, 2007). The grapevine also serves as an early warning system for important organizational change, that is, shifts in the organizational culture. Informal communications travel faster than formal company communication, and the accuracy of the grapevine ranges from 75% to 90% (Crampton, Hodge, & Mishra, 1998; Karathanos & Auriemmo, 1999). Obviously, that 10 to 25% inaccuracy rate leads to internal conflict and unhealthy, "knee-jerk" reactions ("what, we're downsizing? That's it, I'm quitting!") The grapevine can help create common organizational language and culture and facilitate deeper team cohesion, when issues are important, the situation is ambiguous, and the grapevine itself is well-managed (Crampton, Hodge, & Mishra, 1998).

Certainly, the threat of groupthink driven by premature concurrence happens when the decision-making group responds out of impulse, reacting to negative or frightening external data inputs in dysfunctional ways, rather than carefully considering their own motivations, evaluating the information, or searching for alternatives (Chapman, 2006). To prevent groupthink, then, executives and culture monitors like human resource professionals can increase communication by increasing the number and effectiveness of liaison individuals, specifically, encouraging managers to accept what Mintzberg has already proven. The manager's job includes spreading accurate information relative to the company, and that they must compensate for any teleworking employees' isolation by providing them with direct communications (Davis, 1975).

Managers are key communicators, who gather and pass on information important to the team. There are also dead-enders who do not pass along the information they receive, perhaps due to the skepticism they feel toward grapevine information (again, that 10–25% inaccuracy rate). Then there are isolates, people outside the grapevine, who may be excluded from its information – unless, of course, the manager performs the task of compensating for their isolation by reaching out to them directly. Grapevine communications are often "leveled," or trimmed of details that may be important. They may also be "sharpened," hyped up to make the message more exciting. Younger workers (born in 1965 and later) tend to shun grapevine communications and reject office politics, and the rate of litigation over libelous informal communication has risen over the last 20 years (Karathanos & Auriemmo, 1999), so it makes sense that managers may be leery of this particular part of their duty to gather, process, and share soft information from the external and internal environment.

Distortion, noise, and inefficient pattern recognition in communications can lead to poor transmission and comprehension of a message. One study described "noise" as any part of a transmitted message that adds nothing to the intended meaning, and pattern recognition as identifying chunks of relevant information using appropriate descriptors. Distortion happens when, as in their example of the My Lai massacre during the Vietnam War, the content of a message is slightly tweaked from one sender to the next, until the final receiver's meaning is completely opposite from the original sender's meaning (Ferguson & Ferguson, 1987). When a manager communicates his or her expectations in an ambiguous way, or through multiple interpreters, it is possible for an associate or employee to completely misunderstand or misconstrue the message and take action, perhaps detrimental to the team or organization and even career-ending.

The third myth Mintzberg debunked for future managers was the idea that a formal MIS, or management information system, is required for the aggregation of information. Managers must not be given individual data points but instead they should receive summaries, whitepapers, and other documents produced from formal computer systems and programs. The fact is that managers prefer "verbal media, telephone calls and meetings, over documents" (Mintzberg, 1990, p. 3). Let us take a moment to absorb… Mintzberg told us in 1975 that managers prefer verbal communications to written documents and summaries.

And now, some 50 years later, managers still need small, well-informed bites of information presented in a clear and concise manner through a credible channel of communication. The rationale is simple, when you think about it – managers have no time to read ("What do you think this is, college? Why are you handing me a research paper? Just tell me what it says."). When they do take time to read, they skim. Headlines are important and, in our current era of "clickbait" headlines, even those need to convey accurate information.

As for the MIS, it should help managers identify problems and opportunities, answer key questions, and support the mental models promoted by the organization. For example, how do we budget? How do we serve our customers? How do our customers buy? What economic or industry changes are impacting how we do business? But the MIS is not the mind of the organization, not the heart of the organization. The MIS is a computer program bought or built to serve the managers in the organization. The strategic data bank, as Mintzberg called it, resides in the minds of the managers, more contemporarily called human and intellectual capital. In a 1990 reflection piece, a "Retrospective Commentary," Mintzberg himself noted that the threat of technology was its temptation for individuals to sit behind computers isolated in their offices and call that management.

The effect on this dependence on verbal information, which represents intellectual capital gleaned from outside data, peers, and subordinates, is that it makes the task of delegation harder. Many who have led teams have been criticized for poor delegation, poor utilization of the human resources on their teams. Instead of being able to hand over a whitepaper or a file of information on a task, the manager knows that she will have to brief the associate on the history, current state, and desired state of the project. Easier to just do it oneself, particularly when the vision of the desired state only resides in the manager's mind.

Finally, the last myth in Mintzberg's reconceptualization of what management is addresses the idea that management is a science and a profession. It is hard to justify all of the management science classes, the Master of Science in Management programs, when Mintzberg accurately states that scheduling, processing information, decision-making, and influencing others are all the key functions of managers' jobs, and they all reside within the manager. The conclusion is that there are three key sets of roles a manager must play, including the Interpersonal (figurehead, leader, liaison for the team), the Informational (monitor, disseminator, spokesperson), and the Decisional (entrepreneur, disturbance handler, resource allocator, negotiator).

The takeaway here is that managers who want to be effective leaders must address conflict quickly. They must make decision after decision after decision in a relentless series of actions sequenced over time, and attempt to display just and ethical methods in the allocation and distribution of resources. Using technology and information to serve the human needs of the team and the role, managers must gather and disseminate information and delegate tasks effectively to engage associates more deeply. Finally, managers should make time, carve time out of the busy-ness of their schedules, to consciously and deliberately reflect on the issues, problems, and decisions they face along with the resources available to them, to allow innovative solutions (or their own internal blocks!) to surface and be tested against reality.

Antisocial workplace behavior (AWB)

So what? What's the real impact of people behaving in a less-than-friendly manner at work? I'm glad you asked. As I began researching this topic, I found that experiences of AWB distract employees from their work tasks, reduce perceptions of psychological safety, decrease their motivation and energy, and reduce their organizational engagement – because they violate the psychological contract between the employee and the company. Norms of civility in communication may break down in such situations. As a result, employees' levels of trust and organizational commitment decline, leading to negative organizational as well as personal outcomes.

People work because we seek very specific outcomes. We are responding to an inner drive not only to bond with other people, but to be productive contributors to our society. Certainly, we work to earn the means to care for our families. But the psychological and sociological importance of work, and workplaces, has changed. Productive workplaces "require continuous (ongoing) work both on ourselves and our structures" (Weisbord, 1987, p. 256). But the research has shown that individuals are more motivated to work by "inner desire" (Fox, 1994, p. 71) to offer the best of our ideas and our labor, and to improve the condition and lot of our families and neighbors. Work is the way we engage with one another to define our society and social reality, as part of the human condition (Ardichvili & Kuchinke, 2009). Fox (1994) suggested that work represents a means to express "our blessing," and Fritz (2013) called work the manifestation of a good human life. Chalofsky (2003, 2010) described work as an opportunity to develop and reveal our gifts by bringing our "whole self" to work. When we do that, though, we need to feel seen, safe, and valued as contributors, and unfortunately many in the contemporary workplace do not.

Generational and cultural changes play a part; contemporary workplaces bear little resemblance to the industrial factories of the nineteenth and twentieth centuries (Fox, 1994; Weisbord, 1987). The business world formerly represented a highly structured, formal yet friendly, polite environment. But increasing employee diversity, downsizing or rightsizing initiatives, flattening of organizational hierarchies, increased pressure for production and other organizational change variables have been correlated with the increase in uncivil, even aggressive, AWB (Andersson & Pearson, 1999; Baron & Neuman, 1996, 1998). Such behavior includes bullying and aggression (deviant behavior demonstrating intent to harm), verbal and psychological abuse, theft, sabotage, and harassment. The behavior set represents acts "perpetrated by members of the organization, directed at the organization and its members, and [they are] intentional and (potentially) harmful" (Fritz, 2012, p. 5).

Practical applications

How serious is this situation? Well, what represents uncivil behavior in one organization may be normal in another. Some behaviors that are actually *pro-social* may seem uncivil, in fact, like the teammate goading a colleague to higher performance through competitive language and even insults. Specifically *antisocial* behavior must be deviant from the organization's norms and potentially destructive to the organization or damaging to another individual or group. The evidence has shown that experiencing AWB as either target or witness leads to reduced psychological safety (Sutton, 2007). This loss of safety creates a climate of fear, which reduces employees' ability to offer suggestions and learn from mistakes. It also leads to a loss of motivation and energy at work. Indicators of this phenomenon include absenteeism, stress-induced psychiatric and physical illness, increased turnover, or victims may turn into bullying jerks themselves. While often the research does not translate into practice, this book reveals some specific incidents and possible management responses to them. And, as the title suggests, in situations where they have faced AWB, why people stay.

Organizational commitment

Organizational commitment bears a consistent, significant predictive relationship with employee turnover, along with age, tenure, job content satisfaction, overall job satisfaction, and behavioral intent to quit (Steel & Ovalle, 1984). Granted, while people in the workforce might *say* they intend to quit their jobs within the next year or so, there are several moderating factors that will affect that decision: general economic conditions, military or civilian status, blue-collar vs. white-collar job status, and the time interval between the statement of intent and actual termination of employment. It makes common sense that commitment predicts how long an employee will stay in your workplace. But what exactly *is* organizational commitment?

Organizational commitment is the psychological state that binds employees to an organization and makes turnover less likely. Early research focused on the strength of the employee's degree of identification with the organization's values and identity, and the level of the employee's involvement in the workplace (Meyer, Allen, & Gellatly, 1990). Then, Meyer and Allen (1991) continued to focus on "affective commitment" as a more emotion-based concept in which employees stay because they want to, it's their choice, they feel competent at the work they do, and they have strong feelings of comfort and affiliation with the group and organization. The researchers also addressed "continuance commitment," a different type of commitment altogether – this one focuses on the threat of loss of benefits or pension and the absence of alternative options, as in a period of high unemployment. Other researchers have taken these concepts further, as explained later in this book. Suffice it to say that continuance commitment involves maintaining one's activity level in the company based on an economic understanding of the opportunity costs of quitting; it addresses the sunk costs of having chosen this job over some other job, or unemployment. Continuance commitment has been found to explain lower rates of employees offering organizational citizenship behaviors – the "above and beyond, extra mile" types of action that employees can choose to perform on the job (Shore & Wayne, 1993). This, too, makes sense when we consider that employees who are committed to the organization only because they fear sacrificing salary increases, paid holidays and vacations, retirement eligibility, or vesting in the pension plan are not generally going to be people who want to give "extra" of themselves. They do what is required to maintain eligibility for the benefits of employment.

There is a third construct, normative commitment, influenced by early social-ization and role modeling as well as by organizational commitment. This form of organizational commitment manifests when employees stay in a workplace based on the obligation to be loyal, or based on their own work ethic ("I'm no quitter") (Dunham, Grube, & Castañeda, 1994).

Commitment represents an energizing force for work motivation. Affec-tive commitment, or attachment to the organization, shows the strongest positive correlation with job performance (high affective commitment yields high job performance), as well as with organizational citizenship behavior (going the extra mile, doing a little more for the team) and with attendance. Normative commitment, or the obligation to remain ("bloom where you are planted"), shows the second strongest positive correlation with those same or-ganizational outcomes. This type of engagement with the company develops through personal involvement, identification with relevant targets, and value congruence between the individual and the organization. Affective commit-ment and normative commitment positively correlate to favorable attitudinal and behavioral outcomes, but continuance commitment has emerged as neg-atively or unrelated to the same attitudinal and behavioral outcomes. Clearly then, continuance commitment is the least desirable form. It develops through two distinct psychological processes: a "racking up" of factoids reflecting the collection of investments that the employee would lose if he left his current position, and the perception that few alternatives to the current employment relationship exist. The costs of leaving exceed the cost of staying (Sinclair, Tucker, Cullen, & Wright, 2005).

The dark side of organizational commitment: entrenchment

Career entrenchment represents resource allocation and justifying past invest-ments in the light of constricted career options. Possible coping mechanisms include Exit, Voice, Loyalty, and Neglect (EVLN). Carson and Carson (1997) cite the EVLN model of coping responses used to moderate stress caused by work-related dissatisfaction. Exit represents attrition from an entrapping ca-reer. It is often the most rational, but least used, method because it means re-tirement or total withdrawal from the labor force. Voice represents actively and constructively trying to improve conditions by verbalizing concerns when labor force withdrawal is impossible. The voice response is more common when career enhancement is likely and the individual wants to preserve re-lationships with colleagues. The danger of the voice response is the threat of retaliation, loss of reputation, and the emotional cost of confrontation. The individual may express voice internally to the organization or externally to a professional organization. The Loyalty response represents passively, but op-timistically waiting for conditions to improve. The cost of active engagement may be too high for the individual to engage in voice. Dangers of the loy-alty response include skill atrophy, boredom, and depression. An individual displaying the loyalty response may choose to demonstrate their loyalty through organizational citizenship behaviors. Neglect is the final response option, which involves passively allowing the situation to deteriorate. It involves reduced interest and effort in the job, frequent tardiness and absenteeism, increased errors, and inefficient use of work time.

Practical applications

Employees are more committed to organizations that show a demonstrated commitment to their long-term career development (Dessler, 1999). To increase organizational commitment, you should commit to people-first values and put that commitment **in writing**. Additionally, clarify and communicate the organization's mission and ideology; use values-based hiring practices to build traditions; guarantee organizational justice through clear grievance procedures and two-way communications; and provide a sense of community through supporting employee development, celebrating achievements, and enriching employees' work experience.

Rude, disrespectful, or demeaning behavior may indicate dysfunctional group norms or culture, and lead to reduced organizational commitment and trust. Eventual negative personal and organizational outcomes include lower productivity and performance, the increased physical effects of stress and cynicism, and increased turnover intent and actual turnover. Employee turnover as a statistic represents the rate at which the organization's workforce changes due to voluntary or involuntary terminations. This phenomenon carries with it specific costs, including the aggregate of unemployment compensation and continuation of healthcare benefits.

Unpleasant work relationships correlate directly with job satisfaction, satisfaction with coworkers, workplace cynicism, and organizational commitment (Fritz & Omdahl, 2009). Additionally, in workplaces where the organization's ethical standards are clear and widely publicized, managerial adherence to those ethical standards is a direct predictor of organizational commitment. In workplaces where the managers do not adhere to stated ethical standards (or there are none), poor supervisory relations have a negative effect on commitment.

Organizational engagement

A separate construct from organizational commitment, engagement represents a deeper level of commitment, based primarily on affective components but also demonstrating a significant level of impact on organizational and individual outcomes. Additionally, though, employee engagement is a concept already in common parlance in many organizations, and while study participants may demonstrate specific forms of organizational commitment, they are likely to use language and describe initiatives designed to increase employee engagement.

The disciplines of management, psychology, and leadership have deemed organizational commitment and organizational engagement important. They have also validated workplace incivility and toxic workplaces as legitimate constructs. It is of personal interest to me to investigate the linkages between the two sets of constructs.

Alan Saks' study on the factors that lead to and encourage employee engagement, and the organizational effects of that engagement, pretty much represents the foundation of the "engagement" movement in scholarly research. At that point, consulting firms like Gallup, Korn Ferry, and McKinsey were leading the way in terms of identifying this important, but nebulous, intangible asset. Building on research from the previous few years, Saks created a detailed survey to measure job and organizational engagement, identified as separate phenomena. Saks also sought to document the antecedents and consequences of engagement. Somewhat different from organizational commitment (a more established research construct), engagement represents the degree of emotional and intellectual commitment a person is willing to make to their organization, "or the amount of discretionary effort exhibited by employees in their jobs" (Saks, 2006, p. 601). Engagement refers to the amount of **attention** (how much of your brain power and thought energy) and **absorption** (intensity of your focus) you dedicate to your work role. Specific areas of work-life balance that lead employees down the path toward engagement, as opposed to burnout, are "workload, control, rewards and recognition, community and social support, perceived fairness, and values" (p. 603). These components of work-life control the individual's level of engagement at work, or propensity for burnout.

In another study, researchers proposed that there are specific characteristics of a job's design that affected employee engagement. Their model suggests that the demands of the job moderate the relationship between the job's design itself, and the level of employee engagement one has. Further, they suggested that the company's human resource development (HRD) practices have a moderated, rather than direct, impact on employee engagement. This might seem counterintuitive; one more easily accepts that in the workplace HRD initiatives would have a direct impact on employee engagement. But these researchers suggest that relationship is moderated by the demands of the job, which may affect the impact of even the most well-meaning of HRD initiatives (Rana, Ardichvili, & Tkachenko, 2014).

Researchers agree that engagement is a positive phenomenon, and one that is pervasive throughout an organization. It is a mood, and more – a climate, which significantly affects the organization's culture.

Key takeaways

1. People need to feel *seen, safe, and valued* in their workplaces and relationships. When they don't, organizational commitment and employee engagement both drop.

2. Associates leave an organization because of problematic relationships and difficult communications that make them feel unsafe.
3. When associates feel invisible, or ignored, in the workplace, they are prone to engage in more risky, self-serving behaviors and office politics, as well as other antisocial workplace behaviors up to and including theft, sabotage, and corporate espionage.
4. While culture is a complex, layered concept, every organization has a set of cultural norms. AWB violate those norms and make no mistake: AWB are deliberate acts. They are not innocent or accidental.
5. Low organizational commitment leads to high, and potentially expensive, turnover, low job satisfaction, and people spending more time on the job looking for another job than actually working.

Recommended reading

Bradberry, T., & Greaves, J. (2009). *Emotional Intelligence 2.0*. San Diego, CA: TalentSmart.
Chaleff, I. (2009). *The Courageous Follower: Standing Up To & For Our Leaders*. 3rd ed. San Francisco: Berrett-Koehler.
Chaleff, I. (2015). *Intelligent Disobedience*. Oakland, CA: Berrett-Koehler Publishers, Inc.
Lencioni, P. (2000). *The Four Obsessions of an Extraordinary Executive*. San Francisco: Jossey-Bass.

Let's make this #Interactive – Here's a challenge: pick a book, get it, and connect with the author on LinkedIn and/or follow them on Twitter. Let them know you read their book, and ask them a question about it. #Dialogue #WPS #WhyPeopleStay

2

RATIONALE FOR EXAMINING BAD BEHAVIOR IN THE WORKPLACE

Why do people stay?

I told you in the introduction that this book was based on an academic study in the social sciences. Let me also confess now that it will include supplemental scenarios and examples of "bad behavior in the workplace" such as bullying, sexual or psychological harassment, and abusive supervision. This is to provide you with the most comprehensive set of examples of what NOT to tolerate in your organizational culture. I'll give you potential responses and remedies to these doozies from a managerial, human resources, and ethical leadership standpoint at the end of each chapter.

"Nonprofit Nancy"

At one point I worked multiple part-time jobs while I was pursuing my Master's degree in Business Administration. My full-time job as a Marketing Coordinator had been eliminated due to an economic downturn, and rather than take someone else's job (which I was offered, doing work I didn't want to do) I took the separation package and started working on the MBA full time, picking up part-time jobs to pay all the bills. "Nancy" (not her name) hired me after a pleasant interview and asked me to complete a grant application for her organization during my first week on the job. As an experienced professional, former grants manager of a nonprofit myself, I had no problem doing it and… we got the funding.

Only three days later, while working a project that did NOT play to my strengths – making cold calls – I asked Nancy a question about the business, with a prospect on hold. Remember I had only worked there, part time, for just over a week. Her answer to my question was, "What do you think? You need to just FIGURE. IT. OUT." I was stunned! I got off the line with the prospect – that's right, missed opportunity! Then I got up and walked down the hall to her office, and confronted her with, "Do we need to talk?" She actually said no, and thought nothing was wrong. Keep in mind, I was working three part-time jobs at that point, and taking five full-time classes toward my MBA. My stress level was on max from wake up to fall out at night. I ended up quitting the job the next day. I saw a former coworker not long after and she told me that this lady hired low-income women (!), including women just out of prison, to work for her nonprofit under the guise of giving people a second chance, but really, she knew they would take it, the horrible way she talked to people. The coworker told me stories that were much worse than mine; I'm glad I got out when I did. – AD, from summer 2001

Rationale for the study

This study contributed to the cross-disciplinary body of knowledge in management, leadership, and industrial/organizational psychology by allowing participants to make sense of why they do what they do, why they commit and engage in organizations and groups, and why they tolerate (or constrain or ignore) uncivil behavior from their superiors, subordinates, or peers in the workplace. Before 1990, there were 80 to 150 research articles published about this nebulous concept of antisocial workplace behavior, including all of its subtypes of behaviors by organizational members that cause harm to the organization itself or to other employees. From 1990 to 2000 there was a boom in research interest and publication; over 500 articles were published during that decade alone, indicating a much more significant presence in the workplace of these behaviors. Antisocial workplace behaviors (AWB) include theft, sabotage, verbal or psychological abuse, withholding effort, lying, refusing to cooperate, assault, sexual harassment, workplace incivility, bullying, and abusive supervision. Workplace incivility is broken down into rudeness, discourtesy, and disrespect in the research literature.

By now you're saying, "Good gosh, I don't need a study to know that these behaviors are everywhere!" Well, you'd be pretty accurate. I've seen more ugliness at work than I care to remember, so I decided to study it. Not just to study workplace toxicity (been done) or the types of antisocial and uncivil behaviors that manifest in the workplace (been done), but specifically why would people stay in a workplace where they experienced these things? These behaviors are specifically deviant from organizational norms, and

> "No one wants to do a bad job."
>
> A mentoring note given to encourage me and remind me to be merciful in my assessment of others, by someone later identified by others as a workplace bully.

are directed at the organization or its members, and they cause harm, pain, stress, and other very specific outcomes. So why stay?

Assumptions

In order to execute a true phenomenological study, one must identify the assumptions under which she is operating, so I did that. I had to surface and examine my assumptions, in a scholarly manner. It was a requirement of the study that the individuals who participated in the study, and those whose stories have been added since, were gainfully employed at the time of our interview in an organizational context where they experience(d) AWB. I assumed that working adults can and do reflect upon and make sense of their own decisions, and therefore the question, "Why do people do what they do?" actually has an answer. Further, I assumed that workplace associates can identify why it is they commit to, and engage their energy in, the organizations where they work and the groups to which they belong. Finally, I assumed that these same adult workers can also identify why they tolerate, rebuke, or ignore uncivil or antisocial behavior from superiors, subordinates, or peers at work.

Connecting to theory

There are three spheres of leadership: political (including military), business (corporate and nonprofit), and religious. Contemporary leadership studies provide a systematic analysis of specific issues within one or more of the spheres through a defined, goal-oriented process, which includes consideration of the dimensions of leadership in various contexts, or organizational cultures (Hicks, 2003). The researcher and consultant Edgar Schein addressed the dimensions of organizational culture, the analysis of which rests at the intersection of anthropology, sociology, social psychology, and organizational behavior. This is not to be overlooked or taken lightly – there are multiple dimensions of organizational culture, any of which can offer opportunity for poor workplace relations and any of which can derail organizational development initiatives. In the business management sphere, Hicks' key dimensions address the roles of leader and follower, the manifestation of authority and its origins or sources, motivation, ritual, narrative, and communication, while Schein's underlying dimensions of culture allow an investigation of the organization's primary issues of identity and response to external adaptation challenges and internal integration tasks. Schein suggests that studying organizational culture is best done through action research, by directly involving insiders in the research effort. To understand a specific organizational culture within the business management sphere, then, an appropriate research approach involves a qualitative research effort in which participants share their experiences and espoused theories while the researcher compares their input to the organization's published and enacted theories-in-use (Schein, 2005).

Weisbord (1987) expressed concern with the perspective quoted earlier from Fox (1994) and Terkel (1974) focused on the misery of work. Weisbord suggested that leaders (and thus organizations) needed to respond "to needs for dignity, meaning, and community in work" (p. 233). Productive workplaces "require continuous (ongoing) work both on ourselves and our structures" (Weisbord, 1987, p. 256). Contemporary workplaces bear little resemblance to the industrial factories of the nineteenth and twentieth centuries (Fox, 1994; Weisbord, 1987). Hirschhorn suggests that in the contemporary workplace, leaders must draw and maintain internal boundaries between groups, as well as external boundaries that separate the organization from its environment. Unfortunately, these boundaries lead to a psychological violence enacted upon the workplace participants (Hirschhorn, 1988). Employers, managers, and leaders at all levels face a more demanding workforce, one that requires work-life balance (www.shrm.org) and meaningfulness (Chalofsky, 2003, 2010; Chalofsky & Krishna, 2009).

How to handle it...

This chapter started out with the experience "AD" had with "Nonprofit Nancy." But AWB happens all the time. What are some possible responses, or cultural adjustments, that can remedy or address AWB? The answer is, infuriatingly, "It depends."

It depends on whether you are a peer, or a subordinate, or even a superior to the person behaving badly. We'll address possible behavioral responses in a later chapter, in detail. Superiors and culture monitors with titles like HR Business Partner, HR Manager, and Organizational Development Representative have a greater responsibility to monitor and manage the culture and climate in the workplace. Significantly greater, such as if a subordinate is bullying you or creating an atmosphere of rudeness, discourtesy, and disrespect, you must use every tool in your arsenal to address and contain that situation. You must set clear expectations for communication and acceptable workplace and workgroup behavior, and then ENFORCE THOSE EXPECTATIONS. Here are a few other potential managerial responses that might have helped Nonprofit Nancy:

- As a manager, Nancy could have taken the time to listen to the employee's concerns about the unfamiliar task (cold calling).
- She should have trained and prepared the employee, even rehearsed scenarios with her, so the employee would have been able to answer questions posed by prospects.
- Nancy should have answered the questions and encouraged the associate to document and take notes so she would have the answers herself, in future.

What Nancy may have missed is that this associate, still new to the group, was in the storming phase, trying to figure out where she fit and what her contributions might be. In this situation, communication broke down because the associate felt unsafe, doing an unfamiliar task. She also felt unseen and undervalued, because no one asked her if she wanted to make cold calls or if she was any good at it – and it was actually a very uncomfortable task for her. She had achieved a significant win with the grant in her first week, and then being assigned to cold calls and spoken to harshly made her feel undervalued. And, she was already under significant stress, reducing her capacity to manage this difficult interaction.

An HR consultant colleague of mine, Elizabeth Veliz, described it this way in a workshop on giving "the gift of feedback":

> Every single person in a role that is responsible for the outcomes of another human being at work needs to clearly communicate expectations. Job descriptions are not enough; they merely provide a high level overview of responsibilities. "Responsibilities" are NOT expectations. Every single supervisor, manager, director, VP, CEO – or other "C" position – anyone who has another person reporting to them must set the B.A.R. for their direct reports. Clearly explain what Behaviors are expected in the workplace. Outline the right ones and for good measure – talk about the wrong ones. Review the Attitudes that are not only expected of them, but that will lead to their success, the team's success, and the organization's success. Finally, we must deliver a Result at work. Every single one of us has a deliverable. Oftentimes, those deliverables are not exactly tangible – "I expect this to be completed in a timely fashion." We have all heard that one before. When you clearly and explicitly outline the Results you expect from your people, you are setting them up for success. You are making YOUR job easier. You are being a great leader.

I couldn't have said it better, but I will also provide some references for you if you are in such a position and facing the challenge of confronting a bully in your workplace, or a saboteur, or a sniper, or any member of the team who is disrupting the motivation and energy on your team. Why is there so much pressure on the manager or culture monitor? The morale effects of AWB are devastating to organizational engagement, team productivity and performance, and individual feelings of psychological safety. And here's the hard news: you, as the supervisor (manager, director, leader, HR person) are the person who violated the psychological contract between the employee and the company when you either tacitly or implicitly allowed the toxic behavior to occur without correcting it, or worse, allowed it to take root and become the norm. In that capacity, you would be the reason why people leave your team and organization. It really is true that people don't leave organizations; they leave bosses.

Practical applications and consulting notes

AWB appears in general interactions with other people in the work setting, and can affect the stages of team development. Teams are by definition groups of two or more people who are aware that they are mutually accountable for achieving specific goals, and who interact with and influence one another in the process of achieving those goals. Organizational behavior textbooks describe Tuckman's five stages of team development, and contemporary human resources profession-als and organizational development practitioners will tell you that many teams transition or transform rather than adjourn, these days. Teams work best when the characteristics of their task (their charter) are made clear to them and are easy to implement, when the team is just large enough to get the job done but small enough to meet regularly and cooperate, and when the people on the team share some of the same values and competencies.

The stages of team development include, for the uninitiated: Forming, in which the team is created as an entity; Storming, in which the participants strive to establish their roles and expectations; Norming, in which the team gels and creates its identity and affirms its purpose, processes, and tools; Performing, in which the team actually executes its task; Adjourning, in which the team is dis-banded; or Transforming, in which the team composition changes and the team receives a new charter.

Effective teams are comprised of members who want to remain members, who are willing to share information, who share strong interpersonal bonds, and who resolve conflict effectively. Human resource development professionals con-sistently investigate ways to help organizations successfully navigate the ups and downs of team development. To connect the dots for corporate clients, I often point out that high employee engagement is desirable, and this engagement is directly affected by and predicted by team cohesiveness. In order to manipulate and increase team cohesiveness, we must attend to multiple dimensions of di-versity, including surface-level and deep-level diversity factors like generational diversity in the workplace. We also have to accept and create a safe space to ac-knowledge that individuals have different perspectives, and different needs, and due to the very definition of a team, the group of individuals on a team will go through stages of identity and productivity together. At times, conflict will block team performance, so leaders must provide what their followers on teams need to get past their conflicts and ensure effective productivity. One of my favorite authors, Patrick Lencioni, has written a series of consulting manuals in the form of allegorical or fictional short-reads, usually focusing on developing effective teams and improving workplace performance. (He also has a book geared toward consultants called *The Naked Consultant*, which I highly recommend.) Lencioni's most famous book, *The Five Dysfunctions of a Team*, provide a clear-eyed look at how the absence of trust on a team leads to an endemic fear of conflict, because if employees do not feel safe and trust one another, they will not engage in au-thentic, values-based conflict. Then, the team will fail to build real commitment, and as a result, they will refuse to hold themselves and each other accountable to organizational goals. Finally, with no accountability, there is no attention to deliverable results.

Part of the value of working to create effective teams is that they can help to evaluate and encourage performance improvement, even assist in identify-ing and facilitating performance improvement interventions such as training, counseling, policy changes, etc. But to do so the team must include individuals from various parts of the organization, including the group that has the presenting problem and any groups that may be affected by its resolution (Van Tiem, Mosely, & Dessinger, 2012).

AWB and conflict occur throughout the stages of team development, and as teams transition or add new people to the group, they may encounter new conflicts. I have specific recommendations that I provide to client groups for what should happen at each stage of the team development life cycle, although many organizations and groups tend to try and skip from forming to performing with no clear relationship building, ground rules, boundaries, or norms established.

Key takeaways

1. The key question, or purpose statement, is presented in this chapter: Why would people stay in a workplace situation where they experienced AWB?
2. Productive workplaces allow for meaningful engagement in socially valuable work, without fear of verbal or physical attack, or psychological harassment.

Recommended reading

Buckingham, M. (2008). *The Truth About You*. Nashville, TN: Thomas Nelson Publishers.
Leider, R., & Shapiro, D. (2001). *Whistle While You Work: Heeding Your Life's Calling*. San Francisco: Berrett-Koehler Publishers, Inc.
Lencioni, P. (2002). *The Five Dysfunctions of a Team: A Leadership Fable*. San Francisco: Jossey-Bass.
McClain Smith, D. (2008). *Divide or Conquer: How Great Teams Turn Conflict into Strength*. New York: Penguin.

Let's make this #Interactive – Here's a challenge: pick a book, get it, and connect with the author on LinkedIn and/or follow them on Twitter. Let them know you read their book, and ask them a question about it. #Dialogue #WPS #WhyPeopleStay

---

3
THEORETICAL CONSTRUCTS

This chapter could read like a glossary or short dictionary of bad behavior in the workplace, demonstrating the breadth of research that has been done on antisocial workplace behavior(AWB). But do you want to read that?

Let's just talk about what you know is true. And as with any other topic, some of what you know… isn't pretty. In fact it's downright ugly, and you'll be asking me "So what? How do I deal with this, and quickly?!" Or better yet, you'll be raising an eyebrow, saying, "Oh NO, we deal with this *swiftly* in my company." So while this chapter is very firmly based in research literature, its purpose is to reveal to you just how prevalent these issues are, and to make some suggestions for addressing them before they lead to serious psychic damage and organizational destruction. No hyperbole there.

> "In law a man is guilty when he violates the rights of others. In ethics he is guilty if he only thinks of doing so."
> – Immanuel Kant, German philosopher (Roberts, 2016)

Legalese – the black and white/zero tolerance

First, to clarify terms – this book does not address assault and battery in any significant detail. *Assault* is the act of creating the expectation in another person that you intend to harm them, often using words. *Battery* is the actual physical contact done in a harmful or offensive way, that is, with the intent to hurt another person (legal-dictionary.thefreedictionary.com). *Sexual harassment* is usually repetitive, unwanted behavior (it can be just one time, though, if it represents a critical incident). Sexual harassment always has some sexual content, expressing sexual desire. This is different from just being "of a sexual nature," according to the law, because a colleague may simply bear significant animus toward another and approach that person and threaten to perform sexual acts on the target's minor child. This type of incident is bullying and may represent psychological harassment, but may not necessarily fall under the rubric of sexual harassment because it does not indicate sincere sexual desire.

Sexual harassment, as with rape, has its nexus in the power dynamic between two people. Harassment may come in the form of a *quid pro quo* (Latin for "this for that") request ("if you want to move up, you have to…" said suggestively by a superior to a subordinate). In recent months and years, sexual harassment has become more of a buzzword in the news media, particularly regarding the entertainment industry and the behavior of male executives toward subordinates or others dependent on the executive for employment and livelihood. And there lies the power dynamic; it is not possible for the "star" or the network executive to have a fully consensual relationship with a secretary, makeup artist, or intern in his or her organization. Should there be a genuine attraction between them, one of them should change his or her employment status. Unfortunately, in most cases the person who is subordinate may have no other employment options and feel trapped in the situation. Sexual harassment may also come in the form of frequent sexually themed jokes, innuendos, suggestive images, or comments permitted in the workplace that create a generally uncomfortable, unwelcoming atmosphere. This is the phenomenon known as a "hostile work environment." So to clarify, hostile work environment originated as a phrase that immediately and specifically fell under the sexual harassment umbrella. However, it has evolved to include workplace incivility – general rudeness, discourtesy, and disrespect – but if those are the conditions in the workplace, it needs to be addressed within the organization. Filing a "hostile work environment" sexual harassment claim may not stand. Sexual harassment is an equal opportunity offense, and can be perpetrated by men or women of any sexual orientation against men or women of any sexual orientation. It is about the manifestation of power over another. It also, apparently, indicates some degree of laziness. I say this because certain individuals in the news media who have been accused of sexual harassment are using the defense that they had no other way to meet eligible sex partners than to pick from among their subordinates. This is no defense.

In my experience, and probably in your organization it's the same, all production in the affected area stops if there's an allegation of sexual harassment or sexual assault, or if there's an overt threat or act of violence. When I say all production stops, I mean that all parties involved, and witnesses, are pulled off the job and brought to human resources or the equivalent management party. The complainant and the accused are kept separated with escorts who stay with them. Each party and witness is tasked with writing a detailed statement. The complainant is interviewed first, and in the interview I always asked if they felt safe in the moment, and if not, what they needed. If their preference was to leave the premises, we arranged that, after the interview and statements were documented. All of these allegations can shut down more than just a team's productivity for the day. They all could lead to lawsuits, and worse, the complete destruction of the working community that you have created and are working to preserve. With hypothetical but accurate exemplar phrases, let me give you some examples. The threat of violence ("She said she was going to wait for me after work and beat my ass"), actual violence, sexual harassment ("we used to date but now he won't leave me alone; he keeps touching me and trying to get me by myself even when I tell him stop we're going to get in trouble"), sexual assault ("you came in here wearing that dress, let me just get you by yourself girl"), or battery (actual touching of a sexual nature) are all **supremely** destructive.

This is why there's a zero tolerance policy toward this kind of a behavior, and if there isn't in your company there should be. I once heard an employment lawyer say that he encouraged HR professionals to allow a "one kiss" rule – as in, not firing an employee straightaway when there was a sexual harassment accusation against him or her, based on the possibility of "mixed messages." I'm still not sure how I feel about that, but I can tell you this: zero tolerance. Zero. Electrified third rail. WHY do I emphasize this so strongly? Because you set the tone in your company, you lay the rails for the organizational culture, and when any employee is allowed to keep his or her job after an occurrence of zero tolerance activity, it completely destroys feelings of safety and value among your employees.

Management guru Edgar Schein suggested that organizational culture is the nexus, an intersection between anthropology, sociology, social psychology, and organizational behavior. Culture is influenced primarily by what you, the leaders, pay attention to. What you measure and control *matters*. Your employees are watching with a close eye on how managers and leaders will react to critical incidents and organizational crises. On the positive side, how you do role modeling and coaching, and how you set the criteria from the top down for recruiting, selection, promotion, allocation of rewards and status, retirement, excommunication… all of these are the primary means through which you embed culture, or set the rails. In this context, your people want to feel seen, safe, and valued. If a professional employee experiences the loss of personal power and safety that comes with a sexual harassment experience, or an encounter with violence in the workplace, he or she will absolutely not feel valued or safe, and will begin searching for a new environment in which those critical factors can be met. Even your deeply invested, long-term, high-performing employees will jump ship the moment they perceive this betrayal of the *psychological contract* to have taken place. This brings me to our actual topic for this chapter – terms.

So, what are we talking about here?

I'll move in descending order from the most general of terms to the mildest or most specific. The largest overarching theme here is AWB. These behaviors harm an organization or its members and include theft, sabotage, verbal abuse, withholding effort, lying, refusing to cooperate, and even violence. It's personal, and it's business. When it's personal, you note "shrinkage" – your inventory comes up short. Or your company orders office supplies far more frequently than expected and you find that employees are using company supplies for personal projects or taking them home. And of course, the petty cash shortages. All of these are theft. Withholding effort and refusing to cooperate are insidious behaviors in which associates refuse requests for support, ignore parts of their job, or (worse) "fudge the numbers" in order to complete a task. In the latter case, a document requiring accurate documentation is deliberately submitted to an internal or external client with false or misleading information. In my study, this behavior led to rework and significant feelings of betrayal by the employee who observed it, and reported it to management – with no result. It was especially frightening due to the nature of the work – heavy industrial equipment manufacturing. To the end user of the product, mistakes and poor quality essentially amount to life and death risk. And that employee who fails to return phone calls and emails, skips important meetings, declines requests to participate on project teams, and submits reports or presentations to you at the last minute? Refusing to cooperate is also AWB.

The first subcategory under AWB is, fittingly, Counterproductive Workplace Behavior (CWB) – a similar construct nestled under AWB, these behaviors specifically harm the organization and violate cultural norms within that organization. It's strictly business. Any of the actions listed above that only impact the business and do not affect another individual could be classified as CWB. Next we'll get specific about more ways in which the psychological contract between the employee and employer can be violated. Wait, what is this contract? I'm glad you asked.

The psychological contract

Remember that the theme of this book is about ensuring your people feel "seen, safe, and valued." First proposed as the psychological work contract, the concept of reciprocity appeared in the literature in the 1960s. Employees expect salary, benefits, a good work location, opportunities for advancement, and clarity about the nature of their work tasks. Employer expectations center on job descriptions, policies, procedures, and performance standards. Employee vigilance in tracking organizational compliance with perceived terms of psychological contracts has been increasing because of organizational and economic turbulence. Your employees may, cynically, expect violations of the psychological contract as a result.

The psychological contract represents the way organizations fulfill their side of this agreement. It represents an exchange of goods and services in the context of values, beliefs, and norms. Moreover, it represents promises made to the employee by the organization and is the sum total of those promises as the employee understands them. The contract is comprised of multiple, layered expectations brought to the employment relationship by the employee and the basic expectation that the organization holds, namely that the employee will adhere to the stated requirements of the job and that the company will provide compensation for the same. But don't let me understate this - the psychological contract is that critical, implicit agreement between you and your employees in which the employees embed their feelings, their affective commitment to your organization. It is a set of promises that commit the individual (or the organization) to future action. Employees tend to expect not only financial remuneration for their time and work effort, but also career growth, continuance, and advancement. In some cases they also expect personal development and mentoring. There may be other considerations layered into the employee's expectations, such as recognition and special favors based on merit or tenure. Psychological contracts are extremely subjective beliefs and perceptions about what you are offering, what you have promised, and the employee's acceptance of such promises. It changes and evolves over the life of your relationship with the employee, and it requires a significant amount of trust. Unfulfilled promises by the employer deprive the employee of desired outcomes and lead to perceptions of unfair outcomes, perceptions of inequity… these are measured in the management literature focusing on organizational justice.

Distributive justice, procedural justice, and interactional justice all address the employee's perceptions of management's violations of trust. For example, distributive justice is the term applied to employees' perception of the fairness of the outcomes they receive, while procedural justice represents the quality of treatment they experience while organizational processes and procedures are enacted. Interactional justice is the perception of the quality of interpersonal treatment people receive during the enactment of organizational procedures (Forret & Love, 2008; Dayan & Di Benedetto, 2008). Employees seek to experience unbiased consistent and honest procedures. When management fails to honor this expectation, employees experience a sense of wrongdoing, deception, and betrayal, leading to a violation of the psychological contract.

Ira Chaleff (2009) states that trust, according to multiple leadership surveys, is the single most important variable followers use to evaluate their leaders, while leaders use reliability as the reverse variable to evaluate followers. Trust is defined as a subtle state between two or more people formed from an assessment of each other's internal motives and external actions. Each evaluates the other's words and the effectiveness of the other's actions (p. 29). Leaders most highly value followers who have the courage to assume responsibility as much as the other four key follower behaviors combined.

Still other researchers state that justice and fairness issues are not new to the organizational development field and practitioners.

> Justice theory also relates to constructivism (the belief that realities are socially constructed) in that application of justice concepts to an organizational intervention creates the architecture for a socially constructed organizational reality (i.e. openness, trust, commitment).
>
> *(Wooten & White, 1999, p. 16)*

What we're saying here, in scholarly language, is that we're all in this together. I definitely subscribe to the concept that we co-create the roles of leader and follower within a specific context. Social construction of identity is why we so desperately cling to job roles and titles – because we are what we repeatedly do, we find ourselves in and express ourselves through our work roles.

The construct of organizational justice includes distributive justice, procedural justice, and interactional justice. Distributive justice focuses on employees' perceptions of whether they received what they deserved. Specific components addressed in distributive justice include pay outcomes, equity, equality, and need. Procedural justice is defined as the fairness of procedures used to make and implement the decisions and policies enacted by management. Procedural justice includes the concept of voice, or the opportunity to have one's views considered. Interactional justice is defined as "perceptions of how fairly formal agents of the organization treat those who are subject to their authority, decisions, and actions, and how subordinates react to those perceptions" (Wooten & White, 1999, p. 9).

Jong and Avolio (2000) examined the causal effect of transformational leadership on performance, validating the role of value congruence and trust in the leadership process. Workers were more satisfied and more committed when their values were congruent with supervisors' values, and this congruence improved with the supervisors articulating a clear and specific vision with an emphasis on quality. Transformational leadership increases follower trust by showing concern for followers' needs, honoring agreements, demonstrating capability and persistence, and empowering and encouraging followers to make their own decisions.

Robinson and Rousseau (1994) state that the major change in the organizational employment relationship is the psychological contract between employer and employee. The psychological contract is defined as a set of promises committing one to future action: both the promises and the consideration exchange for it form the contract. Psychological contracts are subjective beliefs or perceptions about promises and acceptances. The employee and the employer may have different beliefs "about what each owes the other" (p. 246).

Trust is measured by perceptions of organizational justice. Violations of psychological contracts are related to procedural and distributed injustice. Unfulfilled promises by the employer deprive the employee of desired outcomes and lead to perceptions of unfair outcomes, inequity, or distributive injustice.

Elangovan and Shapiro (1998) state that trust "is important and useful and a range of organizational activities such as teamwork, leadership, goal setting, performance appraisal, development of leader relationships, and negotiation" (p. 547). Betrayal represents "a shadow of trust and loyalty—part and parcel of social life" (p. 547); it includes the abuse of trust and violation of social and organizational norms.

In an effort to conceptualize these psychological contract concepts relative to person-organization fit, for consulting and human resource management (HRM) applications, research suggests that it will be older employees who report higher frequencies of violations of that psychological contract (Bocchino, Hartman, & Foley, 2003). They will be employees who generally just don't fit in with the organization's culture. They may have shorter time on the job than you'd expect – this is sometimes an "alert" flag when I am supporting a client company in a hiring initiative. An older job seeker, with repeated short stints of employment on his or her resume, shows that that person may have a hard time committing to and engaging with the values of an organization. This is low "person–organization congruence" and in an employment relationship, the employee is more likely to report frequent violations of the psychological contract. In other words, that person brings myriad expectations to the work relationships and you cannot, and do not, satisfy them.

Bullying

Next is the old familiar, bullying. Along with incivility, bullying emerges with the highest degree of crossover between academic research in the management and human resource development fields and popular press/applied writing. Psychological abuse includes those behaviors that involve sustained hostile verbal and nonverbal interactions, excluding physical contact. In one study of healthcare professionals, over 90% of those surveyed had experienced verbal abuse in the workplace (Sutton, 2007).

Bullying and psychological or verbal abuse are often grouped into the phrase "toxic workplace environment." The *Oxford English Dictionary* defines "toxic" as having the effect of poison. The popularity of research and popular press exploration of "toxic workplaces" demonstrates the concern and sense of urgency created by those workplaces. Specific to the HRM literature, Daniel (2009) addressed workplace bullying and psychological abuse, using the term "toxic environment." Daniel asserted that over 30% of HR professionals surveyed had observed behavior that violated their organization's ethical standards, company policy, or the law. So if one of your employees uses that phrase, or even the word "toxic," they're probably witnessing or experiencing bullying.

You can identify a department, group, or division in which bullying is likely to take place (the context for bullying) by the presence of chaos, opacity, low accountability, and overstretched capacity (Hodson, Roscigno, & Lopez, 2006). Imagine you're a Director, and you're thinking about one of your marketing managers, Jim. Jim has a team of eight highly skilled professionals of varying tenure and experience. Jim's group always seems to be running just ahead of a deadline, always barely avoiding a crisis. But neither you nor anyone else in the organization can clearly see why, or understand just what that group's priorities and threats are. Perhaps you've allowed Jim too much latitude since he was with you when you first got promoted. You've never really challenged Jim to explain the chaos and tension in the group, or forced him to comply with other organizational development initiatives, because his group *produces*. Your way of dealing with the drama is to deny Jim's repeated requests for an additional headcount, especially because the organizational engagement scores from that group remain consistently low. Here's the thing: stretched capacity, low accountability, low transparency, and high chaos lead to an environment for bullying. Jim's associates are probably having feelings of relational powerlessness, and being bullied on a regular basis – if not by Jim, by someone else on that team. What are they experiencing?

Bullying is the behavior of a person who, because they *can*, puts one or more targets into a submissive position, and seeks to keep the target powerless. The bully enjoys the influence and control he or she has over the target, because influence and control facilitate the bully's own personal objectives (Kusy & Holloway, 2009). Those objectives may serve the organization, and often do, but it happens at the expense of the target's dignity and personal power.

The research has shown that over 10% of all employees, in fact closer to 20%, have reported experiencing being bullied in the workplace (Hodson, Roscigno, & Lopez, 2006). The results of bullying are that targets and witnesses have psychological consequences – the consequences of coming into YOUR organization, every day. Those consequences mimic post-traumatic stress disorder (PTSD)!

Yes, PTSD, exactly the same as that suffered by war and prison camp survivors. This is no small matter. It is not to be brushed aside as "just stress" – stress is caused by long work hours, excessive workloads, or challenging work demands. It can be a normalized state, or it can be distress – but bullying is a very different thing. It is informal, subtle, and covert interpersonal behavior, unidirectional (it's not reciprocated by the target, as that person is usually of lower status or weaker power position), and specifically designed to torment, wear down, and frustrate another person (Hodson, Roscigno, & Lopez, 2006). It's a weapon, only used to hurt, never a tool capable of building. It's the "flexing your muscles" that a diva does, exerting his or her authority and influence or even throwing a temper tantrum unprovoked, simply to dominate others and command attention.

I recently saw a letter, signed, that went out to some 30 people via email. They were full-time employees familiar with the topic, and part-time employees who had no idea what was going on. Bullies require an audience, the bigger the better. When you confront them one-on-one, they tend to wilt, whine, or have something more pressing to do. The letter suggested that the organization would "be open to legal action" if the group proceeded with an agreed-upon action, implied that the people who had agreed on that action were misleading others and potentially behaving unethically, and verbally sneered at the way the action had been taken. It accused the coordinator of the original action of being "transparent and manipulative," putting "peer pressure" on others – when that accusation better fit the bully himself. I've seen such letters and emails a few times in my career. They're often wordy, couching nasty insinuations with formal language, and lots of "in my humble opinion" language. They often come from people my former HR Director would say "need to be kept away from sharp objects... and people." And email.

So what?

When people are the target of bullying, they don't feel seen, safe, OR valued. As a result you'll tend to see high turnover – very high turnover – in departments and on teams where there is a bully. You can reverse engineer it and take a look at where you're seeing high turnover, low engagement or job satisfaction scores on your surveys (you *are* doing regular surveys, right?), and then do some organizational diagnosis in that area. Don't hide from what you find! Your employees, associates, and clients will tell you that fish rots from the head down – in other words, they're looking at you and waiting for you to take the lead. They've already seen the bad behavior (or perpetrated the bad behavior!) and now they want to know what you're going to do about it.

Verbal abuse

"Are you a donkey?" Celebrity chef Gordon Ramsay famously berates contestants on an elimination/competition TV show, but in real life, verbal abuse is frighteningly prevalent in workplace environments. You may be thinking, "Come on, I had to pay my dues coming up, and people need to stop being so fragile and politically correct." In the recent U.S. presidential election, a candidate publicly mocked someone with a physical disability. The journal for the Society for Human Resource Management, *HR Magazine*, has been reporting for the last few years on how gay and transgender people are facing demeaning challenges to their rights to use facilities in their workplaces. The names people call one another in the workplace, and the ways they communicate, become "problematic" when they negatively affect productivity and performance. Employees' satisfaction with their jobs, and with their coworkers, is also negatively affected when they experience unpleasant or problematic workplace communication. Additionally, organizational commitment drops – which makes sense, right? You can hear the clock start ticking down on how long you will be willing to tolerate insults and disrespectful language in the workplace, whether from your boss or from a coworker in a culture where that behavior is tolerated.

I was working as a recruiter in a huge organization with a large HR division. The manager of the recruiting group was known to have been a pretty tough character, and I finally ran into it when I needed help dealing with a situation in which a hiring manager had promised three men promotions with salaries significantly higher than was the norm. After the compensation analysis was complete, I prepared offers for them and then found out that the hiring manager had offered them salaries $4,000 higher. This was outside his realm of authority, as it was the HR manager who approved final offers, as I understood it. But the manager was adamant that the company could find the money to pay them what he had offered rather than what the compensation group had prepared. His words were, "I know your manager, and I'll wait him out." Stumped, I took the requisition files to the manager and left them with him for review, and sure enough within a couple of days he submitted to the hiring manager's demands. I'm sure he was angry about that, but his way of expressing the anger was to bring the three files back to me in my shared workspace with four other contract recruiters present, and toss them onto my table while saying, "Give them the f*^%ing money." I was mortified.

Sofield and Salmond (2003) describe the lived experience of verbal abuse in a large, multi-hospital system, and determine the relationship between verbal abuse and intent to leave the organization. Their sample included 1000 nurses with a response rate of 46% using a mailed questionnaire. Over 90% of the respondents reported experiencing verbal abuse in the last month from physicians, patients, patients' families, peers, supervisors, and subordinates. The amount of abuse and the intent to leave were significantly related. Verbal abuse was directly related to decreased morale, increased job dissatisfaction, and higher turnover. In a healthcare environment, verbal abuse affects nurses' attitudes toward patient care, reduces teamwork, reduces efficiency, and leads to decreased accuracy. Frequent confrontations and general unease on the job result from concerns about safety and outcomes of care. This level of frustration leads to burnout, turnover, and decreased retention of experienced staff. Verbal abuse has been linked to poor long-term relationships, lower job satisfaction, lower relaxation and well-being in the workplace, mistrust, low self-esteem, and low perceived organizational support from staff and superiors. Verbal aggression stresses an individual's ability to use their coping mechanisms. Such ongoing stress is related to global health problems like hypertension, diabetes, coronary artery disease, depression, panic disorders, and PTSD. Sofield and Salmond did find that turnover and intent to leave were linked to verbal abuse.

Sutton (2007) makes the business case against tolerating "nasty and demeaning people" who make it difficult to recruit and retain the best employees, clients, and investors. In a quantitative study of 700 participants, 27% reported experiencing mistreatment by someone at work. A 2003 study of 461 participants working in the healthcare field indicated that 91% experienced verbal abuse. Psychological abuse in the workplace refers to a sustained display of hostile verbal and nonverbal behavior, excluding physical contact.

Some of the woes caused by jerks in the workplace include victims' and witnesses' hesitation to cooperate with them, or to deliver bad news to them. There is also the threat of retaliation from victims or witnesses that can lead to legal costs and damage to the organization's reputation. The actors, or jerks, face humiliation themselves when it comes out that they are bullies and can lead to job loss and long-term career damage.

So what?

Some of the consequences of entertaining bullies in the workplace include that management must spend time appeasing, counseling, and disciplining both the perpetrators and the targets of workplace incivility. There is a cost associated with the time spent calming victimized employees, customers, contractors, and suppliers. Additionally, management must spend time reorganizing the department and the teams so that the offenders do less damage. Finally, there is the time spent interviewing, recruiting, and training a replacement after a perpetrator leaves the company. There are also legal and HR costs associated with an organization's choice to entertain a workplace bully.

Uncivil workplace behaviors/workplace incivility

Hutton (2006) suggested that information about low-intensity uncivil behavior in the workplace should guide HR professionals and line managers to enact policies that prevent escalation of antisocial behavior. Civil, citizenship behaviors in the workplace involve building relationships, supporting one another, and empathizing. Uncivil or "bad" behavior in the workplace is termed "workplace incivility" in the research literature and there are numerous studies of this pervasive, low-intensity negative energy comprised of rudeness, discourtesy, and disrespect. Workplace incivility is a display of disregard for others, often including deliberate mistreatment, and it leads to disconnection, breach of relationships, and the erosion of empathy for others' experiences (Pearson, Andersson, & Porath, 2000). Johnson and Indvik (2001a, 2001b) agreed that anger, stress, and overwork represent significant antecedents to AWB, specifically incidents of rudeness, discourtesy, and disrespect – or, workplace incivility. They further identified costs of incivility that include turnover, turnover intent, decreased work effort, and increased anxiety.

In the last generation, we have seen a dramatic increase in the number of psychological diagnoses. Anxiety and depression are rampant, and many people in the workplace are either medicated or in therapy. This is wonderful – I highly value the field of psychology and support people's need to work through acute, or chronic, issues. I just cannot help but think, though, that the experience of work does not have to be something that wears away at individual identity and self-esteem. The field of psychology has given us several theories of motivation, and when people feel valued in the workplace, that experience increases the likelihood of their committing more deeply to the workgroup, and engaging more deeply in its purpose and values.

Toxic leadership has become a popular topic in the research literature, with Kusy and Holloway's 2009 book on *Toxic Workplaces* and YouTube videos on

Corporate Psychopaths. Janie Harden Fritz has published extensively on *Problematic Workplace Relationships* and Jean Lipman-Blumen has initiated a dialogue on the relationship between leaders and followers, including addressing the possibility of toxic followers. Toxic leaders create a poisonous effect on their environment, and manifest behaviors that are blatantly destructive to the norms, culture, climate, and resources of the organization. Toxic leaders, my friend Jean writes, show dysfunctional personal qualities and behave in ways that may be either intentional, with a desire to harm others in service to enhancing their own situation and image, or unintentional, borne of incompetence, carelessness, or recklessness. When we experience a toxic leader, we may believe or tolerate them when they choose to "mistake," or mislabel, their evil for a moral act.

Toxic followers choose to follow toxic leaders because, like a moth to a flame or an addict to a pusher, these individuals offer grand illusions. Toxic leaders promise certainty. They are decisive. They promise peace and calm, even in the midst of creating chaos and destruction. They represent comfort and the avoidance of pain and heartbreak, for the in-group.

Abraham Maslow (1943) gave us what is probably the most familiar, yet least empirically supported, theory of human motivation. It has endured for decades, so we should probably address it here – it is the hierarchy of needs, with Physiological needs (food, sex) at the bottom of a pyramid, topped by basic Safety needs, then our need for Belongingness (fitting in and being accepted by a group), Esteem needs (recognition by others for our achievements), and then Self-Actualization (recognizing our own completion and our ability to mentor and nurture others). Later two other needs were added: the need to know and the need for beauty. In the workplace, Jean Lipman-Blumen (2005 and 2010) has theorized that we may find that employees are vulnerable and susceptible to toxic leaders because they have unmet psychological needs. Maslow's hierarchy suggests that when lower, more basic needs go unmet, then feelings of powerlessness may lead to a state of vulnerability. In that state of vulnerability and neediness, followers/employees may be willing to accept even the most obvious deception and replacement of parents. This is especially true when a person's parents are departed, or if there are unfulfilled parental relations. In order to fulfill those deep needs of safety, belongingness, and even the perceived esteem of others, followers accept the role of subordinate to a toxic leader. This is particularly true during times of crisis, rapid change, or turbulence in the person's personal life. In order to feel safe and secure, many people will abdicate their own responsibility for effective, moral, ethical, and intelligent decision-making. They accept the "lifeline" of someone else making the decisions, doing the hard things, rather than standing up for what they believe. Instead, they become toxic followers.

My colleague Janie Harden Fritz does research in the field of workplace communication, and she's identified that employee satisfaction and productivity may have increased over time: "professional employees' interaction is marked by incivility to an alarming degree" (Fritz, 2013, p. 5). This incivility has the "potential to ripple out to other spheres of life" (p. 7).

So what?

Research has shown that organizational commitment is negatively correlated to problematic communication in the workplace; the more rudeness and discourtesy you entertain, the lower your people's commitment is to the organization and its values.

Practical applications and consulting notes

I hope that as you've read through these terms and concepts, the practical translations and examples I've given have been helpful to you. Perhaps you've had an eye-opener or two. In Chapter 1, we addressed organizational commitment, which is the desirable factor, leading to low employee turnover and higher productivity, performance, and innovation. Here we've addressed the negative factors that employees face in the workplace, and provided suggestions for how to identify and deal with them. And to revisit Edgar Schein's worthy teaching (1990), there are secondary means and methods that you can build into your organization's design and structure, systems and procedures, and artifacts that can facilitate the culture you want. Artifacts are the visible, tangible components of your organization that convey culture, so physical design and decor, stories, legends, myths and symbols, formal statements like charters, mission statements, creeds, pictures on your website, anything that represents a manifestation of who you are as a group. Culture perpetuates and reproduces itself through socialization of new members, and members can discuss and explain their socialization process. Therefore, the question of why people stay in toxic workplaces finds its context in the definition of a culture and its norms, and in the identification of aberrant or uncivil behavior *for that culture*.

Key takeaways

1. AWB leads to psychological damage at the individual level, and organizational destruction at the group level.
2. Workplace violence such as assault (words), battery (touching), and sexual harassment are all illegal, and if they occur in your workplace, personal liability may attach to those who acted inappropriately as well as to those who knew and failed to act.
3. Key questions in the legal aftermath of such situations include: What did the company know? When did the company know? What action did the company take? And, finally, "Was that action timely?"
4. AWB is the large, overarching category for bad behavior in the workplace. It includes multiple types of behaviors: CWB, bullying, harassment, abusive supervision, verbal and psychological abuse, and workplace incivility.

5. All of these behavior types are violations of the psychological contract between employer and employee. Violations of the psychological contract lowers trust and reduces employees' perceptions of organizational justice.

"I don't know where we should take this company, but I do know that if I start with the right people, ask them the right questions, and engage them in vigorous debate, we will find a way to make this company great."

– Jim Collins, business consultant, author,
and lecturer (Roberts, 2016)

Recommended reading

Grenny, J., Patterson, K., Maxfield, D., McMillan, R., & Switzler, A. (2013). *Influencer*. USA: VitalSmarts, LLC.

Lencioni, P. (2006). *Silos, Politics and Turf Wars*. San Francisco: Jossey-Bass.

Patterson, K., Grenny, J., McMillan, R., & Switzler, A. (2002). *Crucial Conversations*. New York: McGraw-Hill (2nd edition 2012).

Patterson, K., Grenny, J., McMillan, R., Switzler, A., & Maxfield, D. (2013). Crucial *Accountability: Tools for Resolving Violated Expectations, Broken Commitments, and Bad Behavior* (1st ed. titled *Crucial Confrontations*). USA: VitalSmarts, LLC.

Let's make this #Interactive – Here's a challenge: pick a book, get it, and connect with the author on LinkedIn and/or follow them on Twitter. Let them know you read their book, and ask them a question about it. #Dialogue #WPS #WhyPeopleStay

---

4
WHAT THE RESEARCH HAS SHOWN

While this book is based on a real research study, and has a theoretical basis, it is perfectly reasonable to compare why people stay in workplaces where they have experienced antisocial workplace behavior (AWB) to why people stay in dysfunctional relationships. Low self-esteem, lack of other options, financial dependence – all of these are easily understood reasons for why people stay in unfortunate, unhealthy relationships. And all of them appear in the organizational context as well. During the research phase for this book, average people would strike up conversation with me when they saw me parked at a table in Panera Bread or Starbucks and ask what I was working on; as soon as I said I was researching why people stay in workplaces where they've experienced AWB, everybody had an answer. It often seemed that people were all too ready to give a pat response that would (I guess) eliminate the need for any further study. They'd say, "that's easy, they stay for the money" or "they stay 'cause they need a job!" Common sense, right? But you know that common sense isn't all that common.

So, how can you parlay that knowledge into more effective people-management and people-development? How can you ensure that YOUR team feels seen, safe, and valued in your organization? Easy. As Vince Lombardi, legendary professional football coach, said, "Build for your team a feeling of oneness, of dependence on one another and of strength to be derived by unity" (Roberts, 2016). How to do that? Consult the evidence. Observe your team. Document the culture. Interrogate the data. Or read this book and let me do it for you.

> "No man is wise enough by himself."
>
> – *Titus Maccius Plautus,*
> *Roman playwright (Roberts, 2016)*

By the numbers

One study in the late 1980s justified studying AWB this way: with statistics. In a quantitative analysis of almost 200 people, Robinson and O'Leary-Kelly found that 42% of the women in the study had reported instances of sexual harassment at work. If we can generalize from this study – and for the moment, let's do that – then there are some chilling facts to consider here. Think of it – almost half of the female workforce, which is almost half of the workforce altogether, reported having been sexually harassed. As an HR professional you would go straight to "OMG, imagine the work stoppages for investigations." As in-house counsel or a C-suite resident you'd be thinking, "How much is all that costing?" Hundreds of thousands, even millions of dollars. In both cases you'd be on point (see the section on Zero Tolerance in Chapter 3). And that was 30 years ago.

The study continued with data to show that 75% of employees had stolen from their employers. How many associates do you have? One hundred? A thousand? Ten? Just think, most of them (statistically speaking) may have stolen from you. It may have been some small thing, but over time, and across the whole organization, that's a significant impact. Is it an acceptable loss? Shrinkage? Or a destructive and toxic organizational culture, a norm in your workplace?

This eye-opening study used self-report data from surveys to assess the predictive impact of organizational citizenship and loyalty on individual AWB. That means that you are currently relying on associates' goodwill to create norms and reinforce values that prohibit negative behaviors in your organization. Lying, gossip, withholding effort, disengagement, absenteeism, and other behaviors that hurt individuals and/or organizational property are all negatively correlated with citizenship and loyalty. So can you encourage those, the good traits, to counteract the possibility of bad behavior in your workplace? Absolutely. Front-load the group experience with rich, positive, prosocial cultural artifacts and reward behaviors that reflect those values. Encourage managers to support, train, and encourage those behaviors.

The research has proven that this approach works. Creating and managing an ethical culture can prevent and reduce the presence of AWB in your organization. Robinson and O'Leary-Kelly (1988) found that workgroup context does influence the AWB of individual employees. That is, "as the richness of the group experience increases, members become more likely to match their level of antisocial behavior to that of the group.... Groups displaying high levels of prosocial behavior encourage such behavior by their members" (pp. 667–668). The authors state, "A strong work group can be conceptualized as a setting that exists at the intersection of the individual and the organization. The group provides a social context that is critical to the individual's interpretation of organizational level systems" (pp. 669–670). You can design an ethical culture and reinforce it, so that at the individual level your associates are less likely to betray the group norms.

Who is this Norm?

What, not who. *Norms* are the set of expected, acceptable, "normal" behaviors in a specific workplace or group. Kane and Montgomery (1998) offer a description of organizational norms as behavioral expectations of fairness and interpersonal consideration within the group that determine individuals' attitudes and behavior. Their conceptual study of disempowerment as a workplace phenomenon addressed the growing popularity of employee empowerment and its impact on organizational outcomes. In the human resource management literature, Kane and Montgomery (1998) proposed factors related to expectations and norms in the workplace. Specifically, based on procedural and interactional justice perceptions, the stronger an individual's own norm of consideration for others, the more that individual will expect reciprocal consideration from others and experience disempowerment when this norm is violated. Kane and Montgomery (1988) further proposed that trust expectations created norms based on prior experiences of considerate interactions. These would be violated and a state of disempowerment enacted when the employee's expectancy for continued considerate treatment goes unmet.

According to Schneider (1987), the people in the organization define the norms, as an organizational environment represents a function of the persons behaving in it. Members are attracted to, selected by, and remain in a specific work environment; they are not randomly selected or permanently assigned. Schneider (1987) proposed the thesis that individual personality attributes and behaviors contribute more to organizational behavior than do the organization's external environment, technology, or organizational structure. The thesis suggests that a workplace environment, E, is a function (f) of the persons (P) behaving in it (B), such that $E = f(P,B)$. Schneider (1987) proposed that an experimental setting will not suffice for, and is inappropriate for, studying relative contributions of individual traits or situations common in an organizational environment. Additionally, Schneider (1987) proposed that "people are not randomly assigned to real organizations; people select themselves into and out of real organizations" (p. 440). Therefore, if people who do not fit the organization's culture leave, then those who remain will appear somewhat homogeneous and adhere to strong group norms.

Simons (2002) also discusses the potential gap between espoused and enacted values, stating that organizational norms emerge from the employees' experience of trust stemming from word/deed alignment in their leaders and colleagues. In a conceptual paper investigating trust as a highly complex construct which underpins the reciprocal commitments between employees and their employers, Simons enumerates multiple behavioral antecedents which create employee perceptions and combine with their interpretations of those behaviors, leading to specific consequences of a concept that Simons describes as behavioral integrity. Those consequences include specific individual-level organizational outcomes, such as employee willingness to promote and implement change, intent to stay, organizational citizenship behaviors, and employee performance (Simons, 2002). Identifying the definitions and interrelationships between trust, credibility, psychological contracts, and hypocrisy, Simons suggests that behavioral integrity represents a perceived, ascribed trait that shows consistent alignment between a colleague or supervisor's words and deeds. In this dissertation, participants may allude to this construct of behavioral integrity in their descriptions of colleagues' and leaders' enacted work values and ethics.

Forret and Love (2008) investigated the impact of distributive justice, procedural justice, and interactional justice on employee and organizational outcomes, including job satisfaction, organizational commitment, as well as OCB, productivity, and withdrawal behaviors. Forret and Love (2008) further investigated the relationship of perceptions of justice as independent variables (distributive, procedural, and interactional justice) to coworker trust and morale at the group level of analysis. By analyzing survey data gathered from 264 employees at six small companies in the Midwestern U.S., Forret and Love controlled for gender, marital status, education, position, and company tenure. Organizational justice as a concept is based on fairness perceptions. Distributive justice is defined as perceived fairness of outcomes received, while procedural justice is defined as perceived fairness of company procedures used to determine those outcomes. Interactional justice is defined as the manner in which results are explained. It addresses the "quality of interpersonal processes and treatment of individuals (i.e., were they spoken to with sincerity and sensitivity) as well as the extent to which the reasons behind the outcome are explained" (p. 249). The three sub-constructs of organizational justice are interrelated but have been determined to be empirically distinct, accounting for "unique incremental variance" (p. 249). Distributive justice predicts outcome satisfaction, withdrawal, and OCB. It has also been associated with job and pay satisfaction, satisfaction with management, trust in organization, and trust in manager. Procedural justice predicts outcome satisfaction, job satisfaction, performance, organizational commitment, withdrawal, and counterproductive work behaviors, cooperative conflict management, aggression toward management, and trust in management. Interactional justice related to evaluations of authority figures, job satisfaction, OCB, outcome satisfaction, commitment, withdrawal behavior, and performance. Additionally, it predicts supervisor relationship quality, intent to quit, and intent to reduce work effort.

Justice perceptions have been associated with quality of coworker relationships. Trust in coworkers is defined as holding confident positive expectations in situations involving risk with coworkers. Trust has received significant attention in management research, leading to empirical determination of its relationship to increased organizational commitment, overall workplace trust, greater proactive behavior in the workplace, and lower intent to quit. Forret and Love (2008) found support for all of the hypotheses in their cross-sectional field study, with positive associations and regression analyses showing that each variable predicted trust. Longitudinal research would show how justice perceptions influence coworker trust, but this cross-sectional self-report survey study left room for common method variance. Forret and Love (2008) made recommendations for increasing perceived procedural justice, suggesting that managers ensure procedures are fair, involve employee input, and allow for formal appeals mechanisms. They suggest that to improve distributive justice, managers should help employees understand how organizational compensation works so that the employees understand reward allocation. Management should get a better understanding of what their employees actually view as rewards, to make sure that distribution is fair. To improve interactional justice, managers must treat employees with respect and dignity regardless of performance level, employing active listening without defensiveness when questioned.

McShane and von Glinow (2009) suggest that the trust concept can be broken down into three levels: calculus-based, knowledge-based, and identification-based trust. Calculus-based trust, while a mouthful, is simply based on calculating risk; just as one plus one equals two, in the employment exchange relationship there are clearly defined deterrents to certain behaviors, an if-then relationship. If an employee behaves in this or that way, then there will be a punishment to follow. This level of trust is fragile and limited, completely dependent on fear of discipline. In other words, it does not come from the heart of the individual. It is cognitive.

The second type or level of trust is knowledge-based, which invokes the history of the relationship between the employee and the manager, the team, or the organization itself. It starts at a cognitive level, and begins to get to the heart of the individual, in that it is based on the predictability of the relationship. It is a robust form of trust that develops over time and requires consistency and ethical behavior on the part of the superior. Such behavior strengthens the psychological contract and the standing, the level of "credit," that the manager and organization hold in the employee–employer relationship.

The third type or level of trust is identification-based, suggesting that I trust you because we share the same values, we have a common mental model (world-view, or paradigm), we are singing from the same sheet of music. Identification-based trust suggests that the individual takes on the "us-ness" of the team, the organization, and willingly subjugates his identity and personal goals to those of the team or company. This is the deepest and most powerful level of trust, and it is the level at which the most serious injuries occur in the emotional relationship an associate has with the organization. This is where the psychological contract gets broken. This is where the expectations of care and development get neglected, and wither like an unwatered plant. Unfortunately, this can happen rather early in the employment relationship, because contrary to popular belief, employees don't join an organization and get assigned to a team and slowly build trust up from the calculus-based level to the identification-based level. To the contrary! While some people have a higher propensity to trust than others, employees generally come into a workplace relationship with the deepest, most significant level of trust; they come in with high expectations, and then begin to experience "declining trust" (McShane & von Glinow, 2009) over time. This decline may be due to specific experiences of failed expectations and broken commitments, and it may be due to a general atmosphere of toxicity, based on their observations of the workplace overall.

According to Appelbaum and Roy-Girard (2007), a "toxic culture" includes similar artifacts (symbols, language, rituals, assumptions, and behaviors). In their literature review, Appelbaum and Roy-Girard explore the concepts of "toxic leader," "toxic manager," "toxic culture," and "toxic organization" via their effects on the organization and its employees. They describe deviant behaviors such as "absenteeism, theft, unproductiveness and unethical practices" as the retributive effects of layers of toxicity (p. 18). Appelbaum and Roy-Girard suggest that in a toxic culture, the artifacts represent explicit and implicit norms set up to reward uncivil behavior. Toxic organizations, they state, thrive on control, a constant state of crisis, problem-solving procedures driven by fear, and poor internal communications. In Appelbaum and Roy-Girard's literature review, toxic leaders blamed others, covered up their own mistakes, avoided situational realities, only expressed positive emotions, refused to question their duties or operate outside the expectations of their roles, and sought at all costs to protect their image and that of the organization. Appelbaum and Roy-Girard (2007) suggest that toxic cultures engender deviant employee behaviors out of a sense of retribution; employees may engage in theft, sabotage, absenteeism, or withholding effort as a result of their experience of toxicity in the workplace.

Behavioral rationale

Darr (2005) states that civility represents a "rhetorical choice made by speakers within the constraints of normative behaviors" (abstract). In a content analysis of the debates in the U.S. Senate concerning the nomination of John Ashcroft for Attorney General, Darr questioned the commonly accepted norm of civility in Congressional rhetoric and debate. More recently, female U.S. Senator Elizabeth Warren was interrupted and shut down while reading a letter on the Senate floor, causing wide protests of the perceived incivility with which she was treated. Civility may represent an organizational norm, or behavioral expectation within a group implying obligation. As a result, people in organizational groups and teams may report specific norms of communication or civility. Darr suggests that civility relates closely to compromise, reciprocity, and an attitude of respect for fellow participants in dialogue. Name-calling, antagonism, and labeling demonstrate "rudeness and a general unwillingness to cooperate" (2005, p. 318).

Individual values and ethical workplaces

For years, I (like many others) used the terms "values" and "ethics" interchangeably. Once I began teaching Organizational Behavior, I was able to separate the two and differentiate them for others. Values represent a set of relatively stable, evaluative beliefs about what is good or bad, right or wrong, that reside within the individual and govern our preferences for specific behavior or courses of action. Ethics are specific schools of thought which help us to determine what is good or bad, or right or wrong, to which we may subscribe and that guide us in our choices of behavior or courses of action. Still close, right? Schwartz (1992) summarizes five formal features that recur in most definitions of values:

- values are concepts or beliefs;
- values pertain to desirable end states or behaviors;
- values transcend specific situations;
- values guide our selection or evaluation of behavior, people and events; and
- values are ordered by their relative importance.

Ideally, the values we *espouse*, or say we believe in and live by, will match up with our *enacted* values, or those values that we manifest through our behaviors, actions, and decisions. Our habitual behaviors are usually consistent with our values, because we aren't thinking about how we look to others when we follow our habits (yielding the right of way to pregnant women or elders, for example, or holding doors for others). But our conscious behaviors are often inconsistent with our espoused values, because those values tend to be highly abstract constructs. Our decisions and behaviors are obviously and visibly linked to our values when we are mindful of our own values – when we have done the work to surface the top three or four key values by which we choose to live. There is also an obvious connection when we have logical reasons to apply our values in a situation, meaning there is some moral or ethical challenge involved. This is a phenomenon called ethical sensitivity, researched by Rest and others, that indicates the need for our values to be congruent with the ethical principles to which we subscribe.

Gini (2010) suggests that "moral leadership" and "business ethics" represent academic oxymorons, as neither term is credible in popular culture. Both represent ideals rather than reality. For this reason, I am particularly passionate about teaching my business school students about several different ethical perspectives, summarized here, even though I am not a philosopher and do not claim to do justice to them. My only goal is to equip these 19- to 21-year-olds with a nutshell view of ethical perspectives, one or more of which they may encounter in their workplaces and leadership training programs. To that end I encourage you to view the short videos on ethical perspectives available on YouTube, or to look up the names (what did we ever do before Internet search engines...) associated with each perspective and get comfortable with them for yourself.

A brief, adulterated, and wholly insufficient summary of ethical perspectives

- Utilitarianism – the decision maker seeks to achieve a conclusion that represents the greatest good for the greatest number of people. He or she seeks to maximize his/her own pleasure or self-interest; the decision maker will always somehow be counted in the greatest number. This perspective focuses on the consequences of the decision maker's actions, not on the actions themselves. The decision maker will weigh the costs and benefits of different decision options, and select the option that promises the greatest net utility. Although he or she may accept advice, or even consult with others, the decision maker will make the decision largely in isolation. The problem with this approach is that it ignores the morality of the means, which may or may not be justified by the end. *Jeremy Bentham, John Stuart Mill*

- Individual rights/Social perspective – the decision maker seeks to achieve fundamental entitlements in society. Everyone is entitled to certain specific rights and privileges. In this perspective, the decision maker seeks to conform to social norms and cultural demands, largely to avoid punishment or ostracism. He or she will take the action that most closely conforms to the expectations of the larger reference group, or to society as a whole. In essence, the reference group is making the decision, via the decision maker. The problem here arises when we consider different needs and demands – for example, the needs of different stakeholders in an organization, or the rights of one apartment resident compared to the rights of another. *Rawls.*

- Deontological perspective – this is the moral approach to ethics. It suggests that moral and spiritual values should drive decision making. This is the "categorical imperative" about which Kant theorized in the seventeenth century. Some actions are just wrong, and a discerning adult can tell right from wrong. The decision maker in this perspective seeks to adhere to moral and ethical considerations above all else. He or she will use emotion and value judgments to reject courses of action that violate moral and ethical codes by which the decision maker lives. Then, the decision maker will select courses of action that adhere to those codes. The individual makes the decision in the context of the group, guided by moral and ethical principles. Often the deontologist will reference sacred texts or religious figures who have modeled and taught specific behavioral patterns. The problem here is that in a diverse, or tolerant, environment, whose God, and whose rules, apply? *Immanuel Kant*

- Distributive justice – under this perspective, the decision maker feels that people who are similar in relevant ways should receive similar benefits and burdens. Inequalities in society are permissible under a distributive justice perspective, if and only if those inequalities benefit the least well-off in society. *John Rawls*

These are just a few of the many philosophical approaches to ethics and ethics training, but I share them here because perhaps in your organization "things" are done, decisions are made, that make complete sense, but no one has ever given a name to them. Perhaps your organization was formed by, and continues to be led by, people that follow one of these ethical perspectives. Perhaps it would be useful to your employees, the people who follow your lead and for whom you set the tone, to know and understand the ethical perspective to which their organizational leaders subscribe. Just a thought. And imagine the impact of that! I have been pleased to work directly with executives who sought to do what I call "surfacing" strategy days, in which we work to identify individual values, let those settle in, and then move forward to identify and clarify the ethical perspective to which they subscribe (again, using just the barest descriptions, above – this isn't a Master's course on philosophy and business ethics). It can be an eye-opening experience – why should people stay in your organization when you have several different top leaders following several different ethical perspectives? If your organization can state a list of "values," but cannot clearly demonstrate how you manifest those values as a corporate community, you are sending mixed messages to your employees: "This matters. But really, it doesn't." Helping organizational leadership teams get clarity about their ethical orientation has led to some real "ah-ha!" moments. Particularly with regard to why employees feel their companies experience low productivity and performance.

Ethical culture and predictable behavior

Gini (2010), critic of the "business ethics" concept, further states that in a 1990 survey, 68% of participants identified unethical behavior by executives as the primary cause of decline in business standards, productivity, and success. Because of their perceptions of low ethical standards on the part of executives, workers felt justified to respond in kind. This led to increased absenteeism and petty theft, worker indifference, and poor job performance. Respondents indicated that they spent 20% of their time on the job goofing off; one in six drank alcoholic beverages or used drugs at work, and only one in four gave their best effort at work.

Organizational members – both leaders and followers – should have some degree of ethical sensitivity. Just as humans, we are able to recognize the presence of, and determine the relative importance of, an ethical issue. As I ask my students about different scenarios in class, "Is this even an ethical issue?" For example, the student who goes to the professor's office hours, see the prof is not in the office but goes in and sits down only to see the exam master copy out on the prof's desk. The roommate who hates the artwork you've hung in a shared space. Is this an ethical issue? The employee who has a coworker call in and say, "I'm on my way, can you please clock me in, I'm almost there?" The manager who knows that his project is going to come in over budget and late to schedule, which may damage his promotability, so he attributes the lateness and shortcomings to someone else. The colleague who is enjoying a romantic relationship with a coworker. The salesman who hasn't met his quota, but who has access to the sales tracking spreadsheet and can alter it to save his job for another month. Is this an ethical issue?

In addition to a person's ethical sensitivity, there are characteristics outside the individual that influence his or her ethical conduct. The moral intensity of the situation, as with the examples above, for instance. To what degree does each issue demand the engagement of our ethical principles and decision-making skills? If the colleague in the romantic relationship is married, or superior to the coworker, there is some moral intensity involved. The salesman who is tempted to alter the spreadsheet is facing some pressure, but there is definitely moral intensity in that situation. Finally, the situational influences around the person definitely matter. What if the manager facing a late, over-budget project works for a company that loudly proclaims its adherence to honesty, trustworthiness, and supporting its employees? In such a situation, that manager will feel pressure not to blame someone else, but to own the failing.

However, Price (2010) states that ethical failures in leadership represent cognitive malfunctions, not volitional decisions. These cognitive malfunctions are attributable to "mistaken moral beliefs" rather than unethical behavior motivated by selfishness (Price, 2010, p. 402). In some cases, the collective nature of the ends to which the leaders commit on behalf of their group, followers, and organizations justify the means to achieve those ends. The collective good energizes and empowers the leader as well. Leaders may believe they are justified in making exceptions of themselves, and excluding out-group others from the protections of morality. Price offers "an analysis of the challenges to determining what morality demands of leaders, from the perspective of leaders" (2010, p. 403). How ought leaders and influential followers to act, especially when the social norms and group or organizational expectations may be vague? Price suggests that they should restrict the exceptions they allow for themselves, permitting themselves to operate outside the group or social norms only when they do so "to the pursuit of inclusive ends... and publicize their reasons for deviating from the requirements of morality" (2010, p. 403).

Creating, and maintaining, an ethical workplace culture can lead to being able to predict the behavior of your employees and associates. But there are several specific structures you should have in place in order to ensure that your people feel seen, safe, and valued. Employees, in fact I would generalize to say all people, want to feel like they are "good people" working for a "good company." How to establish this goodness, then?

Number one – you need an ethical code of conduct. You must spell out exactly what ethical behavior looks and sounds like in your organization. This may require starting with focus groups to get an understanding of what your employees currently believe and understand about the ethical environment. The recent spate of sexual harassment allegations across the country, primarily in the entertainment industry, is a cautionary tale about establishing and enforcing an ethical code of conduct. Next, you must support that code of conduct through ethics training – companywide, mandatory, and engaging all employees at all levels. There should be, as a policy, a set of ethics officers in place and, preferably, an anonymous ethical complaint system. And finally, there should be a very clear set of behaviors modeled by ethical leaders, and artifacts that document those behaviors. Remember that artifacts are the visible symbols of what your organization believes and preserves, so... plaques, awards, pictures, bonuses, all of these are things that may resonate with employees and represent your organization's ethical culture. And again, reinforce the structure above with frequent, mandatory reviews using the simple four-step ethical decision-making model (Rest's model works well for this and translates easily into workshops and coaching sessions). That is:

1. Encourage/develop ethical sensitivity – Is there an ethical problem here? We can't solve a moral problem until we know it exists. Ask yourself, "Am I *feeling* morally uncomfortable?" This is the emotional level at which participants identify whether someone who will be affected by the decision may possibly be harmed. Is there conflict here between teams, between the individual and the good of the group, between truth and loyalty/respect, justice and mercy? In working with my clients, I help them enhance ethical sensitivity through active listening, role play, imagining unfamiliar perspectives, and other activities. I force them to avoid euphemisms (so I call them on their -isms and their facades!), I do not excuse any misbehavior in our sessions and challenge them to draw similar boundaries for their teams, and I model practicing humility and openness to other points of view. (Note: it's hard to teach humility.) The outcome or deliverables from this phase of ethical decision making is simply a decision on whether or not your roommate's artwork, or your coworker's request to clock him in early, is an ethical challenge.

2. Practice ethical judgment – ask questions about how to handle the specific problem, and analyze each answer for its appropriateness and adherence to your ethical standard. Incorporate others' input to ensure a balanced approach. The inputs for this stage of ethical decision making really just include the decision from stage one. Either you're facing an ethical issue, or you're not. But at this stage of the process, I have my corporate client teams generate and evaluate options for viability and evaluate against the ethical perspective to which you subscribe. At this stage I caution against several ethical blind spots:

    a   We tend as people to overestimate our own ethicality.
    b   We tend to forgive our own unethical behavior.
    c   We tend to follow in-group favoritism, supporting those who subscribe to the same ethical perspective.
    d   We tend to have an implicit prejudice against the perceived "Other" who has caused the situation.
    e   We tend to make our ethical judgments based on outcomes rather than on the process.

Deliverables at this stage primarily involve the one decision response to the ethical dilemma.

Employ an ethical focus – this is where it gets difficult – you selected a decision, now you have to make up your mind to follow through on it, even though it may be hard to do. Challenging one's own intentions is never easy, but questioning how peers and respected others might act may help solidify the position. Inputs to this stage include the decision from stage two, and the motivations, values, cognitive attitudes, as well as the external environmental factors and emotional episodes relevant to the situation. The cautions in this step are that human self-interest and hypocrisy may undermine this stage. It is possible to create an ethically rewarding environment and use it to market your corporate culture to ethically sensitive candidates. Deliverables at this stage are that the individual (client, manager, executive) is focused on a clear decision, and (ideally) motivated to follow through on their ethical decision choice.

3. Finally – TAKE ETHICAL ACTION – the hardest step of all. Following through on a moral decision requires, and shows, courage. It may be uncomfortable or frightening, but if it's the right thing to do, you do it. The input to this stage is a reinforced, considered ethical decision. The process at this point requires follow through; leaders and influencers must work to overcome any opposition factors and resist distractions. I often have to work with clients to proceed through the steps of managing an effective change initiative, because it is at this point that the executive team must develop and execute tactics to reach the goal of a new state of norms and behaviors. The deliverables at this stage are consistent, predictable ethical behavior across the organization and a documented pattern of ethical action.

In the Fritz, Arnett, and Conkel (1999) study described earlier, the researchers state that organizational culture represents "a powerful background influence on employee ethics" (p. 290). They suggested that an ethical culture requires an environment, organizational form, and history that define it as ethical. For the associate level, Fritz et al. found that managerial example and organizational enforcement did predict awareness of organizational ethics, but talking with coworkers did not. At the middle management and upper management levels, managerial adherence to standards, organizational enforcement of standards, and talking with peers each represented significant contributors to awareness of organizational ethical values. Additionally, the researchers hypothesized that these three independent variables would predict organizational commitment, using items from Mowday, Steers, and Porter's (1979) instrument. At the associate level, this hypothesis was partially supported using regression analysis; managerial example and organizational enforcement contributed to organizational commitment, but communication with peers did not. At the middle and upper management levels, the hypothesis received full support.

Toxic managers represent a subset of toxic leaders, in Appelbaum and Roy-Girard's study. These individuals destroy morale, reduce retention, intercept cooperative efforts, and limit information sharing. They may demonstrate unpredictable and disrespectful behavior to staff, and maintain a focus on schedule and budget, allowing no time for feedback or creativity. Toxic managers may be narcissistic, aggressive, or rigid.

In a sample of 307 working adult participants attending undergraduate night courses in a public university in the Southeastern United States, Penney and Spector (2005) found that job stressors linked to counterproductive workplace behaviors such as role ambiguity, role conflict, workload, organizational constraints, and interpersonal conflict. Their quantitative study replicated findings from previous research on counterproductive workplace behaviors (CWB) and the effects of workplace incivility on satisfaction and CWB. Penney and Spector hypothesized that the experience of job stressors, workplace incivility, organizational constraints, and interpersonal conflict at work would all negatively correlate with job satisfaction, but would positively correlate with the incidence of CWB. They also hypothesized that experienced workplace incivility, as reported in existing measures including the Workplace Incivility Scale by Cortina, Magley, Magley, and Langhout (2001) and interpersonal conflict, would be more strongly correlated with counterproductive workplace behaviors targeting other people (CWB-P) than with those targeting the organization (CWB-O). Further, Penney and Spector investigated the relationship between negative affectivity and CWB, and negative affectivity as a moderator between experienced job stressors and CWB. The researchers found that each of the job stressors correlated with the incidence of CWB.

Uhl-Bien and Carsten (2010) suggest that because the predominant message in the ethics discourse is that the responsibility for ethics rests with the leader, then followers may abdicate any responsibility for civil behavior and ethical obligation. Uhl-Bien and Carsten offer a model of upward ethical leadership. Their model teaches employees to display active responses to unethical leader behavior. If followers do not comply with leader directives, then they are considered insubordinate, risking punishment, sanctions, ostracism, and even expulsion from the organization (p. 366). In an unethical climate, a distorted definition of loyalty requires followers to go along and not cause trouble. Followers must not question the decisions of superiors, but only speak to superiors about positive things. Employees experience feelings of powerlessness and have minimal choice of response when they sense a lack of control over themselves and over others. In such situations, followers expect that their own behavior cannot determine the occurrence of desired outcomes (2010, p. 370).

Norms of communication and civility

Davis (1953) explained that top management should recognize the importance of communication as a continuous process both to and from workers. Using a phenomenological approach, Davis explored the paths information took as it spread throughout a single Midwestern U.S. organization with 60 management personnel and 600 employees. Formal communications include lessons learned, white papers, briefings, memos, and reports. The informal communication channel, or grapevine, depended on effective management communications through which the leader could influence the group's point-of-view. Grapevine communications traveled in varying patterns, in either a single-strand chain, a gossip chain, a probability chain, or a cluster chain. In all cases, though, Davis suggested that in informal communications, the expression of attitudes is as important as the transmission of information.

Crampton, Hodge, and Mishra (1998) surveyed 416 public and private employers with 50 or more employees in the Midwestern United States, receiving a 38% response rate; the survey revealed that lower level managers were more aware of the grapevine, and more informed about conditions affecting grapevine activity such as lack of formal communications and threatening or insecure environmental conditions. The majority of managers in the study (86%) agreed that managers should use the grapevine to improve formal communication systems, to provide accurate, adequate information, or to correct false information. Lower level managers recognize the presence of the grapevine the most (92%) and see the effect of the organizational environment on the grapevine's activity, for communicating negative information or to indicate mistrust.

Crampton, Hodge, and Mishra (1998) agree that the grapevine is the major informal communication medium in organizations, representing an inevitable part of organizational life. It demonstrates a natural consequence of people interacting to form informal networks, as the most significant of three levels of organizational communication: the informal grapevine represents 70% of organizational communication, followed by formal organizational communication and leader-level communications.

Guzley (1992) surveyed working adults to gauge organizational commitment related to perceptions of the organizational and communication climate, citing Mowday, Porter, and Steers (1982) regarding the predictive relationship of organizational commitment and organizational factors like turnover, absenteeism, and performance. In a survey of 250 employees with an average length of employment of 4.6 years in a Southwestern U.S. service organization, Guzley hypothesized that organizational commitment correlated with perceptions of the organizational climate, and that organizational tenure might moderate this relationship. Guzley viewed organizational commitment from two perspectives, as behaviorally oriented (externally motivated, such as a pension fund) or attitudinally oriented (internally motivated, as with internalization of organizational goals and values).

The construct of civility has come under investigation in multiple contexts, including Congress (Darr, 2005), the workplace (Pearson, Andersson, & Porath, 2000), and the judicial system (Cortina, et al., 2001).

Pearson, Andersson, and Porath (2000) collected five years of research via interviews and workshops in the United States with over 700 respondents, supplemented by an additional 775 surveys. Pearson, Andersson, and Porath define workplace civility as behavior that helps preserve norms of mutual respect in the workplace. Workplace norms represent the norms, or basic moral standards, of the community of practice at work. Norms differ across organizations, industries, and cultures. Civil workplace behaviors are fundamental to positively connecting with one another, building relationships, and empathizing. The opposite is workplace incivility, defined as rudeness, disregard for others and mistreatment that leads to disconnection, breach of relationships, and erosion of empathy. Norms represent a shared moral understanding among organizational members that allow them to cooperate, while "incivility is a violation of these norms" (Pearson, Andersson, & Porath, 2000, p. 126).

In a quantitative study of workplace incivility including incidents of disrespect, condescension, and degradation, Cortina et al. (2001) surveyed 1,180 public sector employees in a judicial complex in the Southwestern U.S., finding that over 70% of them reported experiences of workplace incivility over the previous five years. Study participants identified "daily hassles," or multiple routine nuisances that they view as threatening and that eventually impair the cognitive well-being of workplace participants.

In a review of the literature on civility and the professions, Fritz (2013) explains that civility in discourse demonstrates "justice in the public sphere… [as it represents] hope for those in positions of low status and power, because civility as a normative practice calls those who have power into account" (p. 2). Civility among colleagues "contributes to the well-being of others with whom one comes into contact in the course of daily life… [it] protects and promotes respect" (Fritz, 2013, p. 3). Fritz identifies "problematic workplace behaviors" that include social undermining, interpersonal harassment, and bullying, as well as backstabbing and swearing.

Organizational commitment

Steel and Ovalle (1984) stated that behavioral intentions represent the single "most direct and immediate cognitive antecedents of overt behavior" (p. 673). Organizational commitment bears a consistent, significant predictive relationship with employee turnover, along with age, tenure, job content satisfaction, overall job satisfaction, and behavioral intent to quit. Their meta-analysis included studies that used empirically established operational definitions of each of these constructs, and they found that general economic conditions might affect turnover decisions and represent a potential moderator between intent and actual turnover decision. Other demonstrated moderators include military or civilian status, blue- or white-collar job status, and the time interval between measurement of intent and actual termination of employment.

Meyer, Allen, and Gellatly (1990) suggested that different views of commitment have emerged, "making it unlikely that any one approach will dominate" (p. 710). Early research led to a definition of commitment that highlighted the strength of a person's organizational identification and involvement, or a person's tendency to maintain a certain level and type of activity once begun. In a quantitative study that triangulated methodology by using three samples of employees from different organizations and both cross-sectional and longitudinal data, Meyer, Allen, and Gellatly collected 337 survey questionnaires

for the first cross-sectional study, and 292 for the second. Then, 308 participants in the longitudinal study provided pre-entry questionnaires about their
work expectations. Then, post-entry questionnaires were administered at one
month, six months, and 11 months on the job. Responses were received from
276, 247, and 210 individuals at post-entry survey administration. Using validated instruments for affective commitment and continuance commitment, the
study sought to provide "clarity in the conceptualization and measurement of
organizational commitment" (p. 716). Confirmatory factor analysis supported
maintaining the distinction between the two kinds of commitment, as well as
for the utility of the two separate scales.

Meyer and Allen (1991) continued to isolate affective and continuance commitment in a review of the literature supporting their conceptual model, showing
that in the former, employees stay in an organization by choice, while in the latter
they stay out of necessity. Affective commitment was "best predicted by work
experiences that promote feelings of comfort in the organization (e.g. organizational dependability) and personal competence (e.g. pension benefits). Continuance commitment, on the other hand, corresponds more highly with measures of
potential loss (e.g. pension benefits) and lack of alternatives" (p. 710). Each of the
two subscales for continuance commitment reflects the "specific source(s) of the
(perceived) cost associated with leaving" (p. 711).

Guzley (1992) surveyed working adults to gauge organizational commitment related to perceptions of organizational and communication climate, citing Mowday, Porter and Steers (1982) regarding the predictive relationship of
organizational commitment and organizational factors like turnover, absenteeism, and performance. Guzley viewed organizational commitment from two
perspectives, as behaviorally oriented (externally motivated, such as a pension
fund) or attitudinally oriented (internally motivated, as with internalization of
organizational goals and values).

In Shore and Wayne's (1993) longitudinal quantitative study involving 276
pairs of employee–supervisor dyads who responded to four surveys over a two-
year period, relationships emerged between affective commitment, continuance
commitment, perceived organizational support (POS), OCB, and impression
management. Data analysis confirmed that continuance commitment explained
a greater amount of OCB than did POS, and that continuance commitment was
associated with lower levels of OCB. Shore and Wayne conducted a quantitative study examining the relationships between affective commitment, continuance commitment, POS, organizational citizenship behaviors, and impression
management behaviors. Their sample of 276 pairs of employee/supervisor dyads
responded to four surveys over a two-year period and yielded support for the
hypothesis that continuance commitment explained more OCB than did POS.
Continuance commitment was also associated with lower levels of organizational
citizenship behaviors.

Shore and Wayne (1993) defined affective commitment as emotional attachment to an organization, such that an individual with strong affective commitment

identifies with, is involved in, and enjoys membership in the organization. Continuance commitment involves maintaining a consistent level of activity based on recognition of the opportunity costs associated with discontinuing the activity, commonly referred to as sunk costs or "lost side bets" (p. 774). Continuance commitment involves the need to belong because of what the employee has already sacrificed or given up in order to remain in the organization, and high levels of continuance commitment correlate with lower job performance. When an "employee's primary tie to the organization is need-based (continuance commitment), the employee engages in behavior that will help guarantee continued employment; nonetheless, such an employee is not likely to exert extra effort on behalf of the organization" (p. 775). Continuance commitment represents employees' "feelings of being stuck" (p. 776).

Dunham, Grube, and Castañeda (1994) performed a quantitative study with nine samples and 2,734 participants, using survey instruments to collect data about organizational commitment, perceptions of others' organizational commitment, perceptions of job dimensions, and participatory management. Their study found strong support for a three-dimensional construct definition of organizational commitment and support for the two separate dimensions of continuance commitment, personal sacrifices, and lack of alternatives. They identified a stronger significant relationship between tenure and lack of alternatives than between tenure and personal sacrifices, but questioned whether the impact of career "sunk costs" was independent of age and tenure. Dunham, Grube, and Castañeda suggest that sunk costs offer greater significance in light of what other organizations can offer to the employee considering a job transition. Some personal sacrifices, such as the loss of a vested pension plan, seem "less replaceable than… others, such as coworker relationships" (p. 378).

Dunham, Grube, and Castañeda (1994) called for further research on the normative commitment construct as a social norm, showing that on the normative commitment scale, six of the eight items focus on moral obligations to remain, two on the obligation to be loyal. They stated that a "theoretical explanation is necessary from both an intra-organizational perspective (i.e., what aspects of the work environment will lead employees to feel an obligation to reciprocate) and an extra-organizational perspective (e.g., the role of parental values). Normative commitment is probably influenced at least as much by early socialization and role modeling as by organizational experience" (p. 379).

Carson and Carson (1997) suggested that employees may want to change careers, but stayed for some degree of security. In the mid-to-late 1990s, 50% of United States companies eliminated jobs, over 400,000 jobs, and 40% of the managerial labor force expressed concern about job security. As a result, many employees reported that they stay in their jobs, perhaps out of desperation, as opposed to commitment. They may not identify with or feel emotionally attached to the organization, but they do nothing about changing their job. Carson and Carson explain this with the term "career entrenchment," defined as the tendency to stay in a vocation because of investments, psychological preservation, and a perception that there are few career opportunities. Some employees stay because leaving would mean sacrificing salary increases, paid holidays and vacations, retirements, and other benefits. "As organizational tenure increases, these economic 'side bets' accrue" (p. 63).

Meyer, Becker, and Vandenberghe (2004) identify several forms of commitment in their research: affective attachment to the organization, normative obligation to remain, and perceived cost of leaving (continuance). Affective commitment showed the strongest positive correlation with job performance, OCB, and attendance, followed by normative commitment. This type of engagement with the company develops through personal involvement, identification with relevant targets, and value congruence between the individual and the organization. Normative commitment "develops as a function of cultural and organizational socialization and the receipt of benefits that activate a need to reciprocate" (p. 994). Continuance commitment, though, develops through two psychological processes in the individual: as a result of side bets, explained as accumulated investments that the individual would lose if he or she discontinued their current job, and as a result of a lack of perceived alternatives to the current employment relationship.

Continuance commitment

"One often hears someone say, 'I work to take care of my family and so I don't stop to ask whether I like the work or not.' It may be that we burden our families unnecessarily by making them the excuse or reason why we hate our work" (Fox, 1994, p. 32).

Obeng and Ugboro (2003) indicate that minimal research exists on public sector levels or determinants of organizational commitment, of any type, at any level of analysis. Obeng and Ugboro (2003) define affective, normative, and continuance commitment. In their study of 289 public transit workers, the researchers found that the antecedents of organizational commitment in the public sector paralleled those in the private sector, e.g., education was negatively correlated with organizational commitment, particularly continuance commitment, because it opens up other opportunities. Affective commitment was found to be negatively related to tenure.

Normative commitment

Work can become a way of "trying to fulfill an unhealthy definition of who we are. For example, many men have been taught that their masculine identity is synonymous with their success as a breadwinner" (Fox, 1994, p. 33). For example, my own grandfather worked from the time he was a young teenager, maybe 14 years old, starting as kitchen help in a hotel and moving on to working at National Biscuit Company (Nabisco) for over 45 years. His entire perspective on work? You work to support your family. If you have to shovel manure from dawn to dark in order to get the paycheck needed to feed the family, that's what you do. He used more colorful language but you get the point. Perhaps you have people in your workplace whose perspective on work is equally... pragmatic, negative, and fatalistic? Those were the ways I viewed his attitude about work, but I kept those views inside. There was no way I'd criticize the man who had worked so hard, for so long, to provide for our family. But I always cringed when I thought about his description of work, and how it had influenced the things his daughter, my mother, said when I would call home and complain about this job, that boss, or some other work experience: "well, that's why it's spelled W – O – R – K, and not P – L – A – Y." Translated? Suck it up, buttercup. I learned that only so much sympathy would come from that source if I was complaining about work.

Actually, a better word than fatalistic or negative would be *normative*, as in, normative commitment. My grandfather, and many others of the Veterans/ Traditionalists generation (our elders) believed that work was a necessity and a privilege. The opportunity to work, to earn money that you could bring home and give to your wife to pay bills or buy groceries, was not to be disdained! It was not a right, it was a *privilege* and an *honor* and a patriotic *duty*. Perhaps you should read that with exclamation points and strong emphasis, because that's how strongly he and others of his generation (or strongly influenced by them) felt about working. It **did not matter** what the work was, or who else was at the work-place. All that mattered was at the end of the day your life, your time, and your contribution counted for something and that you were being compensated for the work you had done. Now your children could eat, your wife might not have to work two jobs, or at all. Work became validation, and identity, and a blessing.

The approach to work epitomized by this attitude is one that leads to a phe-nomenon called "career entrenchment." Career entrenchment represents resource allocation and justifying past investments in light of constricted career options. Possible coping mechanisms include exit, voice, loyalty, and neglect. Carson and Carson (1997) cite Rusbult and colleagues on the EVLN model of coping re-sponses used to moderate stress caused by work-related dissatisfaction. Exit rep-resents attrition from an entrapping career. It is often the most rational, but least used method because it means retirement or total withdrawal from the labor force. Voice represents actively and constructively trying to improve conditions by verbalizing concerns when labor force withdrawal is impossible. The voice response is more common when career enhancement is likely and the individual wants to preserve relationships with colleagues. The danger of the voice response is the threat of retaliation, loss of reputation, and the emotional cost of confron-tation. The individual may express voice internally to the organization or exter-nally to a professional organization. The loyalty response represents passively, but optimistically, waiting for conditions to improve. Cost of active engagement may be too high for the individual to engage in voice. Dangers of the loyalty response include skill atrophy, boredom, and depression. An individual displaying the loy-alty response may choose to demonstrate their loyalty through organizational cit-izenship behaviors. Neglect is the final response option, which involves passively allowing the situation to deteriorate. It involves reduced interest and effort in the job, frequent tardiness and absenteeism, increased errors, and inefficient use of work time.

Workers who focus on traditional career promotions represent linear career prototypes. These include the steady-state prototype characterized by stability in a vocational field. This individual uses minimal information to get a stable career concept that is rarely re-examined. A second prototype is the spiral career prototype in which an individual makes career moves every 5 to 10 years in pursuit of personal growth. This may shorten the time perspective during which an individual might feel entrapped. Third is the transitory career prototype in which individuals change positions more frequently because of the need for variety and stimulation.

Psychological preservation is associated with Festinger's theory of cognitive dissonance. It involves the individual seeking to alleviate the discomfort of inconsistent behaviors and attitudes. Attempts at psychological preservation are likely when individuals voluntarily and publicly select careers that are "sub optimal... Over more fitting alternatives" (Carson & Carson, 1997, p. 68). This is not the case if the individual has taken the only job available. Rationalization efforts and psychological preservation efforts increase as tenure lengthens, or if a career change will require significant time, effort, and money. While a poor labor market "and high unemployment negatively influence organizational turnover, they positively affect career changes" (p. 69).

Dessler (1999) found that organizational justice, specifically procedural justice, consistently correlated with organizational commitment, specifically affective commitment. Organizational justice also correlated positively with OCB. Employees are more committed to organizations that show a demonstrated commitment to their long-term career development (p. 62). To increase organizational commitment, Dessler recommends that organizations commit to people-first values and put that commitment in writing. Additionally, the company should clarify and communicate the organization's mission and ideology; use values-based hiring practices to build traditions; guarantee organizational justice through clear grievance procedures and two-way communications; and provide a sense of community through supporting employee development, celebrating achievements, and enriching employees' work experience.

Meyer and Herscovitch (2001) provided a conceptual model of workplace commitment, demonstrating its functionality as the force that binds an individual to a course of action that is of relevance to a particular target. Commitment can take different forms and have different target foci. It emerges at different levels of analysis, including at the level of team, department or manager, company or organization, occupational field, or directed toward a particular customer or union.

Obeng and Ugboro (2003) used established scales for affective, normative, and continuance commitment in their quantitative study of 289 public transit workers. They found that the antecedents of organizational commitment in the public sector paralleled those in the private sector. Specifically, education negatively correlated with organizational commitment, particularly continuance commitment, because it opens up other opportunities. Affective commitment negatively correlated with tenure.

Meyer, Becker, and Vandenberghe (2004) offered a conceptual paper, promoting a model in which commitment represents an energizing force for work motivation. They identified several forms of commitment in their research: affective attachment to the organization, normative obligation to remain, and perceived cost of leaving (continuance). Affective commitment showed the strongest positive correlation with job performance, OCB, and attendance, followed by normative commitment. This type of engagement with the company develops through personal involvement, identification with relevant targets, and value congruence between the individual and the organization. Normative commitment "develops as a function of cultural and organizational socialization and the receipt of benefits that activate a need to reciprocate" (p. 994). Continuance commitment, though, develops through two psychological processes in the individual: because of side bets, explained as accumulated investments that the individual would lose if he or she discontinued their current job, and because of a lack of perceived alternatives to the current employment relationship. If this is true, then participants in this study will provide insights into their types of organizational commitment.

Sinclair, Tucker, Cullen, and Wright (2005) found that affirmative commitment involves the employee's emotional attachment to their organization. They believe their values match the employer's values, identify with the company, and comply with a social exchange framework. Continuance commitment involves the employee's perception that "costs of leaving the organization exceed the costs of remaining" (p. 1280). Inducements offered by employers include job status, seniority, and benefits. Continuance commitment involves employee side bets, social and economic costs of leaving, such as relocation monies paid and social networks established. Inducements to stay increase continuance commitment but "when companies fail to address poor working conditions (e.g., safety issues, abusive supervision), workers are more likely to judge the costs of staying with the firm as exceeding the costs of leaving" (p. 1281).

Sinclair, Tucker, Cullen, and Wright (2005) suggested that employees with high or strong affective commitment and high continuance commitment are considered "devoted," with significant emotional attachments and many accumulated side bets; these employees have the strongest bond to the employer. Those individuals who have strong affective commitment and moderate continuance commitment have less of a need to stay and may be considered "involved." Attached employees have strong affective commitment and weaker inducements to stay, such as at a low-paying nonprofit job. Invested employees have stronger continuance commitment and moderate affective commitment, and experience more motivation from salary or accumulated side bets than from their emotional attachment. Those employees with some emotional attachment and need to stay are ambivalent, or "allied." Complacent employees are those with moderate affective commitment and weak continuance commitment, those who feel that they are "well-treated...but [they have] no particular need to remain with the organization" (p. 1281). Employees with low affective commitment may be trapped, if they have high continuance commitment signifying a strong need to stay, due to nontransferable job skills or advanced age. Alternatively, such employees may operate as free agents, if they have moderate continuance commitment. This signifies weak emotional attachment with some side bets. They would leave but might find it hard to get a new job. Finally, employees with low affective and low continuance commitment are "uncommitted," or alienated, demonstrating no desire to stay and no significant need to stay. This is the least desirable employment relationship.

Blau and Holladay (2006) proposed a four-dimensional measure of organizational commitment including affective, normative, and two measures of continuance commitment to address the sub-factors of accumulated costs and limited alternatives. In a three-year longitudinal study of 202 medical technologists, Blau and Holladay found affective commitment "based on values and a desire to act in ways that are consistent with being a member" (p. 694) of the organization. They identified a weak positive correlation between age and organizational commitment (all four dimensions) and a weak negative correlation between male gender and organizational commitment (all four dimensions). However, affective commitment represented a "strong positive desire to remain in one's occupation (profession)" (p. 700). Blau and Holladay suggest that lack of alternatives, a sub-dimension of continuance commitment, better fits as an antecedent rather than a component of the continuance commitment construct.

Grant, Dutton, and Rosso (2008) used a multimethod research study to demonstrate the proposition that employee/followers "form attachments to reciprocate what they have received from organizations" (pp. 898–899). This theory ignores the possibility of motivations outside that of rational self-interest. The researchers examined giving-based commitment with a two-part mixed methods study in a Fortune 500 retail organization, finding that affective commitment is strengthened by employees giving to support charitable programs, thus "seeing themselves and the organization in more prosocial, caring terms" (p. 899). The first phase of their study involved 40 qualitative interviews with managers and associates to identify the mechanisms that cultivate commitment. In the second phase, Grant, Dutton, and Rosso distributed surveys to employees of the same company, to test the hypothesized relationship between employee charitable giving and organizational commitment. With a sample size of 249 responses, affective commitment correlated most positively with the most favorable organizational and employee outcomes as opposed to normative and continuance commitment.

Taing, Granger, Groff, Jackson, and Johnson (2011) proposed a multidimensional measure of continuance commitment in an effort to conceptualize the sub-dimensions of lack of alternative job opportunities and perceived sacrifices.

Affective commitment and normative commitment positively correlate with favorable attitudinal and behavioral outcomes, but continuance commitment has emerged as negatively or unrelated to the same attitudinal and behavioral outcomes. Organizational commitment is the psychological state that binds employees to an organization and makes turnover less likely.

Summary

This chapter is important because it reveals, from multiple literature streams, the abundance of research on workplace incivility, AWB, and the substantial impact that these behaviors have on organizational and individual workplace outcomes. The organizational culture and established norms determine the degree of "toxicity" that a group will tolerate, and the results when those norms lean away from ethical and moral behavior such as respectful communication and civility. Power differentials show that the majority of uncivil interactions in the workplace occur with a superior as the actor and the subordinate as the target, although there are abundant uncivil interactions that take place between peers. Organizational leadership and followership behaviors affect how individuals interact and respond to perceived workplace incivility. In an uncivil workplace environment, one rationale for organizational commitment is that substitutes for leadership prevent the supervisor/leader from having significant impact on the employee/follower's work experience at all. This chapter defined incivility and its related constructs, its attributions and antecedents, and specific consequent responses to workplace incivility. Responses included changes in individual levels of trust, perceptions of organizational justice, and the type and intensity of organizational commitment.

Key takeaways

1. Research has shown that 75% of employees have stolen from their employer. Part of this may be due to the fact that the culture of the group influences individual employees toward prosocial OR antisocial behavior.
2. Norms are the set of expected (normal) behaviors in any group. You can prevent the negative behaviors by "front-loading" your group's team identity with positive, prosocial experiences and behaviors. Civil communication is one positive norm you can model and reinforce.
3. There are different types of organizational justice, describing the way employees feel about how they are treated. Procedural, distributive, and interactional justice all address employees' perceptions of fairness.
4. There are also three different types of trust, based on the threat or knowledge of rules and procedures, based on the history and consistency of a relationship, and based on shared values and respect.
5. Toxic workplaces feature frequent crisis, deviant behaviors such as theft, unproductiveness, and unethical practices. Ethical workplaces involve leaders

who model an example of high moral standards for their associates to follow, galvanizing the group's movement toward positive, inclusive goals.

6. Three types of organizational commitment are also covered in this chapter – affective (emotional), continuance (based on sunk costs and probably losses), and normative (based on socialization and values). Career entrenchment is the result when employees stay out of desperation rather than desire.

Recommended reading

Fritz, J. M. H., & Omdahl, B. L. (Eds.) (2012). *Problematic Relationships in the Workplace.* New York: Peter Lang.

Lencioni, P. (2007). *The Truth About Employee Engagement* (previously published as *The Three Signs of a Miserable Job*). San Francisco: Jossey-Bass.

Rath, T. (2007). *StrengthsFinder 2.0.* New York: Gallup Press.

Rath, T., & Conchie, B. (2009). *Strengths-Based Leadership: Great Leaders, Teams, and Why People Follow.* New York: Gallup Press.

Let's make this #Interactive – Here's a challenge: pick a book, get it, and connect with the author on LinkedIn and/or follow them on Twitter. Let them know you read their book, and ask them a question about it. #Dialogue #WPS #WhyPeopleStay

---

PART III

The study – executive summary

"If only one didn't know that at the secret heart of all such organizations, corporations and governments alike, it still came down to a finite number of fallible people talking to each other ..."

– Lois McMaster Bujold, author (from her book
Cryoburn, 2010) (Roberts, 2016)

In this section, I'll share with you the inspiration for this book. This is the root, the golden nugget, the why behind what I have to say. First, "what I have to say" is that employees have a clear, demonstrable need to feel seen, safe, and valued in the workplace. I've reverse-engineered that fact by examining the data that show how people think and behave when they *don't* feel seen, when they *don't* feel safe, and when they *don't* feel valued. I shared that information in the research review in the previous section. And, employee engagement is the key to all three. Now, why I say that? Because I have heard firsthand – both anecdotally and empirically – from people who remained gainfully employed in a situation where they had experienced antisocial workplace behaviors (AWB), often counterproductive to the goals of the organization, and often hurtful and personally demoralizing incidents. But they stayed. Why? Why would people stay in a situation where they are insulted, reduced, minimized, ignored, disrespected, even harmed? Doesn't that go against professional and personal values, common sense, and self-preservation? What could be so powerful as to keep people in that kind of situation and allow them to survive, even thrive in it? We'll get to that in this section of the book, detailing the research study that supported these assertions.

5

WHAT, WHY, WHO, AND HOW

While empirical studies of antisocial workplace behavior (AWB) in its various forms lend generalizability and credibility to the constructs, they may not address the specific issues present in a particular workplace. They do not plumb the lived experience of the employee who has stayed in a workplace where he or she has experienced specific AWBs, the narrative of that experience, or the nature of the staying. This qualitative study invited participants to tell the stories of their experiences, counterbalanced with the stories of why they value their positions, and why they stay there.

What

The experience of work is a real thing – it is, often, what defines us as people for many years of our lives. Fox (1994) has suggested that in the "Green Era," these postmodern days after the Modern/Machine era that saw the Industrial Revolution and the advent of large-scale technology, we no longer work and learn by objectivity, but instead understand that people work and learn by participation and creativity. In the past, indeed over the last 300 plus years as Fox indicates, the anthropocentric metaphor of work as a machine has prevailed. We have treated our bodies, our groups and teams, and our organizations as machines, seeking to ensure smooth operation and proper placement of all the "parts." Fox prefers the metaphor of an organism, though, suggesting growth and mystery and welcoming the creative process of relationship-building and productive service. While work consisted of effort and force, work resembled "pushing... drudgery...conflict" (Fox, 1994). The only motivation acknowledged was compensation, incentives like paychecks, benefits, parking spaces, promotions, and raises. Fox hints though that perhaps the universe overall, and the experience of work in particular, is more about attraction than forcing reluctant components "into place" – he suggests then that perhaps our work is more accurately defined by inner desire, by what we love, by the service we seek to offer to others in our community and in the world when we gain specific skills and bring them to the marketplace. This openness, this offering of skills, requires a willingness to make oneself vulnerable to the needs, the desires, even perhaps the whims and cruelty of others. That vulnerability is the definition of trust. It is, more specifically, a state of being in which one person is willing to accept the risks of making himself or herself vulnerable to another person. McShane and von Glinow (2009) posited that it really has to do with one's *expectations* of another person, that is, one's belief in the positive intentions of the other person. Thus, there is a trust required when contemporary employees enter into a psychological contract with their employer. We examined these concepts of the psychological contract, trust, organizational commitment, and organizational justice in Chapter 4 if you'd like to go back and examine the theoretical background. In this study, individuals representing three classes of employment (management, salaried, and hourly) from seven professions and five departments across three major program divisions shared over 70 unique critical incidents of AWB. Those occurrences (63 reported in interviews, 11 in journals) were then sorted into subcategories from the literature: abusive supervision, workplace incivility (rudeness, discourtesy, and disrespect), bullying and aggression, and verbal or physical abuse. An additional category, poor work performance, emerged as an important form of AWB as well. In this small group, no participant reported incidents of sexual harassment.

Participants attributed these incidents to motivations of equity, emotional content, social identity, self-preservation, retaliation and self-protection, malice, and a general environment of entitlement (us vs. them). They reported outcomes and results including feelings of helplessness, decreased self-efficacy, psychological distress, emotional exhaustion, work-family conflict, turnover intent, decreased job satisfaction, decreased organizational commitment, and general perceptions of injustice. Yet, in most cases, they stayed in the same position, same workgroup, same company. Without judgment, I sought to understand why.

Why

Why? Why is precisely the question here. Why people stay, why they choose to go on trusting their careers and their lives to employers, bosses, supervisors, and peers who make them feel invisible, or unsafe, or less than valuable… but first, why do this study? Aren't we just dwelling on the frustration and disappointment of difficult work situations by looking closely at the lived experiences of select individuals who chose to stay? The answer is no, a resounding and joyful no! This study, and this book as a result, is an opportunity to do what many upper-level managers and executives seem to have forgotten to do over the last several years, even become afraid to do: LISTEN.

The more I worked in corporate America, the more I observed that managers seemed to hate addressing the needs, desires, thoughts, and opinions of their associates. Employees were parts to be put in the right place, given their "marching orders," and avoided as much as possible. Highly interactive managers were rarely rewarded other than with the hard work and loyalty of their employees. As their teams developed in terms of maturity and tenure of working together, they developed a deeper level of interpersonal knowledge among themselves and with the managers, and trust developed such that the individuals were willing to *endure*. Whether that meant enduring the boss's bad day, or the boss's boss handing down some inconvenient tasking, or the poor work performance of another teammate, those individuals had confidence that their work mattered, that *they* mattered. With this study, I questioned the effects of antisocial workplace interactions on organizational commitment, e.g., why do people stay in toxic workplaces? How do they situate and make sense of their experience(s) of workplace incivility relative to the desire, or need, to remain in the work group and organization? These questions led to multiple propositions, and questions, about the effects of workplace incivility on the individual employee.

Level of analysis

Being the **target** of antisocial workplace behavior affects individuals' employee engagement. Of course, right? But when you present a scholarly research proposal, you really do have to lay out all of the assumptions and propositions you intend to explore. When we talk about "level of analysis," or LOA, we're talking about the difference between analyzing a problem at the macro, or organization-wide level, in which we might administer a quantitative survey and aggregate the data. From the aggregated statistical information, we can make generalizations about other environments and recommend treatments and interventions based on those generalizations. Then there is a median level of analysis, the group and team level, in which we conduct quantitative or qualitative analyses and discuss their results and impacts based on subgroup reporting within the organization. Finally, we have the individual level of analysis, at which we do better with qualitative interviews. This was the approach I took for this study. The group level of analysis did show up in my interviews, though. You see, being a **witness** to AWB affects employee engagement and organizational commitment as well. The indirect effects of AWB.

To identify these effects, I needed to create a safe space for employees of the organization at which I was conducting the study. I gave them a place to talk about their experiences of rudeness, discourtesy, disrespect, bullying, abusive supervision, and peers' poor work performance. Because I'm not a psychologist or counselor, I ensured that the participants knew we were just having a conversation, and I invited them to simply share their experiences. This leads to another of my initial propositions, that organizational members can define and understand the constructs of organizational commitment, employee engagement, and organizational engagement, within their own organization's context. Further, those same employees can describe the effects of AWB on their own level of employee engagement, and they can discuss organizational commitment in real-time, in real terms. Those employees can also describe the effects of AWB on other employees, down to identifying a general culture and feeling. My questions based on organizational LOA included asking, how does being the target of AWB affect a person's organizational commitment? How does it affect that person's level of employee engagement? I assumed that both would decrease, but I needed evidence. I asked, how do organizational members define, and make sense of, the concepts of organizational commitment and employee engagement? How do employees describe the details and the effects of AWB on their own organizational commitment and employee engagement? How do they perceive and make sense of the effects of AWB on others' organizational commitment and employee engagement?

Followership orientation

Another set of propositions I had, going into this project, centered on the individual employee's followership orientation. The word "follower" means different things in different contexts. In an organizational context, followership orientation and the tendency toward courageous follower behavior may emerge as a driver for organizational commitment and engagement in the presence of AWB. Self-identified follower orientation, using Chaleff's (2008) two-by-two matrix typology, permits employees to take ownership of their own role in the dynamic leader-follower-context relationship.

In the present study, of 11 participants, five self-identified as Partner, four as Implementer, and one as a Resource. One individual declined to self-identify. During their interviews, study participants were shown Chaleff's matrix (Figure 5.1) and asked which descriptors best described them. Their responses in Chapter 10 offer some insight as to how each follower type sounds. Chalofsky (2003, 2010) suggests that organizational members act to improve one another's lives, and Gini (2010) paraphrases St. Augustine, stating that "the first and final job of leadership is… to serve the needs and the well-being of the people led" (p. 349). But followers make up the majority of organizational members, participating in the mission and functions supporting the company's goals. Followers serve their own goals and, ideally, those of the group and organization. Chaleff (2008, 2009) suggests that both leader and follower serve the same organizational purposes, not one another.

In the present study, 11 participants provided rich descriptions of their experiences in a large, diverse workplace, with only minor excerpts shared here. Ten identified a follower "type" using the descriptors from Chaleff's model. Their

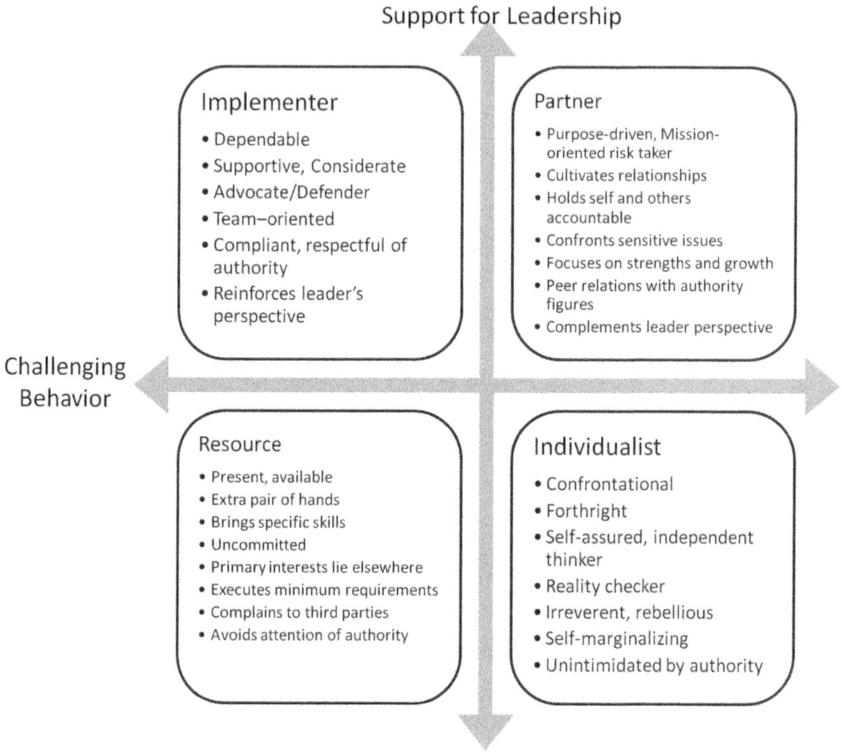

Support for Leadership

Implementer
- Dependable
- Supportive, Considerate
- Advocate/Defender
- Team–oriented
- Compliant, respectful of authority
- Reinforces leader's perspective

Partner
- Purpose-driven, Mission-oriented risk taker
- Cultivates relationships
- Holds self and others accountable
- Confronts sensitive issues
- Focuses on strengths and growth
- Peer relations with authority figures
- Complements leader perspective

Challenging Behavior

Resource
- Present, available
- Extra pair of hands
- Brings specific skills
- Uncommitted
- Primary interests lie elsewhere
- Executes minimum requirements
- Complains to third parties
- Avoids attention of authority

Individualist
- Confrontational
- Forthright
- Self-assured, independent thinker
- Reality checker
- Irreverent, rebellious
- Self-marginalizing
- Unintimidated by authority

FIGURE 5.1 Chaleff's model.

self-descriptions provide some insight as to what these follower types might sound like, in their own words. These participants' language and use of story illustrate three of the four types and the relationship of that type to communication behaviors (Fritz, 2002, 2012; 2013), perceptions of and responses to AWB, and descriptions of organizational culture (Schein, 1990, 2005). Therefore, the propositions I started with were that individual followership orientation affects the experience of AWB. Further, followership orientation affects organizational commitment. And the individual practice of Chaleff's five courageous followership behaviors would affect organizational commitment as well. Individuals' courageous followership behaviors affect the experience of AWB as either a target, or as a witness. My questions around followership and its impact on perceived AWB and organizational commitment abound. But primarily, how does a person's followership orientation affect the experience of AWB? How does followership orientation affect a person's organizational commitment? And how does the individual's practice of Chaleff's five courageous followership behaviors affect their organizational commitment? How does the practice of courageous follower behaviors affect their experience of AWB as a target? As a witness?

Organizational culture, perceptions of justice, and norms of civility

The next set of research propositions for this study addressed my expectations about organizational culture, and the norms of civility, norms of ethical behavior, and norms of communication that would be enacted in the organization where participants worked. First, I suggest that organizational culture affects organizational commitment in ways that can be identified, explained, and documented. Second, I suggest that organizational norms (described earlier) affect the experience of AWB in similarly observable ways. Next, organizational members' understanding of the power differentials in their organizational culture will influence their experience of AWB. Finally, organizational members' understanding of the power differentials in the workplace will affect their perceived organizational justice and organizational commitment. I asked, how do organizational culture and norms affect organizational commitment? Do those norms activate in some specific way when they are violated and AWB are manifested? How do power differentials in the organizational culture influence group members' experience of AWB? And how does this understanding of power differentials in the workplace impact employees' organizational commitment? Finally, I asked, how are employees' perceptions of organizational justice affected by their experiences of AWB?

Trust (separate from organizational justice)

As my exploration of why people might stay in a workplace where they had experienced AWB went deeper, I found that trust as a concept that influenced workplace interaction needed to be treated separately. I defined it separately from organizational justice, and suggested that the experience of AWB and workplace incivility negatively impacts employee trust toward managers, as well as trust in the organization overall. I wondered, How does the experience of AWB impact an individual's level of trust? Specifically, does the individual hold "the organization" accountable for violations of the psychological contract? Or is culpability more directly placed on the manager of the agent or bad actor in the AWB scenario?

Who

Twenty-five individuals employed in the same organization at different levels and in different divisions and occupational fields were invited to participate in this study. Eleven took the time to share specific experiences of AWB that they had lived through and had still chosen to stay in that same workplace. The profile of the participants was diverse enough though, with individuals from hourly, salaried professional, and management positions; there were men (7) and women

(4), Black (4), White (6), and Latino (1); and there were members of three generations (Millennial – 1, Generation X – 7, Baby Boomer – 3). Their education levels ranged from high school, to some college, to graduate degree, and their backgrounds included retired military, career switcher, and single employer/single career.

Specifically, there were ten salaried employees and one hourly employee. The group included seven professions: technical instructor, instructional designer/training developer, systems engineer, production planner, production scheduler, procurement specialist, and welder. These individuals represented five departments, three different program divisions, and all three employee classes (hourly, salaried, management). Two had worked in the environment they described for five years or less, five had worked there for between five and 10 years, and four had been there from 10 to 15 years. None had over 15 years' tenure.

How

For this particular study a process called empirical phenomenological research was used, with mixed purposeful sampling. Translated, mixed purposeful sampling was the process that allowed me to vary the demographics and professions across the organization. This way, I ensured that I got at least a minimal cross-section of representation from different levels and divisions within the organization. But because the research question was a "why?" rather than a "what?" or a "how many?" it was necessary to get deep, rich data – individual, thoughtfully considered comments and responses. Knowing that self-report data is by definition somewhat tainted, it's appropriate to spend significant quality time with the participants and get as much detail from them as possible to sift through and make sense of – this is the empirical phenomenological part.

This study summarizes the findings of several in-depth interviews with employees in a single large manufacturing employer, using a semi-structured format so that the participants could explore for themselves their own experiences of AWB and/or toxic leadership. In the present study, over 25 employees in a single large manufacturing company in the southeastern United States were solicited for interviews about their experiences of AWB. Eleven actually completed the process, representing three employment categories (hourly/production, salaried/professional, and management), five divisions, and seven different professions. Some of the responses specifically addressed experiences of toxic leadership and the effects of these experiences on the participants' level of organizational engagement and organizational commitment. Because organizational commitment has been established as a theoretical construct, it was used to balance the interview protocol, but what emerged was that participants were familiar with the Gallup Q12 survey and the term "organizational engagement," although it addresses different criteria than the commitment construct.

Participants were further asked to consider and share their levels of organizational commitment and organizational engagement, based on their tenure and other factors. They revealed that while their commitment to the organization or to its management might be low or nonexistent, their engagement with the mission of the organization, the canon of their profession, or the needs of their customers might be quite high.

How – from the participant's perspective

To get multiple "layers" of data, I invited (required) study participants to keep a journal and fill it with at least three entries following a particular outline. Specifically, each entry had to be dated (so, fresh incidents). Each entry had to fit the description of AWB: "behavior that harms the organization and/or its members" and could range from rudeness and disrespect to verbal and psychological abuse, bullying, aggression, and violence. The participant had to write a brief description of the event, and indicate if it had happened to him or her personally or if it was something they had observed. Finally, the participant had to finish the sentence, "as a result of this incident I definitely thought/felt…"

Then, we scheduled an interview to discuss the journals and to go through a prescribed set of questions, called an interview protocol. The protocol was my script for managing the interviews, so I followed it very closely – capturing names and contact information to send transcripts for approval, age range, and job information first, and confirming the confidentiality steps I had taken and would continue to take to protect their information. The protocol also listed my open-ended questions, and as they answered I tried to take notes as I could – but I relied on the fact that I was recording the sessions (with their permission) so that I could engage with them in the dialogue. These were people whom I had either known or who had been referred to me for the purpose of this study, and I wanted them to feel safe sharing these experiences. The questions they were asked about their experience of AWB included:

1. Please describe a time when you experienced antisocial workplace behavior at work. (this includes violence, aggression, verbal/physical abuse, bullying, abusive supervision, rudeness, discourtesy, and disrespect).
2. What happened just prior to that event? (antecedents).
3. Regarding the example you described, was it verbal/physical; active/passive; attempted/completed; intentional/unintentional? Who was the perpetrator? Who was the target? What was the action? Consequence? Intention? (O'Leary-Kelly, Duffy, & Griffin, 2000).
4. What was the outcome for you personally? (helplessness, decreased self-efficacy, psychological distress, emotional exhaustion, work-family conflict, turnover intent, decreased job satisfaction and organizational commitment, general feelings of injustice).
5. What was the impact on the group from the incident or environment you describe?
6. How did communications, trust, organizational commitment change, if at all?

7. How did your group deal with it? (self-evaluation and group cohesion; criticism of others who leave).
8. What have you found most troubling or surprising about the examples that you've observed or experienced?
9. What response options did/do you have to address the antisocial workplace behavior? (Feel powerless? Lack credibility? No autonomy? Participative decision making? Ethical climate?).
10. What do you think was the motive behind that episode? (equity, emotional, social identity/self-preservation, retaliation, self-protection).
11. What job stressors create or support the environment? (role ambiguity, role conflict, workload, organizational constraints, interpersonal conflict).

I also prepared specific question sets for follow-up lines of conversation, particularly about organizational commitment. Those included:

12. How would you describe your level of organizational engagement?
13. Do you feel more committed to the organization, to your immediate superior, or to the workgroup? Why?
14. How long did you stay/have you stayed in the environment you describe? What do you think is the main reason you stayed (as long as you did/ have)?
15. When you think about your commitment to the Company, what comes to mind? (feelings, identification with the company's values; stay because that's what you do, that's how I was raised; or money, sunk costs, benefits).

There were other follow-up questions I prepared, too, but they were very specifically tailored to certain cues that the participants would have to have given me in our dialogue up to that point. Each interview lasted from 90 minutes to 3 hours, and at the end of each interview I made sure to provide a debrief in which I reassured the participant that whatever they had shared would be kept confidential, and that the experiences they had described were definitely not unique to just them, but that many other people had had similar experiences. I also asked:

16. How was the experience you described here valuable to you? What did you learn from it?
17. How has thinking and talking about it been valuable? What can you take away from this?

As each participant prepared to leave our one-on-one encounter, I gave each of them a laminated card as a handout with appropriate responses to experiencing incivility in the workplace, whether as a target or as a witness:

- report the incident;
- speak up when you witness incivility;
- reinforce the knowledge of consequences for incivility;
- set clear expectations for communication and acceptable workplace/workgroup behavior;

- reinforce those expectations through recruiting, selection, orientation, and feedback; and
- know that organizations that condone incivility will attract uncivil recruits.

(Pearson, Andersson, & Porath, 2000)

And, finally, each participant was given a choice of thank-you gift: restaurant gift certificate or spa massage coupon. The whole idea was to thank them and give them some respite from their constant endurance of work as toil and difficulty.

How – from my perspective

Empirical phenomenological investigation invites the participant to explain and share a specific experience, or phenomenon, invokes the feelings and thoughts it created or caused, and allows the researcher to experience it with the individual. Groenewald (2004) suggests (as does Creswell, 1998) that for a phenomenological study, two to ten participants engaged in long interviews should lead to the researcher's achieving "saturation," the point at which participant themes begin to recur. The researcher must continue data collection until participants introduce no new perspectives on the topic. The researcher may balance interviews with focus groups and essays; data triangulation to contrast the reports permits the researcher to identify similar findings. Groenewald cites Kvale's 1996 instruction on developing the research question for interview protocols, suggesting that instead of a leading question, I should ask "How would you describe your most challenging workplace or job? What made it that way? What impact did this environment have on your commitment to stay at this job?" The findings of the study may or may not illustrate the research question at all; the research may not yield any "answers" whatsoever. Husserl's term, "bracketing," signifies that the inquiry is performed from the researcher's point of view, asking participants to reflect on the value of the identified experience. Bracketing also indicates that the researcher puts her own experiences and preconceptions aside, and enters into the participants' world to interpret their story free from all suppositions. That part was challenging, but I had to do it in order to fully receive whatever the participants shared. I did not want to communicate any judgment or criticism for how they responded to the situations they had experienced.

It's critical that the participant feels only acceptance, and safety, in the interview, and (to me) it's equally critical that they do not leave feeling worse than when they came in to share their story. That is, questions like "why did you stay in a workplace where you say you experienced antisocial workplace behaviors" might have left participants feeling stupid, or full of self-doubt. Thus, the questions had to be modified, and it had to be a dialogue, a processing through, of the motivations behind their commitment. Moustakas provided structure for the empirical phenomenological approach, explaining that there must be two levels – first, a gathering of original data from the participant through open-ended questions and dialogue, and second, my (the researcher's) description of the experiences that had been shared, based on reflective analysis and interpretation (Moustakas, 1994).

There was also a debriefing at the end of each interview to help participants find the value in the interview experience as well as in the lived experiences they were reporting. I followed Moustakas' recommendations closely, utilizing a systematic three-step approach in this study: formulating the question (Why do people stay in workplaces where they have experienced AWB?) was step one. Step two involved gathering descriptive narrative material from participants – individuals who actually become partners in the inquiry, querying their own reports right along with me; they wanted to know why they and others stayed in such a situation too! This step provided an extra validity check for me though, called "member checking," to ensure that the participants agree that I had captured the essence of their experience. Finally, the third step is the "explication" step, the interpretation of the data (some would call it data analysis, but that sounds too quantitative for my purposes here). In this third phase, I explored the material before me, seeking some kind of structure, pattern, and coherence. That is, making sense of it all.

Ethical considerations and assumptions

Attempting to investigate why people stay in an environment where they have experienced verbal and psychological abuse, bullying, and even physical threats does not lend itself to the neat administration of surveys for quantitative analysis. The ethical considerations relevant to having participants share these difficult memories are summarized in this chapter. And, the focus is here is on why people *stayed*, after experiencing the incidents they described. If it was that bad, you'd leave… right? Who would stay, why would they stay, in an environment where behaviors occur that harm the organization, or harm organizational members, and you witness that? Where you experience the "casual cruelty" of rudeness, discourtesy, and disrespect on a regular basis? This study allowed each individual to examine how he or she interpreted, and adapted to, those experiences, relative to his or her position and team membership. There were two key ethical issues to be addressed in this study, that of confidentiality, and then the impact of self-examination in the process of the study itself.

Confidentiality

Issues of confidentiality were addressed via multiple assurances both oral and in writing. I provided informed consent documentation both orally and in writing. I developed a carefully designed interview protocol approved by a Human Subjects Review Board, and undertook formal documentation of my own issues and biases going into the project (called bracketing, this involved my own walking through the protocol and journal tasks based on my own experience) so that I could process and set aside those issues and biases. Additionally, I coded all

participant files, both hard copy and digital, to protect the identity of my participants, and I kept all materials in a locked office. Any excerpts used identify participants only by initials, and the organization is masked along with the identities
of any specific group or manager. I explained this to each participant so that they
would each feel safe sharing their experience with me.

Impact of self-examination

Any time a researcher, coach, instructor, or consultant (I work in all of these
roles) asks threatening questions, we run the risk of putting our audience, client,
or participant on the defensive. To avoid this, as mentioned above, I carefully
refined the phrasing of the questions on the interview protocol, so that at no
time did the language imply judgment of any of my participants. For individuals
who are already remembering and sharing with me their painful memories of
workplace experiences, I felt strongly that I owed them a nonjudgmental and
receptive space in which to process these memories. I wanted to extend to them
the care and respect that, at least for a few specific moments in their careers, they
had been denied.

Ethical leading and following

Smircich and Morgan (1982) state that leadership as a concept "permeates and
structures the theory and practice of organizations and hence the way we shape
and understand the nature of organized action" (p. 257). Organizations struggle to find a balance between people being disorganized and lacking any clear
leadership and situations in which the organization seems full of current leaders,
developing leaders, and wannabe leaders, or leaders in training. Unfortunately,
as my friend Gene Dixon has stated, contemporary business organizations focus all too much on leadership, leader development, and the role of the leader,
which activates a shared cultural error of attribution in which the leader becomes
all-important (Dixon, 2009). He's got a point – and it's an important one.

   Under the current, popular paradigm in which everyone is expected to be a
leader in his or her organization, we devalue the role and importance of the effective, ethical follower. Executives and HR managers do this to the peril of the
organization's culture! This is a self-destructive psychological schema. In essence it
creates a duality within the culture, an environment of "us" and "them" consisting
of those who serve as the Resource people, consistently present and available, or
the Individualists who confront and challenge the policies, practices, and decisions
of management. These forthright reality checkers are absolutely necessary in an
organization, because they represent a subculture, sometimes even a countercul-
ture, of emerging values in the company. Managers and executives would do well
to listen carefully to these team members, rather than validate their sometimes
self-marginalizing perceptions by ignoring them in favor of the "emerging leaders"
who never confront, challenge, or oppose. Diversity of thought is a tremendous

asset, but what it looks like is conflict, and all too often executives and top leaders want no part of conflict. But ethical followers will find themselves compelled to offer opposition when it means standing up for, and protecting, the shared, organizational values to which they have committed, and the purpose to which they have linked themselves and their own personal reputations.

Chaleff's other two categories of followers may offer greater support for leadership, and may also be included in the "emerging leader" category. The Implementer is respectful of the leader's authority and reinforces the leader's perspective, advocating for and defending it. This is the true believer, the dependable team player who may experience the resentment of colleagues because of that support for leadership. The Partner is the follower on the team who will confront uncomfortable, sensitive issues. She complements the leader's perspective, agreeing and supporting in principle but moving toward goals as a peer. The Partner will definitely hold the leader and the rest of the team accountable to the organization's values (often unstated, and woven throughout the culture) and ethics (often clearly stated, but ignored).

What happens, then, when followers stray from the moral, ethical high ground? It is generally not something that happens deliberately. As a coworker once told me, "no one comes to work intending to do a bad job." I find it is the same with toxic followers, people who contribute negatively to the workplace culture and climate. No one comes to work intending to cause pain to others, intending to disrupt productivity and make work a miserable place. So how do followers become "toxic?" Mourdoukoutas' (2014) *Forbes* online article painted a picture of toxic leaders as workplace psychopaths, operating from an evil core. The image is offered of a leader "with a dark inner side, hidden motives and identities." But everyone has a dark side, as Kets de Vries (2006) noted, and Kusy and Holloway (2009) showed that a toxic environment is a function of leader behaviors, *follower behaviors*, and environmental contingencies. Where anecdotal or observational research depicts evil, morally disengaged individuals, Zimbardo's (2007) empirical research from the Stanford Prison Experiment and from consulting with those involved in the Abu Ghraib military trials shows that toxic behavior by members of an organization may emerge out of necessity or cultivation in a toxic work environment. That's right, out of necessity.

Ethical following is as important as ethical leading, perhaps more so, because leaders cannot constantly monitor what each follower does and how he or she represents the organization. Trust is involved on both sides; followers have expectations of their leaders, and vice versa. But when employees' unmet psychological needs become too great, they may become vulnerable to the lure of safety, belonging among the "leader" class, the possibility of amassing greater personal power (again, safety), or the feelings of esteem that come from recognition by one's higher-ups. Jean Lipman-Blumen talks about this human susceptibility, addressing the turbulence we face in regular, daily life as a source of vulnerability as well. A toxic leader, or a coworker with an unethical shortcut idea that seems like it may save money, time, effort, or the company's image, can offer the lure of job security if the follower goes along, and thus a toxic follower is born.

"Evil is knowing better but doing worse" – Philip Zimbardo, 2007

Ethical following means avoiding the temptation to do what Zimbardo has called "evil." He says, "Evil consists in intentionally behaving in ways that harm, abuse, demean, dehumanize, or destroy innocent others – or using one's authority and systemic power to encourage or permit others to do so on your behalf" (2007, p. 5). Ethical following, then, means governing oneself, in each situation, within the system that currently exists. These three components – self, situation, and system – offer significant opportunity for vulnerability to the temptation to act in self-serving, or even harmful ways, as Zimbardo's TED Talk on the psychology of evil shows. In my own education and research I have always wondered why people do what they do, and Albert Bandura's social cognitive theory gives a comprehensive response to that question, complementary to Zimbardo's embedding of Self within Situation within a System. Bandura simply showed us that there is a triadic reciprocal causation to all human psychosocial functioning. What a fun sentence… in essence, Bandura stated that there are three factors that interact to predict how people function with one another, in social contexts. Those three factors are equally important, and equally powerful. They are Personal Factors (the personality, nature and nurture, and experiences that shape who you are), Behaviors (how you enact, or manifest, your espoused beliefs about what is good or bad, right or wrong), and Environmental Factors (as Zimbardo has stated, the Situation and the System). See Figure 5.2.

The internal personal factors include our individualized needs, as McClelland described as far back as 1975, for achievement, affiliation, and power, and how

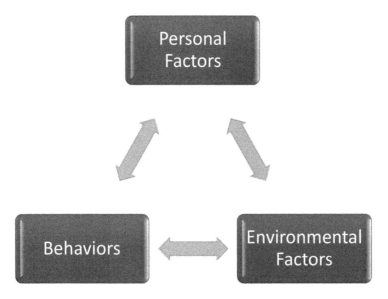

FIGURE 5.2 Factors and behaviors.

that need for power manifests in terms of orientation – is it a personalized need for power OVER others, or is it a socialized need for power WITH others? Is it destructive, or supportive, to the culture and community?

The environmental factors include the preexisting power relations in the organization, department, and team (the System). There is also the significant influence of organizational culture, including tolerance of power distance – is a great deal of inequality the norm in your organization, or do even the lowest level employees feel like valued equals? Finally, there is the impact of role theory, also attributed to Philip Zimbardo from 1973, which tracks with common sense when we think about it: we behave according to the role we play. In Zimbardo's Stanford Prison Experiment, as well as his documentation of American soldiers' behavior at Abu Ghraib prison in Iraq, the research showed a hideous deterioration in the behavior and judgment of people who may have been morally good, ethical, positive influences on their groups prior to the situation and system in which they found themselves. Certainly they were responsible for their own behavior! Zimbardo just identified that ethical following is significantly impacted by the external factors, the Environmental Factors in Bandura's Social Cognitive Theory.

Bandura himself attempted to explain what we call unethical, evil behavior, in a study of moral disengagement (2002). Your employees and associates have something called "moral agency." A *moral agent* has the power to intentionally cause harm to another person, and the power to choose not to do so. This is an individual employee's ability to make moral judgments based on a *commonly held notion* of right and wrong, and to be held accountable for these judgments and their ensuing actions. When there is conflict in the workplace, when we are facing ethical challenges and finding toxic followership at the root of them, that signals discord between the personal factors, environmental factors, and behavioral options available to your associates. Conflict manifests in two primary ways: task conflict, which is healthy and problem-based and can lead to greater creativity and team cohesion, and relationship conflict, which is unhealthy and person-based, and thereby destructive to the culture.

Ethical following, in essence, involves individual acknowledgment of our own values and the fact that others have values which may agree or differ but which are equally important and worthy of respect. It involves taking ownership of our moral agency. Zimbardo offered a ten-step program to resist unwanted influences, which I think can be translated into a set of habits and hashtags (for the social media savvy) to remind ourselves of the power of that moral agency, that social and personal responsibility. If any of the hashtags resonate with you, do share and let me see you tweet them (@DrSpranger) or post them on Instagram (sprangerangela). The list is shown below, as adapted from pages 452–456 of Zimbardo's book, *The Lucifer Effect*:

1. **ENCOURAGE admission of our mistakes, first to ourselves, then to others.**

    a   **Habit:** Give yourself permission to acknowledge the truth: you may have made an error in judgment, made a wrong decision. I once had a supervisor who trained me out of "paralysis by analysis" in quite a dramatic way. He banged on my desk and said, "Make a decision! If you don't like that decision, make another decision! If that's a bad decision, make another decision! But MAKE. A. DECISION." I would offer that in the case of acknowledging a bad decision, a wrong decision, or a decision that may have caused negative repercussions, it becomes even more critical to just Make. A. Decision. Move forward from it, learn from it, and own it. Maya Angelou famously said, and was quoted by Oprah Winfrey and Lisa Nichols to millions of people around the world, "when you know better, you do better." After a decision turns out differently than you planned, you will do better by owning it and failing forward, rather than pretending it never happened. Now you know.

b **Hashtag:** #IKnowNow.

2. **NOTICE the obvious situational clues, and reflect on the meaning of the immediate situation.**

   a **Habit:** Be mindful. While that word, "mindful," and its variations have become increasingly common and thus perhaps lost some impact, I encourage you to consciously, intentionally, *see* and *question*. When you question what you see, you may find that there's nothing to worry about, or perhaps there is an ethical challenge that needs your attention. It's important and valuable to reflect on the meaning of the immediate situation. Every interaction has meaning.

   b **Hashtag:** #IAmMindful

3. **OWN IT – recognize your own personal responsibility for your actions, even in response to the actions of others.**

   a **Habit:** We become more resistant to ethically questionable temptations (an opportunity to make oneself look better at a colleague's expense, for example) when we hold ourselves accountable for our actions. Apply the sunshine test – is this behavior one that would be acceptable in the bright sunlight, in front of an audience? Always imagine a future time when today's actions will be published on the front page of the newspaper your grandmother reads. Or, for a more current metaphor, is the action something of which you would be proud if it were covered in a story with photos on your favorite Internet news site? If your action were going on trial, would it be found ethical?

   b **Hashtag:** #OwnIt

4. **BE YOU, uniquely you.**

   a **Habit:** Assert your individuality. Politely state your name and credentials whenever necessary. As an executive, a leader, an influencer, you know that you have responded to a call, an internal summons to offer the world your very best, to share the gifts and talents with which you have been endowed. Do it, be you, skip the temptation to imitate others whose success and influence may have come to them at a younger age, or faster, or with flashier results. Being uniquely you empowers others to do the same; it frees them and encourages them to acknowledge their own deeply held beliefs and values and to walk confidently in an ethical path.

b **Hashtag: #BeYouDoYou**

5. **HONOR just authority.**

a **Habit:** As adults, leaders, and influencers, we have a responsibility to model correct behavior for the students, children, employees, associates, members, and other followers who are constantly watching us. Rather than teach anyone to challenge authority, or (as I have commonly heard) teach anyone that "respect must be earned before it is given," I would encourage all to respect *just* authority, and rebel against *unjust* authority or authority that has been usurped. Let me explain. I find it offensive when a young person says to an elder or a new hire says of a superior, "respect must be earned before it is given." The audacity! However, I do not recommend or encourage anyone to mindlessly follow any authority, much less the self-appointed authority, whose priorities are clearly not in the best interests of the follower.

b **Hashtag: #HonorJustAuthority**

6. **FIND COMMUNITY that demands no sacrifice of values.**

a **Habit:** Too often we find ourselves sacrificing our own morals and values for the privilege of membership in specific groups. It is sometimes appropriate to step away and seek opinions from others outside the membership group, team, or organization as a whole. Intentionally testing the opinion of the desired group means breaking out of groupthink and creating conflict, which can be horrendously difficult to endure ("why are you always the one who goes against the team? You're not a team player"). But while we may want group acceptance, it is infinitely more important to value one's own independence. There will always be another, different, better group with which to unite.

b **Hashtag: #OKAlone**

7. **CHECK the frame.** Be vigilant about how issues and situations are framed in your organization. The way this is done is often more influential than the persuasive arguments within the frames themselves. If a situation is set up and sold to associates and followers as a loss, I remember learning in my graduate marketing classes, then those associates and followers may scramble to prevent the loss, comply, act fast, respond to the call to action. If that same

situation is framed as a gain, an opportunity, they may respond differently. Similarly, humans may be attracted to the scenario presented as a gain, even when the net effect is nil.

a   **Habit:** Be more frame-vigilant. Pay attention to how you structure things, what tone you set, and when you are on the receiving end of internal messages, listen carefully to the tone being set for you.

b   **Hashtag: #FliptheScript #FrameIt**

8. **BALANCE your perspective.** Understand that past commitments, whether met or unmet, are past. Future liabilities or assets are future. Whether you are hopeful or cynical about what the future holds, choosing to address bad behavior in the present allows you to step away from the bondage of "going with the flow."

a   **Habit:** Recognize that time is fluid, and that different people have different perspectives on past, present, and future.

b   **Hashtag: #TimeMatters**

9. **REFUSE to sacrifice freedom for security.**

a   **Habit:** Know that it is indeed a tradeoff when we allow personal or civic freedoms to be co-opted for the sake of some additional degree of "security." In our workplaces, this may look like an accommodation of the increasingly frightening reports of workplace violence. We install additional locks, codes, doors, keypads and badges, cameras, and passwords on our technology… and we create an atmosphere in which the lure of security and safety are underlined by fear, and willingness to surrender our own personal information, others' information, or privacy.

b   **Hashtag: #FreeAndSafe**

10. **SAY I CAN oppose the unjust system.**

a   **Habit:** We as people, and workers, tend to wilt in the face of an overwhelming adversary like a representative from the military, a phone call threatening to engage the justice system ("we may serve a warrant on you, unless you pay…"), or even the "good old boy" system in our corporate environment. But one person, one voice, can stir up others for positive change and cultural evolution. We must encourage one another to oppose unjust systems, wherever we find them.

b   **Hashtag: #Evolve**

Again, these ten steps are gratefully repurposed from Philip Zimbardo's book, *The Lucifer Effect*.

As a shared, interactive social practice (Weick, 1979), leadership is a "process whereby one or more individuals succeeds in attempting to frame and define

> Character is who you are when people are looking; Integrity is who you are when no one's looking.
>
> TESTIMONIAL: Patient X is a Spanish-speaking patient with no prescription insurance. I have helped this patient by signing her up for patient assistance after multiple conversations. Her income was about $1000 a month, and she was spending $500 a month on ONE prescription medication, so I got her signed up for patient assistance and she was given one year of *free* access to that one medication. She was very thankful. My company has a policy that as a member of management and an hourly associate, you are not to accept gifts, period, ever. However, sometimes we do accept cookies, we don't want to be rude. This patient brought me a letter telling her that they're extending her patient assistance, and she was so thankful. She brought me a Christmas card and asked me first if I celebrated Christmas. When I said yes, she gave me the card and I threw it my bag. I held it for two weeks, and I didn't open it. When I did open it, I saw she had included TWO $50 gift cards to XYZ fancy restaurant at the beach. Wow. That was nice, but… I knew what I was supposed to do, so I returned the gift cards with a very nice thank-you card, and I put them in her prescription bag so no one else would see. But I knew what my company required, and I did it.
>
> *– Senior Pharmacist*

the reality of others… an obligation or a perceived right on the part of certain individuals to define the reality of others" (Smircich & Morgan, 1982, p. 258). Gini (2010) paraphrases St. Augustine, stating that "the first and final job of leadership is… to serve the needs and the well-being of the people led" (p. 349). Other researchers suggest that leadership is better defined as the relationship wherein leaders and followers collaborate because they are mutually invested in a direction and because they are inherently interdependent (Howell & Mendez, 2008; Rost, 2008). If this relationship holds, then both leaders and followers "do" leadership.

However, Kelley (1998) found that research over the last two decades has shown American follower -employees as extremely dissatisfied with the quality of leadership in their organizations. Survey data revealed employee perceptions that 40% of their bosses had questionable leadership abilities, and the employees surveyed did not perceive their leaders as people worthy of emulation or trust. They instead experienced their leaders as people who were threatened by talented subordinates, who needed to act superior to others, and who were unwilling to share credit for successes (Kelley, 1998, p. 193). In such an atmosphere, when immediate supervisors represent the organization to their work groups, employees are unlikely to internalize or identify with the values and behaviors that they observe. They are more likely to comply with the basic requirements of the organization, completing tasks and adhering to procedures in order to satisfy their perceived obligations in exchange for pay or benefits.

In workplaces where employees perceive uncivil or toxic, rude behaviors, more often than not it is manifested downward. Leaders model accepted norms and enact behaviors on followers, who then replicate behaviors with colleagues, peers, and customers. Both leaders and followers do leadership, and both leaders and followers contribute to the creation of an ethical, healthy environment or an unethical, toxic one.

Healthy, ethical workplaces, and honorable leaders

Bass and Avolio's work on transformational leadership theory balances the more exchange-based transactional leadership theory. The transformational approach to leadership suggests that the leader's role is to inspire followers to perform in ways that benefit the follower personally, as well as the organization.. Both leaders and group members act to improve one another's lives, under this paradigm (Chalofsky, 2010, p. 95). The approach focuses on empowering followers, rendering them less dependent on the leader and his or her power to reward or punish. Instead, the emphasis is on delegating authority and ownership, developing follower skills and self-confidence, and sharing information across the work group (Yukl, 2006, p. 271).

Transformational leadership leads to superior results because leaders deploy what Bass and Avolio call the "four I's" – idealized influence over colleagues and followers, inspirational motivation of others toward a mission or vision, intellectual stimulation of others to challenge and grow their ability and competence, and individual consideration of each member of the group (Bass & Riggio, 2006, p. 136). This set of behaviors is associated with high-quality leadership, based on empirical testing of the theoretical constructs (Mancheno-Smoak, Endres, Polak, & Athanasaw, 2009, p. 10). Effective leaders motivate higher job satisfaction, employee commitment, better performance, and fewer turnover intentions (2009, p. 12). Edwards and Cable (2009) empirically demonstrated that when followers share the values of their leaders and the organization, the ensuing value congruence leads to lower turnover costs and increased frequency of organizational citizenship behaviors.

Congruent values and transparent communication, moral leadership, and an ethical culture create a fulfilling workplace that inspires and encourages followers. Lipman-Blumen (2005) suggests that honorable leaders promote noble visions. Non-toxic or constructive leaders create noble visions by articulating an achievable reality. They offer a cooperative venture in which leaders and followers struggle together to achieve goals. Their primary goal is to help humankind, never harming others or enhancing one group at the expense of another. Noble visions such as this call out the best in the leader and followers. The characteristics developed include "integrity, truthfulness, courage, strength, ethics, compassion, love, generosity, altruism, kindness, reliability, flexibility, resilience, dedication, intelligence, imagination (and) creativity" (p. 34). Pursuing a noble vision may require a paradigm change, though; a leader who casts a noble vision may deliberately disillusion followers and share with them, "the burdensome responsibilities of leadership" (p. 35).

Price (2008, 2010) offers a formula for how leaders ought to act, especially when the social norms and organizational expectations seem vague. Leaders should first restrict the exceptions they allow for themselves, permitting themselves to operate **outside** the group or social norms only when they do so "to the pursuit of inclusive ends" (2010, p. 403). Second, leaders should be transparent in their communications, willing to make public their rationale any time they choose to deviate from "the requirements of morality" (2010, p. 403).

Davis (1953) explains that top management should recognize the importance of communication as a continuous process both to and from workers. The informal communication channel, or grapevine, depends on effective management communications through which the leader can influence the group's point of view. Greenbaum (1972) suggests both oral and written mechanisms for internal communications at the individual, small group, and organizational levels. Crampton, Hodge, and Mishra (1998) identify a consensus in the literature that managers should not try to control or restrict the grapevine, but would better serve their organizations by seeking to manage it with accurate information, as employees may be more likely to believe information received through the grapevine than through formal communications. Two additional factors affect grapevine operations: whether the organizational environment is insecure or even threatening, and whether there is a lack of trust in the formal communications.

Ethical failures in the workplace no longer solely due to leadership

Gini (2010) reported that in a 1990 survey, 68% of participants identified unethical behavior by executives as the primary cause of decline in business standards, productivity, and success. Because of their perceptions of low ethical standards on the part of executives, workers felt justified to respond in kind. This led to higher absenteeism and petty theft, worker indifference, and poor job performance. In fact, respondents indicated that they spent 20% of their time on the job goofing off; one in six drinks or uses drugs on-the-job and only one in four gives their best effort at work. Gini (2010) states that regarding an organization's ethical environment, "Followers share responsibility for the overall conduct and culture of an organization" (p. 346).

Key takeaways

1. "Work" can be conceptualized as mechanical, with great effort and force applied, or as organic, with creativity and relationship-building involved.
2. The most important thing leaders can do is listen to their associates and ensure that they know you see them, that they believe you will do all you can to ensure their safety, and that you value their individuality and contributions.
3. When initiating a conversation around topics that may be threatening or uncomfortable, be prepared with tools and statements to restore the other

person's (and your) sense of equilibrium. Let them save face. Don't let anyone leave your presence feeling stupid, useless, or otherwise worse than when they came in to speak with you.

4. More often than not, uncivil or toxic behavior is manifested downward. If you observe it, it was probably learned from a superior, past or present.
5. AWBs, and a cultural tolerance of them, violate the psychological contract, and reduce organizational engagement.
6. Learn more about transformational leadership and encourage these behaviors in your organization's managers and directors: Inspirational motivation, Idealized influence, Intellectual stimulation, and Individualized consideration.
7. Does followership type affect employee tolerance for AWB? What if you are the supervisor of employees who reflect the ambivalent, "I love this place, I just hate working here" attitude?

6

WHAT ACTUALLY HAPPENED (AND IS HAPPENING IN YOUR WORKPLACE)

My manager made clear to me more than once where I stood by saying, "have you checked the org chart lately?" My supervisor, who didn't think that way automatically but who knew how to survive in that atmosphere, later said to me, "OK I know you might be thinking that this is a good idea and it's out of the box but, we need you to get back in your box. Remember the org chart." Later, at my second performance review, I asked what I could do to go from a 2 (on a 4-point scale) to a 3, because all of the "outside the box" initiatives I thought would get me there were getting shut down. I was told, "You can't, and it's not that simple." I felt crushed and completely demotivated.

– AS

Throughout my own career I **have felt compelled** to observe, listen to, and encourage colleagues who constantly complained about the job, the work site, the supervisor, upper management, and other factors. I began to challenge others to say positive things about why they stayed in the workplace. I earned a reputation for not accepting whining, complaining, and moaning. Instead, I maintained numerous resources and contacts internal and external to the organizations where I worked, so that if colleagues expressed willingness to change or improve their situation, I could help them. This became a mission, and I help people either change their declarations, or change their situations. This chapter offers a review of the concepts, and a consideration of the environment in which the participants worked from a structural and a cultural standpoint.

Overview: what led me here

In 2007, during graduate work in Human Resource Development, I learned that researchers had studied workplace incivility for some years. The construct included bullying (Hodson, Roscigno, & Lopez, 2006), verbal and psychological abuse (Sofield & Salmond, 2003; Sutton, 2007), workplace deviance (Dunlop & Lee, 2004; Warren, 2003), workplace incivility (Pearson, Andersson, & Porath, 2000), and antisocial workplace behaviors (AWB) (Robinson & O'Leary-Kelly, 1988). The phenomenon had been, and continues to be, empirically studied using various instruments; researchers quantify, generalize, and summarize results into diagnoses and offer organizational development initiatives (Dessler, 1999; Sofield & Salmond, 2003). But the research does not often translate into practice.

> I worked in the human resources specialty area of Labor Relations, handling grievances, discipline, and discharge at a unionized heavy industrial manufacturing facility. One case involved a female trades worker in her twenties, who had verbally abused and threatened to physically assault a colleague for moving "her" ladder. The colleague was a 30-plus year employee, a man who could have been her grandfather. Still, all involved agreed that there was a very real threat and that the woman needed anger management assistance, after being physically escorted off the company property. Even the union rep put up no argument.
>
> *– AT*

It is both personally and professionally motivating to me that I capture the lived experiences, the essential themes, of people's own stories about why they continue(d) working in environments they perceive as toxic or uncivil. When I question why any follower would choose to remain in a situation that numbs, dulls, or weakens them, the most frequent ad lib response is "for the money" or "because they need a job." But as Vroom (2007) suggests, I seek to address the real, as opposed to a perceived, audience and their practical concerns.

Vroom (2007) states that a researcher takes a cautious stance about making statements about the world, only making statements tempered by statistical significance and acknowledgment of uncontrolled variables, and measurement error. As a researcher, I choose to dig deeper into the subject of organizational commitment and workplace incivility than quantitative analysis and experimental distancing will allow. I choose to give people an opportunity to talk about the environments in which they work, why they perceive that environment as toxic, and why they choose to stay there. No other empirical research study, aside from Kusy and Holloway's 2009 mixed-methods three-stage project, offers such an approach to this subject matter. Most studies apply quantitative methods to encapsulate and summarize the phenomenon of workplace incivility (Harvey, Stoner, Hochwarter, & Kacmar, 2007; Tepper, 2000; Tierney & Tepper, 2007), when it can only truly be understood through the eyes and language of individuals who experienced it. This leads to a qualitative, phenomenological approach.

Giorgi (1985) states that the purpose of phenomenology "is to do justice to the lived aspects of the human phenomenon, and to do so, one first has to know how someone actually experienced what has been lived" (p. 1). Such descriptions are fruitful despite the objections to their use (people lie, honestly distort, or provide inadequate information), and any problems can be addressed and corrected with additional description.

Lester (1999) explains phenomenological research as gathering deep information and perceptions through inductive methods such as interviews, discussions, and observations. Lester (1999) asserts that modern humanist and feminist researchers insist it is impossible to start a qualitative research exploration without bias, and suggests that the researcher should place herself "in the 'frame' of the research as an interested and subjective actor rather than a detached and impartial observer" (p. 1). I am neither dispassionate nor disengaged in this work. Having been an employee subjected to uncivil conditions and inappropriate behaviors, I chose to exit the situation when I could. In my jobs in the field of Human Resources, I discouraged or disciplined such behaviors whenever possible. I continue to wonder why so many choose to stay in their own "psychic prisons" (Morgan, 1998).

The psychic prison metaphor

Introduced by Gareth Morgan in his 1998 book, *Images of Organization: The Executive Edition*, the metaphor emerges from Plato's allegory of the cave, "in which Socrates addresses the relations among appearance, reality, and knowledge" (p. 182). The allegory involves a literal underground cave, in which people are chained to the cave wall. There is a fire burning in front of the mouth of the cave, which illuminates the wall in front of the prisoners. Shadows of people and objects are thrown onto the wall by the firelight, and the prisoners come to associate outside sounds with those shadows. The prisoners give the shadows names and characteristics, and talk about the shadows in real time. They have created a reality based on their observations of the shadows.

In the metaphor, though, if one prisoner were released and allowed to see different aspects of reality, her vision would be completely altered, and she would be unable to accept the same confinement and limited reality again. And if she tried to share her new views on what was actually causing the shadows, and sounds, she would likely be ignored or ridiculed by the other prisoners, for whom the shadows represent the entirety of what is real. Those prisoners would cling desperately to their reality, and view the outside reality as dangerous and to be avoided at all cost, and by extension view their former comrade as dangerous as well.

People who learn new things and try to share them with a group bound by a strong organizational culture and shared reality may find that the new thing is opposed, and that they, too, are opposed, because they represent something new and potentially dangerous. It is possible to make change in your organization and eliminate antisocial workplace behaviors. But one cannot underestimate the power and significance of the unconscious in the organization's culture. As Morgan states, "it is possible to release trapped energy in ways that may promote creative transformation and change and create more integrated relations among individuals, groups, organizations, and their environments" (1996, p. 206).

We cannot ignore the unconscious dimension of human reality in the workplace. As you consider your own organizational culture, and ways in which it might be adjusted to eliminate any toxicity, I encourage you to review the strengths of the psychic prison metaphor:

- The idea of our own organization as a psychic prison is challenging and provocative. That's good. That means you have to take a good hard look at the basic assumptions about how you, and your employees, see and experience the world. Granted, you don't want to focus so much on the unconscious and psychological that you ignore other forces that control individual behavior and results (motivation, ability, role perceptions, situational factors, etc.).
- The possibility that our organization is operating as a psychic prison gives us a clear insight into how and why organizational development and change initiatives may have failed in the past, or may be so difficult to facilitate. You can't just mess with people's *reality*. They will fight you for it. Seriously, it is to your benefit to identify the status quo, and who has a vested interest in maintaining the *status quo*. Those who have deeply vested interests may represent potential champions for a change initiative, but it will take work to show them the benefit of releasing their current reality in favor of something foreign and new.

On a deeper level, I question the followership orientation that binds people to jobs and organizations where they observe workplace incivility. Some people take the position of "I can wait you out – you can't outwork me or outlast me" with regard to difficult colleagues and abusive supervision. One long-service employee, a manager, said to me directly, "I've been working here some 26, 27 years now, and man I've seen 'em come and go. Some of the managers, bosses I've had, whew. Real pieces of work. Yell at you, cuss you out. But at the end of the day, we got the job done, and I'm still here. Some of them aren't."

My years of observing and listening show that individuals' beliefs about their own ability to endure workplace challenges may be a factor in the decision to stay. Mosley, Boyar, Carson, and Pearson (2008) define self-efficacy as people's judgments of their capability to organize and execute courses of action required to attain designated types of performance, from Bandura's 1986 research. Successful performance equates to a person recognizing that he or she has the skills and abilities necessary to accomplish the task. If the task is to remain with the organization until retirement, or until a child covered under the organization's health plan graduates, then the employee may simply focus on that and determine that nothing will deter them from the goal.

Appelbaum and Hare (1996) investigated the impact of social learning theory, specifically self-efficacy, on work performance. I discussed this theory at some length in the previous chapter. Bandura described this construct as pervasive and central to the choices people make, their goals, how much effort they apply to a task, how long they persevere at a task in the face of adversity, how much stress they experience, and their susceptibility to depression. Self-efficacy correlates with and is predictive of burnout, stress, supervisors' performance ratings, and role adjustment, including acclimation and acculturation. Still, human resource management as a field has been slow to integrate social learning theory and self-efficacy concepts into the field. Perhaps those colleagues of mine who believed they could "wait out" bad leadership, rudeness, and incivility have since adjusted their roles, or even burned out. Fox (1994) states that work has the greatest influence on national health, more so than diet or lack of exercise. When people feel in control of their lives and their work, they live longer and have a better quality of life. Those who experience high levels of job dissatisfaction and disengagement experience a "joyless striving" that leads to more heart attacks than does poor diet. Fox even cites research that shows more heart attacks occurring between 8:00 and 9:00 am on Monday mornings than any other time.

Results of the study

The initial study was based on two assumptions: first, that those individuals can identify the varying personal reasons why they stay; and second, that staying leads to specific individual and organizational outcomes. These outcomes may include decreased creativity and innovation, reduced discretionary effort, and dysfunctional internal competition. In this book, excerpts from participant interviews are incorporated to illustrate theoretical concepts. Some participants reported leader or organizational negligence and oppression as a unique type of antisocial work behavior (AWB), while others identified specific toxic leader behaviors that led to negative individual and organizational outcomes. Overall, participants reported 74 unique incidents of AWB; of those, 21 specifically involved abusive supervision and 31 referenced bullying (Table 6.1). In 25 of the 74 reported incidents, management or a specific manager was identified as the perpetrator or agent of AWB.

TABLE 6.1 Frequency of occurrence by type of AWB

Description	Interviews	Journals
Abusive supervision	17	4
Violence	0	0
Bullying/aggression	27	4
Physical abuse/altercation	1	0
Verbal/psychological abuse	22	10
Rudeness, discourtesy, disrespect (workplace incivility)	56	16
Poor work performance	10	3
General environment	6	0
Total occurrences of AWB, by report type★	139	37
Total occurrences reported from target workplace	176	

★Including duplicate.

TABLE 6.2 Frequency of occurrence by descriptor and perceived intentionality

Descriptor	Frequency
Verbal/physical	41/22
Active/passive	52/11
Attempted/completed	2/61
Intentional/unintentional	53/10

Using Baron and Neuman's (1996) table as a guide, the frequency of participants' experiences as reported in interviews and journals was determined (Table 6.2). This set of frequencies showed whether the participant described an incident that was verbal or physical, active or passive, attempted or completed, and whether the participant had made an attribution about the actor's intentionality in the incident.

Antisocial workplace behavior

Robinson and O'Leary-Kelly (1988) identified a good reason for American managers and organizational researchers to study the prevention of AWB of all kinds. That reason is that **42% of women have reported instances of sexual harassment at work, 75% of employees have stolen from their employer, and 33% to 75% of employees report a range of AWB from insubordination to sabotage.** Robinson and O'Leary-Kelly's quantitative study used data from 187 full-time workers, evenly balanced between men (52%) and women (48%) from 35 work groups across 20 different organizations. Employees had an average tenure of 5.93 years in their company and 3.87 years in current job. Their study relied on survey instruments to assess the predictive impact of organizational citizenship and loyalty on individual antisocial behavior, the dependent variable. They defined AWB as negative behaviors in organizations, inclusive of a wide range of actions that have a harmful nature and offer the potential to hurt individuals and/or property. The data produced moderately negative correlations in each of the two relationships, lending support to the construct validity of the antisocial behavior scale they developed and used. So what? Well, the evidence shows the powerful and significant impact of AWB on workplace productivity, performance, and morale.

The superior boss–subordinate relationship is the pivotal environment through which work gets accomplished. Subordinates either affirm and support, or withdraw their affirmation and support, isolating the superior. Zaleznik (1970) identifies as a common executive mistake the confusing of compliance with commitment; compliance represents an "attitude of acceptance when a directive from an authority figure asks for a change in an individual's position, activities, or ideas… [the individual] is indifferent to the scope of the directive and the changes it proposes [and offers] little difficulty in translating the intent of directives into actual implementation" (p. 50). Commitment, though, represents "strong motivation on the part of an individual to adopt or resist the intent of the directive." If the individual is supportive, he or she will use ingenuity to interpret and implement the change, and work to assure success. If not, the individual may think and give lip service to "compliance," but find ways to sabotage the initiative.

In an early conceptual paper, Ashforth (1994) used similar terms to describe the petty tyrant, stating that these toxic leaders and managers may find support, even encouragement, for uncivil behaviors from targets and followers who lack the necessary means to respond appropriately. Ashforth suggested that powerlessness, lack of credibility, and the absence of autonomy limit followers' response options in the face of petty tyranny. As one participant in the present study stated, a peer used verbal abuse, profanity, bullying, and public shaming via group email to gain his compliance. He cited the shame and dismay of being cursed and insulted in front of his entire team in an email:

> when I questioned her in the email about what she wanted to do, here, of course she didn't have a good answer so she lashed out. And you know of course it was sending it out to the whole department and you know, name calling, which… that was very unprofessional to swear in an email and call somebody names.
>
> – K

> …this woman's manager… and the HR rep… they told me I had to drop it or there was going to be a letter put in *my* file. And I was like, but I didn't *do* anything, I was just trying to stick up… for how we do things, but evidently they don't want to create any waves, and, so I said "OK." And then they wanted me to be friends with her and take her to lunch but I didn't do that.
>
> – K

The peer's bullying was followed up by management coercion and Human Resources complicity, using positional power and coercion to stop his making "waves." While the suggestion for K. to take the adversarial peer out to lunch was never enforced, K. did continue to experience incidents of betrayal and bullying in that workgroup.

Trust, revisited

Toxic leaders "have poisonous effects" on their workplaces in which intent and impact are intertwined. That is, the leader tells a lie, but that leader has an inherent character flaw that makes it acceptable to lie. In the present study, leaders represent company policy one way to their employees, discordant with published corporate requirements, and then coerce the employees into submission. A female participant (T.) demonstrated knowledge of corporate policy and business unit practices borne of over 25 years' experience in the organization, indicating concern with her manager's supervisory practices:

> I think this is illegal and against the time and attendance policy… she's verifying my time and has no idea what I'm doing.

I'm charging to (temporary department) charges, but she's (home department supervisor) verifying my time. And I think that's illegal, according to the little training that I had. Because how does she know if I'm even putting in the right time?

Then she questioned me about my time and I said, "no that's what they told me to put in" and she said, "but I don't think it should be that." How do you know?

…So to me it's just… lies, liars. They go against anything that corporate says. If corporate says do not verify salaried employee time, they want you to send them an email, when you leave, when you get there. If it's outside of 7 to 3:30. To me, that's how she knows if my time is not within that 7 to 3:30 time frame, with that email. Because she's tracking my time. Which corporate says don't track time for salaried employees.

And if you call the HR guy, he's going to inform them on your whole conversation with him. And give them ammunition to go against you on anything.

– T

Followers are poisoned, or suffer from toxicity when leaders focus on their own well-being and power above the needs of the follower. Both followers and the organization suffer as a whole when leaders act without integrity. Managers who withhold support, "leave you hanging," or otherwise betray the employee's psychological contract create an atmosphere of distrust:

trust changed a lot, because at the time, the manager, I really had a lot of respect for the manager and when he didn't stand by me… [*hangs head*]

When nobody stood up for me it was like, well, then you don't value the employee as much as you value your false sense of calmness and everybody getting along, and it's a "happy place to work" instead of dealing with the conflict.

– K

In the present study, a line manager (M.) reported conflict with a high-ranking customer. He stated:

But this guy is one of our top performers and he gets the job done even though he's rude and crass and causes a bunch of waves and he's the squeaky wheel. At the end of the day he gets the job done so we can only be so tough on him. And it seems that it recurs about every two to three months. Just had another one last week. Same individual.

– M

Toxic managers represent a subset of toxic leaders, who erode trust in the organization and its management. They destroy morale, reduce retention, and intercept cooperative efforts and information sharing. Toxic managers take credit for departmental successes, but are unpredictable and disrespectful to their staff members. They focus on schedule and budget, ignoring opportunities for feedback or creativity. These individuals may be narcissistic, aggressive, and rigid.

Fritz (2002, 2013) sought to construct a typology of "troublesome" bosses, peers, and subordinates to understand how individuals think about them. Fritz found that unpleasant workplace relationships cost managerial time and energy through mediating disputes and dealing with problematic subordinates, leading to a crisis of incivility (Fritz, 2013). This crisis influences the professions and organizational lives of employees as it gains momentum in society. The study participants cited here, K., T., M., and D., reflect the influence of this crisis in their reporting of abusive events with only periodic episodes of emotional content. They have become inured to it, used to it. They endure.

Prior to the present study, one long-service employee in a management role shared thoughts on how the workplace used to be much more severe than at present:

> I've been working here some 26, 27 years now, and man I've seen 'em come and go. Some of the managers, bosses I've had, whew. Real pieces of work. Yell at you, cuss you out. But at the end of the day, we got the job done, and I'm still here. Some of them aren't.
>
> – B

Perseverance, an attitude that "no matter what, they can't break me," emerged in several participant accounts. Reasons for staying in the toxic workplaces or in relationships with toxic leaders included "I'm stubborn," "just plain hardheadedness," and "I don't quit." But the perseverance factor does not mask the actual outcomes of the toxic exchanges. The manager, M., identified the outcomes as frustrating to his own self-efficacy and self-esteem as a manager:

> *Interviewer: How has this experience impacted you in your job as a manager?*
>
> Couple of things. One, wearing. You know, just frustration of having to deal with, having to spend man-hours on something that shouldn't even be dealt with.
>
> And then having to, you know, hopefully the message getting across to my folks was hey I've got your back. And you know, you guys shouldn't stand for this and I don't stand for it either.
>
> So it's kind of twofold, one is you know hey I want him to recognize that I don't appreciate the comments, not needed not professional, change your attitude. Spending time dealing with all that. And then also, you know making sure that my folks understand that I'm not complacent about it.
>
> – M

This manager tries hard to reinforce the trusting relationship he has with his team, attempting to show them that he supports them, represents their interests, and will defend them as needed. But he walks a narrow path of protecting his own job security and fighting for his team members.

Civility, incivility, and toxicity – a review

The social and behavioral sciences focus on human behavior associated with toxic leadership, addressing how group pressures encourage or discourage conformity in group members, but not specifically focused on toxic leaders. Social scientists like Fromm, Becker, Asch, Festinger, and Sherif all sought to investigate the nature of obedience to toxic leaders (Lipman–Blumen, 2010). Perhaps the most famous study resulted from Milgram's investigation of obedience to a toxic leader, finding that "a large percentage of individuals can be intimidated into obeying a malevolent authority… [But there was no], focus on why, even without intimidation, many of us yearn for, are attracted to, and sometimes prefer toxic leaders" (p. 385). Lipman–Blumen (2005) states that followers are vulnerable to toxic leaders because they "choose to live by illusions" which offer comfort, or exhilaration, over the realities of our humble painful challenging lives (p. 29).

Lipman–Blumen (2010) defines toxicity as an act of commission or one of omission. The traditional definition of the word toxic involves acting as or having the effect of poison.

A study participant, D., indicated a pervasive undercurrent of toxic leadership:

> management creates an oppressive environment. It's subtle, and it's pervasive, so it affects everybody without them realizing it. Let me give you a for instance. They will call together a meeting of the entire group at a conference room. They know how many people are in their group, they know the capacity of the conference room, and they will go out of their way to deliberately schedule everybody in the conference room at one time knowing they will not all fit.
>
> The heads will be at the table with reserved seats, and everyone else can stand around like cattle. That happens so routinely, and you have to go out of your way to do it. The only possible conclusion is that they are doing it deliberately.
>
> *Interviewer: Is there any consistency in who's left standing?*
>
> Well it's always people that aren't management. Whereas if they were to split the meeting up into two sections, everybody could come and have a seat and be comfortable for the hour-plus presentation.
>
> And that's how pervasive it is. They literally no longer think about the impact of the way they routinely do business. The question just never crosses their minds, "is this the way you treat human beings, or is this the way you treat cattle?"
>
> – D

Toxic leaders "have poisonous effects" on their workplaces in which intent and impact are intertwined. That is, the leader tells a lie, but that leader has an inherent character flaw that makes it acceptable to lie. Toxic leader is defined as an individual whose destructive behavior and dysfunctional personality characteristics generate serious and enduring poisonous effects on those they lead. Intentionality plays a part in determining an individual's level of toxicity. For example, an intentional toxic leader will "deliberately harm others or enhance themselves at others expense" (Lipman-Blumen, 2010, p. 29). Unintentionally toxic leaders "cause serious harm by careless or reckless behavior, as well as by their incompetence" (p. 29).

> Leaders can be "toxic in some situations and not in others."
>
> – Jean Lipman-Blumen

The inimitable Dr. Lipman-Bluman goes on to describe how followers are poisoned, or suffer from toxicity, when leaders focus on their own well-being and power above the needs of the follower; both followers and the organization suffer as a whole when leaders act without integrity. Most books on leadership focus on leaders rather than followers, but there is "no shortage of bad leaders to chronicle" (p. 384). So why stay? Jean identifies specific barriers to exit, including the financial, social, political, psychological, and existential impact to an individual choosing to change his or her career and exit a relationship with the toxic leader. This would fall squarely under the "continuance commitment" category described in Chapter 4; I stay because I can't afford to leave, whether that means I can't afford to lose the salary, the social network or esteem, the political capital I've accrued in the organization, or other psychological investments I've made in this identity. According to her, there are six aspects of the human condition that render followers vulnerable to toxic leadership. These include existential anxiety, psychological needs, feelings of powerlessness, crises, rapid change, and turbulence in our lives, special to the special terrors and challenges of our era, individuals longing for leaders to help address the infinite possibilities ahead, and recognition of the unfinished and unfinished of the world which leaves room for heroic action. Followers want their leaders to project certainty and confidence, characteristics that they sometimes lack themselves. But leaders sometimes project an altogether different image, that of an abusive boss.

Tepper (2000) defines abusive supervision as a manifestation of dysfunctional workplace behavior involving tyrannical, ridiculing, and undermining actions by one's superior. Such behavior is likely to continue until the target terminates the relationship, the agent the relationship, or the agent modifies his or her behavior. The behavior has an enduring quality because the target remains as long as they feel powerless to take corrective action.

Further, Harvey, Stoner, Hochwarter, and Kacmar (2007) describe abusive supervision as a phenomenon affecting a substantial number of organizations and their members, stating that 10 to 16% of American workers report experiencing abusive supervision on a regular basis. These numbers have increased in recent years. Abusive supervision is defined as a sustained display of hostile verbal or nonverbal behaviors excluding physical contact. Some of the resultant undesirable subordinate outcomes include turnover stress, emotional exhaustion, and perceptions of organizational injustice.

What does abusive supervision look like?

Many workers have had the experience of a "horrible" boss or supervisor, but never really have we had to delineate exactly why we viewed that person as a horrible leader. If nobody comes to work – no rational person, at least (see Clive Boddy's work on Corporate Psychopaths) – with the intention of doing harm to another person, then certainly we must stop and consider what it is these people do that is so abusive. Perhaps by naming it, we can eventually reshape that behavior and reduce its presence in our workplaces.

It includes public criticism, rudeness, coercion, loud, angry tantrums, and other inconsiderate actions. While similar to early constructs like petty tyranny, abusive supervision definitely involves hostility as well as indifference. NOTE: Abusive supervision may not be deviant if it conforms to organizational policies or norms. It is in these cases that the associate or employee experiencing or witnessing abusive supervision as part of an organizational norm must decide for himself or herself whether or not to stay and tolerate it, and become a part of the reason the norm continues.

While similar to petty tyranny and social undermining, abusive supervision includes hostile behavior, both violent and nonviolent (Harvey, Stoner, Hochwarter, & Kacmar, 2007). Employee outcomes include feelings of helplessness, decreased self-efficacy, psychological distress, emotional exhaustion, work-family conflict, turnover intentions, decreased job satisfaction and organizational commitment, and general feelings of unfair treatment. Harvey, Stoner, Hochwarter, and Kacmar (2007) found that abusive supervision directly predicted tension, emotional exhaustion, and intent to leave. It is definitely a form of psychological abuse – and, generically, abusive supervision is just one person behaving like a jerk. Psychological abuse in the workplace refers to a sustained display of hostile verbal and nonverbal behavior, excluding physical contact. One author in the HR field states that the total cost of jerks, or TCJ, must include the cost of overtime, turnover costs for assistants to that individual, potential legal costs, and anger management training, all on top of salary and benefits. And, unfortunately, being a jerk is contagious (Sutton, 2007). Seriously.

The concept of emotional contagion emerged in the literature in the early 1990s, and suggests that disdain, anger, and contempt spread quickly throughout a group or team. If one person such as a supervisor demonstrates such behavior then others will emulate that behavior, creating a vacuum of civility. Sutton provides a list of uncivil behaviors in the workplace called the dirty dozen: personal insults, invading coworkers' personal territory, uninvited physical contact, threats and intimidation, both verbal and nonverbal, sarcastic jokes and teasing used to deliver insults, withering emails, status slaps intended to humiliate victims, public shaming or status degradation rituals, rude interruptions, two-faced attacks, dirty looks or glaring, and treating people as if they were invisible. Why would you stay in that kind of environment? Why *not*?

Turnover costs in particular should scare you; in some industries and for certain positions, it can cost nearly twice as much to recruit, select, hire, onboard, and train a replacement for the employee who decides they've had enough and resigns. In another study, Sofield and Salmond (2003) describe the lived experience of verbal abuse in a large, multi-hospital system, and determine the relationship of verbal abuse to employees' intent to leave the organization. As you'd expect, the amount of abuse and the intent to leave were significantly related. Verbal abuse was directly related to decreased morale, increased job dissatisfaction, and higher turnover.

Deviant, uncivil behavior

Dunlop and Lee (2004) define workplace deviant behavior as voluntary behavior of organizational members that violates significant organizational norms. That is, it's a choice the individual employee makes to go against the cultural expectations of that organization and group. In doing so, the individual employee threatens the well-being of other employees, of the team, or of the organization overall. Deviant behavior is dangerous and corrosive to organizational culture; employees who observe occurrences of deviant behavior tend to feel unsafe and begin to take precautions to protect themselves. The researchers state that at the unit level workplace deviant behaviors affect the organization's functioning and conceal multiple hidden costs that reduce efficiency.

The management literature focuses on **negative** organizational employee deviance such as stealing and embezzling, but lacks any discussion of **positive** forms of employee deviance, such as dissent, tempered radicalism, whistleblowing, and functional disobedience. Any of these might be considered employees exercising their voice (as opposed to the exit option) in the workplace. Employee deviance is defined as behavioral departure from norms of a reference group that can cause disastrous consequences for the group, organization, or society (Warren, 2003).

"CIVILITY MATTERS." [emphasis mine] - Pearson, Andersson and Porath (2000)

In the workplace, common, everyday incivilities "taint the office and the factory" (p. 123). Types of rude or uncivil behavior include demeaning language or gestures, innuendos, and physically hovering while the coworker is on the phone. The authors defined workplace civility as behavior that helps preserve norms of mutual respect in the workplace. These behaviors are fundamental to positively connecting with one another, building relationships, and empathizing.

> Our innate drive to bond requires that when we work, we have the opportunity to connect with others and build relationships with them.

The opposite then is workplace incivility, defined as rudeness, disregard for others, and mistreatment that leads to disconnection, breach of relationships, and erosion of empathy. Workplace norms represent the norms of the community of practice at work; basic moral standards norms differ across organizations, industries, and cultures. Norms represent a shared moral understanding among organizational members that allow them to cooperate; "incivility is a violation of these norms" (p. 126). Workplace incivility is defined as social interaction between two or more parties at work that can be interpreted differently by different observers, but the event is often ambiguous regarding the initiator's degree of malicious intent. Workplace incivility includes unexpected behaviors that go against workplace norms for mutual respect. How employees treat each other affects their ability to work together, their interactions with other colleagues, and their interactions with bystanders. The results of a sustained culture of workplace incivility include increased absenteeism, reduced commitment, decreased productivity, and higher turnover. Of course. Might be worth avoiding those consequences, and investing in some team development work, eh? Then again, some organizations condone behavior that may get the job done using uncivil means. Uncivil acts occur, and no one is taken to task for rude behavior. One participant in the mixed-methods (some quantitative surveys for analysis, some qualitative interviews) study asked, under such conditions "how do we find respect for our leaders, let alone enthusiasm for our organization?"(Pearson, Andersson, & Porath, 2000, p. 136).

Time to pay attention

> One pharmacist in my department has a tendency to get overly anxious, and she sends herself into work that other subordinates can do, others who are in positions like Technician. The other pharmacist will see the first one NOT working on pharmacist duties, and so as soon as pharmacist 2 sees pharmacist 1 walk away like take a break or go to lunch, then 2 will say, "then I'm not going to do any work today." Now, number two can't (won't) say anything to the first one, so this game persists. And the pharmacy suffers. Every team member in the pharmacy suffers. Every single one. All of the cashiers are

getting yelled at by the customers who want their prescriptions, the techni-
cians can't get to the prescriptions because the pharmacist hasn't checked
them, and the second pharmacist refuses to do the work because she believes
the first pharmacist hasn't done her share of the work. And how does that
affect the organization, in terms of being the manager? Well, the manager
gets called whether on duty or not, and has to try to sort this mess out. And
you don't know if it's a customer that called the manager, or the next level
up – the manager's supervisor. So now you've gone outside the group, and
everybody knows your dirty laundry.

Robinson and O'Leary-Kelly (1988) state that there is good reason for
American managers and organizational researchers to study the prevention of
AWB. That good reason is that 42% of women have reported instances of sexual
harassment at work, 75% of employees have stolen from their employer, and 33 to
75% of employees report a range of behavior from insubordination to sabotage.
AWB is defined as negative behaviors and organizations. It is inclusive of a wide
range of actions that have a harmful nature, with the potential to hurt individuals
and or property. Using Bandura's social learning theory, individual and environmental antecedents have been identified, predicting AWB. Justice theory has
been used to explain AWBs like theft and retaliation. The research is generally
focused at the individual level of analysis that can be considered at the group level
as well. Robinson and O'Leary-Kelly (1998) found that work group context does
influence the AWBs of individual employees. If a work group exhibits antisocial
behaviors, this predicts individual antisocial behaviors, supporting group level
analysis.

In this mixed-methods research study, the interviews identified five key issues
which led to construction of the survey: the toxic person's character and behaviors, the leader's reaction to the toxic behaviors, the leader's strategy for dealing
with the toxic person, the effects of toxicity on the system, and the role of the
organization's culture on toxicity (Robinson & O'Leary-Kelly, 1988, p. 8). They
found no significant differences in gender of toxic individuals, stating that individuals with the manipulative interpersonal style "have been using problematic
behavior for years to get what they need from others" (p. 9). One domain within
toxic personalities is that of incivility, defined as employees' lack of regard for
one another. Approximately 50% of those who experienced incivility at work
reported that they lost time worrying about the incident and its future consequences. Over 25% of individuals who were targets of incivility cut back their
work efforts, and 50% contemplated quitting after being the target of incivility;
12% of those actually quit (p. 14). Other studies indicate that 20% of American
workers report having been the target of incivility at least once a week, while
10% reported witnessing workplace incivility daily. Another domain within the
toxic personality involves bullying, defined as the behavior of "someone who

places targets in a submissive, powerless position… Easily influenced and controlled, in order to achieve personal or organizational objectives" (p. 15). Experiences of bullying in the workplace lead to higher turnover and less favorable attitudes toward both the job and the organization (p. 15).

Kusy and Holloway (2009) also researched toxic people and toxic workplaces, from the angle of the toxic person's behaviors and the effects of those behaviors on the organization's outcomes, including how leaders react and how organizational systems sustain the behaviors. I'm not alone in my curiosity about employees' perspectives on their workplaces, and why they stay in the presence of toxic behavior and toxic people.

Workplace bullying

Hodson, Roscigno, and Lopez (2006) state that 10 to 20% of all employees report being bullied, with psychological consequences equivalent to PTSD from war and prison camp experiences. Little research exists identifying the organizational contexts likely to promote bullying behavior. Two specific dimensions of workplace context affect the likelihood of bullying: weak targets or low level employees with relational powerlessness, and a state of mismanagement or poor leadership, which damages organizational coherence. Bullying is defined as a form of informal subtle and sometimes covert workplace behavior; it includes repeated attempts to torment, wear down, or frustrate another person; it further includes treatment that provokes pressures, intimidates, or otherwise causes discomfort (p. 384). Bullying can include blatant emotional abuse, violations of interpersonal norms, and other means of inflicting damage to another person's sense of dignity and self-worth. Bullying emerged as a topic of interest around the same time as trust "was identified as a core concept in organizational analysis" (p. 385). Bullying represents a subcategory of conflict in organizations, but is defined by a unidirectional nature and intentional use as a weapon to hurt others. Organizational context is a factor in individuals' perceived ability to exercise their own relational power to dominate others.

> I have a person in my office, we'll call her Sheila. She varies in her moods, as most of us do, and if she doesn't thinks that you've handled past situations in a positive light or if you've approached her with constructive criticism of her job, she will hold on to that until a later period to use toward her superior. The superior will then feel bullied, manipulated into situations where Sheila can have the upper hand. For instance, she'll make friends with the customers. She's not friendly with coworkers, or superiors. But she'll take the customer's side in a dispute, even vocally arguing against company positions and leaving the superior in a situation where they're standing alone and unsupported, telling a customer "no." It's a tough situation.

Unethical leaders/followers

Uhl-Bien and Carsten (2010) state that the predominant message in contemporary ethics and communication research is that the responsibility for ethics rests with the leader. If you, the executive, the leader, or influencer, do not model ethical behavior then why should followers act in an ethical manner? The authors offer a model of upward ethical leadership to yield more active responses by followers to unethical leader behavior; if followers do not comply with leader directives, then they are considered insubordinate, they risked punishment sanctioned disregarding ostracism, even expulsion from the organization (p. 366). Studies have shown people cite reasons of futility, fear, and concern about labeling as a troublemaker, as well as retaliation as reasons why they do not object in the face of leader unethical behavior.

In an unethical climate, there is a distorted definition of loyalty, requiring employee followers to go along and not cause trouble. Followers must not question the decisions of superiors, but only speak to them about positive things. Employees experience feelings of powerlessness and have minimal choice of response when they sense a lack of control over themselves and over others. In such situations, followers expect that their own behavior cannot determine the occurrence of desired outcomes (p. 370).

Key takeaways

1. Workplace incivility is a real thing, and when it involves threats of violence it must be taken very seriously.
2. As Morgan stated, "strong … cultures can become pathological" and that can lead to increasingly dangerous blind spots, areas of individual and organizational vulnerability. That is, ignorance is not bliss. What you don't know can hurt you, and it's likely that there are things you don't know because of what your organization chooses to focus on and chooses to ignore. More specifically, as the leader, you may see some components of your organization's culture, and miss others.
3. We are all vulnerable to toxic leadership, and to becoming toxic followers.
4. Abusive supervision, bullying, and workplace incivility may be the norm in some workplaces.
5. Emotional contagion can cause disdain, anger, and contempt to spread throughout a work group.

7
STRUCTURE AND CULTURE

Organizations are social entities, existing solely for and comprised of individuals. We as people fulfill our own goals by participating in organizations. They are constructed, artificial things, designed by people. The difficult decision is how to design tasks and break them down into units that individuals can manage. There are three specific criteria for robust organizational design: effectiveness, efficiency, and viability. Effectiveness suggests that the organization (the group of people working together) "realizes its purpose and accomplishes its goals... An organization is efficient if it utilizes the least amount of resources necessary to obtain its products or services... [and] An organization is viable if it exists over a long period of time" (Burton & Obel, 2005, p. 4). Over time, organizations tend to become larger, more cumbersome, more formalized, and departmentalized creations.

> "If you give two employees a block of stone each and ask them to carve a square out of it. If you tell one of them that his stone is going to become a part of a large castle whereas you only ask the second person to carve a square, the first person is for sure going to like his job better."
>
> (Carlzon, quoted in Burton & Obel, 2005, p. 89)

Organizational structure

Jan Carlzon, former president of SAS Group, understood the connection between leadership style and organizational structure. In fact, Carlzon sought to decentralize the organizational structure of SAS decision making, so that employees (once educated) could be empowered to handle more problems in real time. Because of this increased employee engagement initiative, SAS associates began to help one another more, look out for one another's safety and success, and focus on giving superior service and products to their customers rather than focusing on claiming credit for good performance (Burton & Obel, 2005).

In the organization where my study took place, the structure is a large, 100+ year-old, mechanistic, and highly formalized company. McShane and von Glinow (2009) offer a great outline of organizational structure, and I used it to analyze the environment in which my study participants worked. Formal decision-making authority resides at the top levels of management, at the primary corporate location. The organization has a tall hierarchy, with multiple layers of management and a clear "chain of command." Staff generally feel minimally empowered, and management is a highly desirable placement merely due to the positional power it offers. The hierarchy depends on those within the span of control of a manager submitting to that manager's legitimate power, and on formal communications and processes to coordinate work. The grapevine, or informal communication channel, is "thick and quick," but the organization itself depends on a high degree of standardization through processes, formal instructions, procedures, work packages, and work breakdown structures to transform its inputs (whether material or technological) into outputs, measured by clear goals and metrics. The skills required to perform specific tasks are trained into employees using formalized systems and processes.

As McShane and von Glinow (2009) noted, as firms get older, larger, and more regulated, they encounter many of the issues my study participants identified: significant rigidity and clinging to "how we do things," resistance to change or even global market conditions due to an inflexible set of systems that support the existing structure, reduced work efficiency as numbers of employees grew over the decades / redundancy; and, finally, significant job dissatisfaction and work stress.

In this organization, there is a highly departmentalized (think: silos) organizational environment. There is a clear chain of command, and common mental models or paradigms are shared, which leads to a pervasive sense of "us, for better or worse – this is who we are." The culture in this organization is definitely not weak, perhaps not as adaptive as would be desirable, definitely strong.

Staff coordinate through informal coordination – grapevine – more than management might like, but that is one of the side-effects of extreme departmentalization and information control. Metrics are created to measure just about everything in this workplace. The structure is a mix of functional (organized around specific skills and services provided) and divisional (organized around major product type) structures – there are finance and supply chain departments, for example, that serve the entire organization, but there are professionals in each major program division and on each major project, representing the functional departments. In some cases this approximates an actual matrix structure, in which employees answer to two different managers at the same time – causing additional workplace stress. Matrix organizations, such as those shown in Table 7.1, are popular in corporations and publicly held organizations like this one, because

TABLE 7.1 Sample of matrix configurations

Company	Function/Division	Supervision
American Bankers Association	Administration, Corporate planning, Finance, Information services, Investor relations, Legal	By project – Utilities, Auto Industry
Booz Allen Hamilton	Worldwide commercial business, Worldwide technical business	By market teams – Aerospace, automobiles, defense, financial services, energy, health, information technology, organizations, and management
Nestle	Finance and control, Marketing, Production, Technical, R&D	By region – Americas, Asia, Europe, Oceania, and Africa

(Burton & Obel, 2005)

functional specialization and efficiency is desirable and a project focus allows the organization to clearly communicate to its stakeholders its objectives, metrics, and milestones. In some respects this organization behaves as a matrix organization, and it is worth conceptualizing that idea with a sample listing.

The matrix structure is justified when the organization seeks to focus on the customer, product, or specific market, and when organizational leaders desire agility and responsiveness to market conditions and customer demands. However, this structure requires comfort with uncertainty, shared leadership and authority, and team result accountability. This setup is expensive, requiring many specialists and managers to coordinate their work.

The divisional structure, exemplified in companies shown in Table 7.2, does create an environment for redundancy and duplication of resources, and some silos of knowledge. Employees can spend an entire career in this one workplace and, potentially, move from one division to another, but it is unlikely. The benefits of a divisional structure are that it accommodates organizational growth, and it allows for coordination in a diverse market, but this organization does not function in a diverse market.

"Organizational theory is a positive science that focuses on understanding organizations."

– (Burton & Obel, 2005)

The organization in which my study participants worked faces a complex external environment in which there are many stakeholders – the community where the facility is located, the employees themselves, local and distant supplier

TABLE 7.2 Sample of divisional configurations

Bank of America	Global asset management, retail banking, wholesale banking
Bayer	Additives and rubber, animal health, biologicals, coatings and colorings, consumer care products, diagnostics, fibers, industrial chemicals, pharma, plastics, specialty metals
Hewlett Packard	Computing systems, embedded and personal systems, finance and administration, HP labs, human resources, imaging and printing systems, strategy and corporate operations
KPMG US	Assurance, consulting, financial services, healthcare and life sciences, manufacturing, public services, retail and distribution, tax
GE	International, aerospace, aircraft engines, medical systems, transportation systems, lighting, plastics, industrial and power systems, motors, supply, appliances, information, corporate R&D

(Burton & Obel, 2005)

organizations, multiple unions, an internal trades and professional educational program, local workforce development centers, and a political contingency that seeks to protect the interests of the organization as a major employer in the region. When the external environment is complex, the recommendation is to decentralize (Burton & Obel, 2005; McShane & von Glinow, 2009). However, this organization tends to remain largely centralized.

The company faces relatively stable external environmental conditions, in which change is fairly predictable and regulation is consistent. These factors support the organization's use of a mechanistic structure, in which there is generally a narrow span of control (managers of salaried associates and supervisors of hourly employees tend to have groups of no more than 12–15 employees reporting to them); a high degree of formalization, and a high degree of centralized decision making.

The company functions in an integrated external marketplace; that is, as an organization it primarily produces two to three products, serving one to two primary clients and operating in two to three locations only. This would argue for a functional structure, particularly as the external environment is complex, lacking significant segmentation, and presuming a static condition (not dynamic). The organization does use a mixed functional structure, as described above. The functional structure, as shown in Table 7.3, is "the most prevalent in many industries" (Burton & Obel, 2005, p. 51). The rationale for this structural approach is that it leads to efficiencies of scale and specialization. However, this configuration tends to lack flexibility and innovation. A company configured this way will function best in a stable environment requiring minimal change or responsiveness, using known technologies. Such an organization benefits from job specialization and product specialization, and allows coordination to work with minimal information processing needs (Burton & Obel, 2005, p. 54).

TABLE 7.3 Sample of functional configurations

Coors Brewing Company	Administration and finance, corporate affairs, engineering and construction, human resources and communication, marketing, plant operations and technology, sales
Fiat Auto	Environmental and industrial policies, logistics, marketing and sales, manufacturing, personnel and organization, purchasing, quality, research and development
General Semiconductors, Inc.	Corporate development, E-business, finance, information technology, general counsel, operations

(Burton & Obel, 2005)

This organization faces a varying environment with regard to munificence versus hostility. That is, in a munificent external environment, organizations enjoy plenty of resources and high product demand, and can settle into a mechanistic structure without as much concern about becoming obsolete. However, in a hostile external environment ("the red ocean") in which there is a great deal of competition and resource scarcity, organizations should employ a more organic structure for responsiveness. Legal regulation and political impacts tend to reduce the stability of resources and product demand for this company, which would argue for a more organic structure, but the company remains highly mechanistic. Large, resistant to change, slow to address the ethical and subcultural needs of its people.

With regard to size, organizations tend to increase job specialization as the company grows larger, to accommodate greater and greater division of labor even to a granular "assembly line" approach. Standardization of processes increases, and there is more hierarchy and formalization. Decentralization generally increases as well (McShane & von Glinow, 2009).

Technology in an organizational context includes the mechanisms, processes, and tools used to generate the products or services an organization provides. Burton and Obel (2005) explained two key contingencies that help performance management and organizational scientists determine the appropriate organizational design, or structure, applying an if/then rule. First, what is the number of exceptions to standard procedures that tend to occur in this organization? This is an organization's *variability*. Second, what is the degree of predictability, or its opposite, non-routine difficulty, in the work required to generate the products and services in the organization? This is the organization's *analyzability*. If variability is routine and analyzability is non-routine, undefined, then the organizational structure is known as "craft." If the variability is routine and problems are highly analyzable, the structure is known as "routine." In the organization where my study participants worked, according to the two key contingencies, task variability is high and problem analyzability is analyzable, then organizational structure is known as "engineering." The effect of technology on a manufacturing business such as this is significant, and has caused opportunities for employee disengagement and cultural rifts.

> "Structure follows Strategy."

While organizational structure should always follow strategy, sometimes the structure takes root and engenders a maladaptive culture, preventing the agility needed for environmental responsiveness. An organization that offers a cost leadership strategy should be open to ideas from any employee for how to better capitalize on competitive advantages like pricing and low-cost production. An organization that, like the one my participants worked in, is more focused on differentiation, should ensure that it provides unique products and attracts clients who want greater customization.

Cultural orientation

Organizations can take one of many different perspectives – the stakeholder perspective, the open systems perspective, the high-performing work groups perspective, the organizational learning perspective. In the latter, the company focuses on improving its knowledge base through gathering human, intellectual capital (what's in the minds of employees) as well as knowledge capital (stock and inventory of stored knowledge). According to Burton and Obel (2005, p. 11):

> organizational learning involves four constructs: knowledge acquisition, information distribution, information interpretation and organizational memory... Knowledge management is developing the knowledge base of the organization; organizational learning is improving that knowledge base for increased value to the organization.

Schein (2005) states that while still a relatively recent concept, organizational culture is at the intersection of several social sciences – anthropology, sociology, social psychology, and organizational behavior. Primary embedding of culture is influenced by what leaders pay attention to, measure, and control; how leaders react to critical incidents and organizational crises; how leaders facilitate deliberate role modeling and coaching; organizational criteria for the allocation of rewards and status, and the operational criteria for recruitment, selection, promotion, retirement, and excommunication. Secondary articulation and reinforcement of organizational culture happens through organizational design and structure, organizational systems and procedures, physical design, stories, legends, myths and symbols, and formal statements of organizational philosophy like creeds and charters. Culture perpetuates and reproduces itself through socialization of new members, and members can discuss and explain their socialization process. Therefore, the question of why people stay in toxic workplaces finds its contexts in the definition of a culture and its norms, and in the identification of aberrant or uncivil behavior *for that culture*.

Organizational culture is comprised of shared attitudes, behaviors, values, beliefs, and assumptions, which demonstrate how employees in the organization respond to organizational challenges. There are three specific levels of organizational culture; the first involves that which observers can see from the outside, or artifacts. Self-reported, self-managed marketing information like the company website, annual reports, financial statements, and press releases all provide some basic artifact data. Additional artifacts may require a closer look at the company, such as organizational stories and legends ("Chainsaw Al," for example), rituals (how we celebrate earning a contract), ceremonies (the 40-year employees' dinner banquet), and organizational language used (Clients or customers? Explosive head-on conflict, or tactful, respectful dialogue? Jargon?) And finally the structures and décor in the organization's physical location.

The second, deeper level of organizational culture is the set of shared values that may be invisible to the external observer but that comprises the tacit beliefs and attitudes around what is right or wrong, good and bad, in an organization. Many organizations publicize their values, so this information may be available to the casual researcher. Due to new technologies and internet platforms in our contemporary culture of sharing that allow employees to reveal more about their employers than might have happened 50 years ago, organizational researchers and social scientists can now also get an idea of the internal climate in an organization. Employees post on social media, professional networking sites, and job and salary comparison sites what they think about their organizations and their leaders, and how well (or poorly) those individuals manifest the company's stated values.

The third and deepest level of organizational culture, impossible to identify without significant time either as an organizational member or through prolonged interaction with organizational members, is the level of *shared assumptions*. This level represents the unconscious beliefs, the attitudes that are taken for granted and presumed. This is the level of paradigms, worldviews, and mental models – this is where assumptions like "that's just professional behavior" or "that's just common sense" get formed. It's the "How we do things around here" level of understanding.

McShane and von Glinow (2009) summarize the dimensions of organizational culture, as based on seven dimensions: Innovation, Stability, Respect for people, Outcome orientation, Attention to detail, Team orientation, and Aggressiveness. The organization where my study participants worked is one that does not welcome experimenting and opportunity-seeking behavior, is risk-averse, has many rules, and has high cautiousness; thus, it is low on the Innovation dimension. The company values predictability, security, and rule-orientation, so it is high on Stability. Its espoused values include respect for people, and efforts are made originating in the human resources division to ensure fairness and tolerance, but study participants identified poor work practices and sufficient incivility to cast doubt on these key organizational justice principles.

The company is results-oriented with high expectations and a significant quality orientation due to the high-risk nature of the work performed there, so it has a high Outcome orientation. Attention to detail is required and failure to adhere to precise, analytic standards can lead to extreme product failure, discipline, even discharge. The individual climate or mood of employees is collaborative and people-oriented, but overall the employees did not indicate that they felt the *company* was collaborative or people-oriented. They dissociate themselves and their workmates from The Company. Finally, the company places significant emphasis on social responsibility at the same time as on its competitive positioning, seeking to maintain high barriers to entry for any other potential market entrant. This would indicate a midrange position on Aggressiveness.

Why they stayed: letting the data speak

In this book we've reviewed the previous knowledge on antisocial workplace behavior (AWB) and its many subtypes: verbal and psychological abuse, abusive supervision, bullying, and workplace incivility (rudeness, discourtesy, and disrespect). We've looked at workplace toxicity, the psychological contract, norms of communication, values, and ethics (and unethical leaders and followers). In my consulting business I spend a lot of time looking at organizational design and structure, organizational culture, and employee engagement, and I spent a bit of time on those topics as well here. Now, I'll share with you what my participants actually said.

In an empirical phenomenological study, it's important to establish "validity" (a mostly quantitative concept applied to qualitative research) by demonstrating faithfulness to the key topic. The phenomenon I investigated here with these participants was, specifically, why employees might choose to stay in a work situation where they have experienced AWB. Rather than attempting to generalize, or do a lot of counting to prove the frequency of this phenomenon, we rely on weight and intensity for explicating the data here. While the study may seem small by quantitative standards, its depth compensates for that, and each participant was invited to recommend another potential participant ("Snowball sampling"). However, saturation occurred at ten participants, which matches what the literature on this qualitative methodology stated – two to ten participants engaging in long, in-depth interviews will usually yield saturation, the point at which participant themes begin to recur.

My study participants described unique incidents of AWB that had happened to them, or that they had observed. Their reactions included feeling disrespected and abused, bullied and treated aggressively, challenged to the point of violence, undervalued, and betrayed. In some cases participants felt obligated to help the actor understand facts and information about the situation, in the hope of getting the actor to change his or her behavior or attitudes.

TABLE 7.4 Frequency of occurrence by type of AWB

	Interviews	Journals
Abusive supervision	17	4
Violence	0	0
Bullying/aggression	27	4
Physical abuse/altercation	1	0
Verbal/psychological abuse	22	10
Rudeness, discourtesy, disrespect (workplace incivility)	56	16
Poor work performance	10	3
General environment	6	0
Total (including duplicate) occurrences of AWB, by report type	139	37
Total occurrences reported from target workplace	176	

In addition to their journal entries, my study participants shared 63 independent incidents of experiencing AWB as target, witness, or even agent/actor. And what's worse is that by type of AWB, the breakdown gets even more dramatic, as shown in Table 7.4.

The incidents that were reported included verbal attacks (41), physical threats or contact (22), active aggression (52), and passive behaviors or refusal to act (11). Sixty-one times the AWB was completed, twice it was attempted but not completed, and 53 times the participants stated that the behavior was intentional versus 10 unintentional incidents. Most commonly the actor/agenda was a specific peer (30 times), a specific manager or supervisor (15 times), or Management as an entity, in general (9 times).

As a result, these participants described feelings and outcomes as listed in Table 7.5:

TABLE 7.5 Frequency of outcomes reported

Outcome indicated	Frequency
Feelings of helplessness – "I was powerless"	4
Decreased self-efficacy	1
Psychological distress	5
Emotional exhaustion	4
Work-family conflict	1
Turnover or turnover intent – "my time (on loan) had expired …and I left;" "Leave"	5
Decreased job satisfaction	4
Decreased organizational commitment – "Yes. (whispered) Sad"	2
General feelings of injustice	3
Other: Felt Empowered - "my faith sustained me… strengthened my faith… I'm nobody's victim"	1
No impact at all: "just another day at work"	3
Other: Self-reflection – "guarded in conversation now"	2

Key takeaways

1. Structure follows strategy, and culture is pervasive.
2. Organizational structure affects everything, from coordination of work to communication tools and types to products and customer relationship management.
3. Organizations tend to decentralize, increase job specialization, and standardize more as they get older and larger.
4. Over time, organizational culture can become entrenched and maladaptive.
5. Organizational culture is influenced by what the organization's leaders pay attention to, measure, and control. It's also influenced by how leaders react and respond to critical incidents (positive or negative) and crises. Culture is transmitted by leader role modeling.

PART IV

Composite themes – executive summary

"People are definitely a company's greatest asset. It doesn't make any difference whether the product is cars or cosmetics. A company is only as good as the people it keeps."

– Mary Kay Ash, founder of Mary Kay Cosmetics (Roberts, 2016)

8

SENSEMAKING

"Equality, justice, fairness – all this is missing in our culture."
– Matthew Fox, author

Fox (1994) suggested that "instead of a burden with a paycheck at the end of it" (p. 42), work could become a place, a space, a community in which the full capacity of a person can be honored and celebrated. That's not making the workplace "touchy feely"; instead, it's simply offering an alternative to the old way of thinking that work is by nature and definition a place, a hardship, and a burden. Instead, we can choose to make sense of our workplaces and create the community we need to get specific tasks done while ensuring that the people who are doing the tasks know that we (you, as leaders and executives) see them, acknowledge who they are and what they bring to the situation. That we will make them feel safe, to the best of our abilities, in the physical and professional and emotional senses. And that we value them, we recognize that the knowledge, skills, and abilities they bring to our organization is important, useful, and unique. That they have talent over and above their knowledge and skills, talent which leads to specific strengths which we value and will pay a premium to cultivate and maintain.

In the study I conducted, antisocial workplace behaviors (AWB) were reported dozens of times. The constructs of bullying and petty tyranny, verbal and psychological abuse, and workplace incivility were the most commonly identified. The organization had some reverse norms of communication, such as the habit of bantering and speaking informally (even a little rudely) with colleagues indicated trust and confidence, while "overly" polite language indicated distrust and caution. Some participants reported cases of extreme profanity and abusive language, though, which caused them discomfort in the workplace. The study participants identified that there is a high degree of organizational bureaucracy in their workplace, as well as a significant degree of organizational chaos. It seemed curious that both could coexist, but participants were adamant that amid all the hierarchy and chain of command, there were situations and policies that seemed to engender a level of chaos and unpredictability. When there is a great deal of chaos, bullying and abuse can occur without rebounding badly on the agent behaving in those ways. Low accountability means that some workplace participants remain relatively powerless, while others use organizational politics to gain power. People stay because of the barriers to exit that Jean Lipman-Blumen identified, tolerating toxic managers and co-workers, and watching their job satisfaction decline.

People also stay in this particular workplace, though, and perhaps in others like it, for deeper, more positive reasons. There were communication and behavioral norms that participants share that revealed high esteem for peers who demonstrated a work ethic dedicated to excellence. Those who did not share such a high work ethic were reviled. Some participants indicated an abiding respect for the mission of the organization, even to the point of quoting the mission statement. Shared values and shared assumptions definitely emerged in this study, and participants referenced their own morals as well as the ethical perspectives – or lack of – that they had observed during their tenure in the organization. One participant called the company "despicable," but continued working there. One stated, sadly, that Management (capital M, generalized to all leaders in the organization) was hypocritical because they did not adhere to the mission statement as a body.

Sociologist Karl Weick talked about "sense making" as a phenomenon (Weick, 1979), and that's exactly what we do in our workplaces. Psychologically we *find ways of making sense* out of the situations we encounter at work, even if those situations are uncivil, horrendous, and even repulsive. For example, one of my participants described a colleague who had "mastered" an "act" – that is, behaving as if there were some mental illness involved. The participant was absolutely convinced of the peer's deceptiveness, and while it horrified me in the interview that someone could pretend to have severe psychological issues, it was even more disconcerting that the participant could describe the scenario with a detached coolness, and acceptance that the situation would not change under the current management – or ever. Change would only happen as the other employee retired or resigned. Another employee described – and was moved to tears by – the extreme feelings of betrayal and frustration caused by a colleague's poor work performance. The fear expressed by that study participant was palpable, and I understood completely that if the poor worker falsified records and sabotaged work product, it could potentially lead to destruction of equipment and even loss of life. Another participant described bullying and rudeness, and feelings of disrespect to the point of invisibility, having developed courses to train colleagues, and personally trained another employee who was then promoted, all while being overlooked for promotion and called incompetent. Yet another victim of bullying and verbal abuse in this company dealt with profanity and insults from an internal customer, and was told afterward to take her to lunch and smooth things over with that department. And one additional participant had others take credit for work performed and ideas submitted, as well as receiving verbal abuse and physical threats. This last participant chuckled while sharing the part about physical threats, stating that as a black-belt level martial artist, it was lucky nothing had ever happened.

All of these shocking incidents represent AWB for this culture and disrupt the flow of work on a daily basis. Culture is not just dependent upon the buildings and artwork, but on the language we use with one another and the ways we work to manifest the company's mission and vision. When employees know the mission statement verbatim, but candidly state that "we don't mean it," there is an indication of some cultural illness that needs attention. Employees make sense out of their environment by comparing their experiences with the organizational artifacts, the legends and stories that they've heard about their workplace. People who go above and beyond their normal duties, who support and help their colleagues, earn high esteem. But these employees are all savvy and attentive, and they have identified behavior that gets rewarded and that which goes unnoticed (even willfully) by management. And at the end of it all, while turnover *desire* might have been high in this study, turnover *intent* – the act of planning to leave the organization or group within the next six to twelve months – was virtually nil.

So... they stayed because they wanted to see management step up and turn things around. They stayed because they had a pugnacious determination to do the best job possible, despite management's passivity. Some stayed because of their faith in God, and their belief that they had been divinely placed in their jobs. Others stayed because they felt they owed it to their end user customers to do an excellent job, despite the input or impact of others in the workplace.

> "Relationships are the only thing that matter in business [and] in life."
> – Jerry Weintraub, movie producer (from his book *When I Stop
> Talking, You'll Know I'm Dead: Useful Stories
> from a Persuasive Man, 2010) (Roberts, 2016)*

Key takeaways

1. People stay because they value and connect with the mission and purpose of the organization, and/or with the needs of the customer.
2. People stay because of the many barriers to exit.
3. People stay because they have internalized the shared, implicit values and assumptions of the organization and choose to view experiences of AWB as aberrant and non-representative of the organization or themselves.

4. People stay because they have hope and expectation that management, or HR, will intervene and turn things around. (Personal takeaway for you: DO something. Don't wait.)

5. People stay because of the positive interpersonal relationships they've formed in the workgroup. (Personal takeaway: Be respectful of that.)

9

WHY PEOPLE *ENDURE*

"Company cultures are like country cultures. Never try to change one. Try, instead, to work with what you've got."

— *Peter F. Drucker, management consultant, educator, and author (Roberts, 2016)*

Well, I respect Peter Drucker's work immensely. Still, I think that you can, and probably should, try to change organizational culture when necessary. Incremental changes are more likely to succeed over time. But you set the tone. When it becomes obvious that you have people enduring rather than choosing to commit, it may be appropriate to make some adjustments that encourage and increase organizational commitment and engagement. I chose that chapter title because during my research, a colleague strongly urged me to change the title of my work from "why people stay" to "why people *endure*," and passionately shared with me his challenging work experience of simply enduring. Tolerating the experience of work, basically, and that experience was largely connected to the kind of leadership he had experienced.

Reliably measuring leadership and its relationship between organizational commitment and productivity has interested social scientists for decades (Posner & Kouzes, 1993, p. 191). Leadership, and leader-follower dynamics, constitutes a major portion of business research in contemporary business literature, both scholarly and popular. A simple Internet search of the term "leadership" yields over 52 million results, while "followership" yields a still-noteworthy 55,800 results. Followership orientation has not yet been studied as a predictor of organizational engagement, or in relation to perceptions of organizational justice (trust). Posner and Kouzes (1993) state that without followers in any organization, the structure, mission, and vision of the organization are moot, and without effective leaders, the organization is prone to disorder and lack of focus.

My study investigated followers' perceptions of their workplaces and their own understanding of why they have stayed in them.

This study continues an established line of research into the construct of psychological attachment, popularly called organizational engagement. By identifying leader behaviors that contribute to the aspects of work that define people's engagement in their organizations, we can understand how employees define meaningful work (Chalofsky, 2003, 2010), or as entrenchment (Carson & Carson, 1997) in a psychic prison (Morgan, 2003). Instead of testing specific hypotheses regarding the impact of leader behavior on engagement, this study qualitatively explores the impact of leader behaviors and organizational decision-making processes on followers. By incorporating the moderating influence of substitutes for leadership in a consideration of how leadership interventions and decision-making processes may affect engagement, this study may lead to organizational development interventions that enhance psychological attachment by promoting specific leader behaviors (Kouzes & Posner, 2007; Kouzes, Posner, & Biech, 2010).

Organizational commitment

Organizational science and practice has long shown interest in employee motivation and commitment based on the belief and evidence that there are benefits to having a motivated and committed workforce (Meyer, Becker, & Vandenberghe, 2004). Fox (1994) notes that if we are aware, "we praise God by our work" (p. 23), suggesting any work that has meaning and contributes to the common good, if fairly compensated and performed in safe conditions, is an opportunity for meditative, sacred expression. However, O'Reilly and Chatman (1986) identify that although the concept of organizational commitment has received significant research attention in the organizational behavior field since the late 1970s, there are over 25 commitment-related concepts and measures.

Meyer, Allen, and Gellatly (1990) agree that different views of commitment have emerged, "making it unlikely that any one approach will dominate" (p. 710). Early research led to a definition of commitment that highlighted the strength of a person's organizational identification and involvement, or a person's tendency to maintain a certain level and type of activity once begun. And Obeng and Ugboro (2003) define affective, normative, and continuance commitment, finding affective commitment *negatively* related to tenure in public sector jobs while continuance commitment correlated negatively with education, because education opens up other opportunities. In previous studies, continuance commitment has emerged as less than desirable, as it has no effect on attendance, task performance, and organizational citizenship behaviors. This is the "enduring" from the chapter title. It is akin to inertia, and offers you little to nothing in terms of engagement, synergy, or initiative. There are clearly documented positive relationships between organizational commitment and performance metrics, and between organizational commitment and prosocial behaviors. There are also clearly documented significant negative relationships between organizational commitment and turnover, as well as turnover intent (Kirkman & Shapiro, 2001). Zigarmi, Nimon, Houson, Witt, and Diehl (2009) explored the relationships between leadership, employee satisfaction, customer satisfaction, and organizational performance. Their model for employee engagement was developed after a massive literature review – a reading of all the articles they could find from academic journals, consulting firms, and training companies. The researchers found a lack of any agreed-upon definition of employee engagement. Engagement is usually associated with job commitment (wellbeing or burnout) or organizational commitment (intent to stay, endorsement), but not both.

Organizational engagement, or employee psychological attachment to the organization, has been conceptualized as organizational citizenship (Dessler, 1999) and affective psychological attachment (Blau & Holladay, 2006; Dessler, 1999). Multiple studies have explored the impact of various antecedents on psychological attachment including organizational fairness (Chiaburu & Marinova, 2006), antisocial workplace behaviors against the organization (Zoghbi-Manrique de Lara & Verano-Tacoronte, 2007) and employees' perception of victimization, whether direct or indirect, in the workplace (Aquino, Grover, Bradfield, & Allen, 1999). The literature indicates that employees' perceptions of their treatment in the workplace by their organizational leaders predict their level of organizational engagement. This treatment specifically includes how leaders respond to employees' observations of antisocial behaviors by peers and colleagues. Supervisors' treatment of their subordinates "shapes the nature of the relationship and influences an array of subsequent work outcomes" (Yang, Mossholder, & Peng, 2009).

By identifying leader behaviors that contribute to the aspects of work that define people's engagement in their organizations, we can understand how employees define meaningful work (Chalofsky, 2003, 2010), or as entrenchment (Carson & Carson, 1997) in a psychic prison (Morgan, 2003). Instead of testing specific hypotheses regarding the impact of leader behavior on engagement, this study qualitatively explores the impact of leader behaviors and organizational decision-making processes on followers.

Engaged employees maintain their positive mood throughout the whole week, are more productive, maintain better health, are immune to stress from commuting, and are more likely to be thriving in general (Harter, 2012). Disengaged workers experience worse workdays and worse weekends; those individuals' work experiences carry over into their home life. Low levels of organizational commitment manifest through artifacts, language, and rituals of communication within the group. This sad image is borne out every day:

> Whenever I would ask a former work acquaintance, "how was your day," he would always, always respond with a curse word along the lines of, "crappy." If I asked, "how are you doing," or "what's up," he would say, "I'm just trying to get through the day." I wondered how he survived in any work environment, with such an extremely pessimistic attitude. It was depressing, honestly.
>
> – *AD*

And you have the power to change that kind of attitude. Sure, there may be people in your organization, or on your team, who aren't giddy about coming to work every day. But you can, through transformational leadership practices, inspire a positive expectation in your associates. You can ensure that they feel seen, safe, and valued. Gini (2010) describes power as the capacity to control or direct change, stating that "all forms of leadership must make use of" it (p. 352). The question is whether that power will be used well, for the good of the group, in a "non-coercive manner to orchestrate, direct, and guide members of an organization in the pursuit of a goal or series of objectives" (p. 352). Leaders and followers in a totalitarian system, for example, must all conform to the organization's norms in order to contribute to the self-preservation of the system.

People *endure* in a work situation because they've been conditioned in a certain way. Perhaps they believe that that's all they can get, that's all they're qualified for, or that's what work is – remember my own family anecdote that work wasn't supposed to be enjoyable. And then there is the influence of our leaders. We may be conditioned… by the negative behaviors of those who hold power over our career or current livelihood.

Dutch psychologist Manfred Kets de Vries addresses the concept of leadership by terror, or leadership that "achieves its ends and gains compliance through the use of violence and fear" (2006, p. 197). Citing the work of social scientists such as Asch, Schein, and Milgram, Kets de Vries states that "The explanation is disturbing: studies of human behavior indicate that the disposition to violence exists in *all* of us; *everyone* may have a despot in his or her basement" (p. 196; italics in original). The author references the quote attributed to Lord Acton, "All power tends to corrupt, and absolute power corrupts absolutely" (p. 196). Not to be intrusive here, but have you found yourself vulnerable to the corrupting influence of power? Needed to reach out to a peer or a "cold-water" partner, someone who isn't afraid to throw cold water on an idea or impulse you may be having? Or just needed a private moment to recalibrate those impulses, by yourself? Every leader should ensure that there are both internal and external moral foci that keep him or her from being swept up in the waves of power and influence that may lead to modeling less than transformational behaviors. Otherwise we may become caught up in the mindset of scarcity, and lack; we begin to believe that there is a scarcity of power, requiring competition to accumulate it. It reinforces the idea that people tend to compare themselves to others as a result of early life experiences when dependency yielded benefits in terms of time, attention, and affection from caregivers.

The superior boss-subordinate relationship is the pivotal environment through which work gets accomplished. Subordinates either affirm and support, or withdraw their affirmation and support, isolating the superior. Scholar and author Abraham Zaleznik identifies as a common executive mistake the confusing of compliance with commitment; compliance represents an "attitude of acceptance when a directive from an authority figure asks for a change in an individual's position, activities, or ideas… [the individual] is indifferent to the scope of the directive and the changes it proposes [and offers] little difficulty in translating the intent of directives into actual implementation" (Zaleznik, 1970, p. 50). Commitment, though, represents "strong motivation on the part of an individual to adopt or resist the intent of the directive." If the individual is supportive, he or she will use ingenuity to interpret and implement the change, and work to assure success. If not, the individual may think compliance, but find ways to "negate the effects," sabotaging the initiative. You've heard of self-sabotage, right? That's what we're talking about here – and you've probably seen it happen in your workplace. It's rooted in a lack of organizational commitment.

Employee organizational commitment has also been examined as an independent variable, determinant of job performance and organizational citizenship behaviors. Commitment involves psychological attachment to social foci. Meyer and Herscovitch (2001) provided a model of workplace commitment, demonstrating its functionality as the force that binds an individual to a course of action that is of relevance to a particular target. Commitment can take different forms and have different target foci. It can be identified at different levels of analysis, including at the level of team, department or manager, company or organization, occupational field, or it can be specifically targeted toward a particular customer or union. Similarly, Gallup found organizational engagement measurable at the team, department, and organization levels. Both identified through empirical studies that higher commitment reduces the likelihood of turnover, or employees utilizing their Exit Option.

Entrenchment

Carson and Carson (1997) suggest that employees may want to change careers, but stay for some degree of security. In the mid-to-late 1990s, 50% of United States companies eliminated jobs, over 400,000 jobs, and 40% of the managerial labor force expressed concern about job security. As a result, many employees reported that they stay in their jobs, perhaps out of desperation, as opposed to commitment. They may not identify with or feel emotionally attached to the organization, but they do nothing about changing their job. Carson and Carson explain this with the term "career entrenchment," defined as the tendency to stay in a vocation because of investments, psychological preservation, and a perception that there are few career opportunities. Some employees stay because leaving would mean sacrificing salary increases, paid holidays and vacations, retirements and other benefits. "As organizational tenure increases, these economic 'side bets' accrue" (p. 63). That's sunk costs, or continuance commitment. Again – inertia.

Psychological preservation is associated with Festinger's theory of cognitive dissonance. It involves the individual seeking to alleviate the discomfort of inconsistent behaviors and attitudes. Attempts at psychological preservation are likely when individuals voluntarily and publicly select careers that are "sub optimal… Over more fitting alternatives" (Carson & Carson, 1997, p. 68). This is not the case if the individual has been forced into the only job available. Psychological preservation is likely when individuals believe that their persistence and course of action will increase the possibility of need fulfillment. Rationalization efforts increase as tenure lengthens. Psychological preservation is also likely to increase. A career change will require significant time, effort, and money. While a poor labor market "and high unemployment negatively influence organizational turnover, they positively affect career changes" (p. 69).

Key takeaways

1. Leaders need followers, and a context in which to collaborate.
2. Organizational engagement is a manifestation of psychological attachment to the organization. It's a good thing, a form of intangible equity.
3. Organizational commitment is a much-researched concept involving employees' tendency to maintain a certain level and type of activity.
4. Career entrenchment is based on continuance commitment, a form of professional inertia, where we stay because we don't want to lose what we have (pension, salary, medical benefits, etc.) as opposed to staying because we want to.
5. Psychological preservation is a set of actions we take to resolve cognitive dissonance, and alleviate the discomfort of behaviors that don't match our attitudes and beliefs.

10
FOLLOWERSHIP

It's a funny word, followership. I was once even confronted by a manager who insisted that it wasn't a "real" word, but in the workplace context where we worked, I was able to point out several context-specific jargon words that did not show up in the online dictionary searches, while followership did, and he accepted that. Followers are not necessarily always employees, and all employees are not necessarily followers, so I use the words as appropriate here. In many cases, employees perceive that while leadership and followership are interrelated and symbiotic, each position requires specific skills, motivations, abilities, and role perceptions (Agho, 2009). Both the leader and the follower influence the performance and productivity of the work group, and without followers, a leader is unnecessary. A leader requires followers who accept his or her influence and direction. Indeed, followers have equal, if not greater, power in the leader-follower dyadic relationship, as they are the component without which the leader cannot function. Potter, Rosenbach, and Pittman (2001) suggested that a shared, partnership orientation toward developing effective relationships and driving high performance represent two key elements in encouraging such a partnership orientation.

And this is a conscious process; the leader and follower roles are both socially constructed identities, born of implicit leadership and followership theories. Implicit theories are those which we bring with us into the relationship, representing the expectations and perceptions we have of the role. So, if I am hired into a company and assigned to a team, and I am told that my role is a Specialist role, and I will report to a certain Manager or Director, then I will bring certain implicit theories-in-use into that situation. I will have expectations about what my role is, what my contributions should be, and what I can offer to the group as a follower, as one of the ones not-in-charge. I will also bring a set of expectations about the leader of the group to the relationship. I will consider how leaders have behaved in my previous employment situations, and develop theories-in-use about how my current leader *should* behave, and then probably generalize those expectations, suggesting that "that's just common knowledge," or discussing what the leader should do with other employees. Unless I take a more assertive approach, and choose to talk directly with the leader about my expectations in a nonthreatening way that expresses no demands or judgment, which is unlikely. Both parties, the leader and the employee-followers, use their implicit theories and expectations of self and other to create a dynamic process based on the role performance and conformance of both Leader and Follower, in their specific context. The theories evolve over time with various interactions, and researchers are finally delving more deeply into this ongoing, relational construct (Shondrick & Lord, 2010).

Early understanding of followership as a concept

Robert E. Kelley (2008) states that despite the contemporary Western view that leadership is better than followership, in the original, Old High German word origins, followers took care of leaders in an equal, symbiotic relationship. Each relied on the other "for existence and meaning" (p. 182). The early "great person" leadership notion is ascribed to Thomas Carlyle, an early nineteenth-century British philosopher whose leader-centric worldview suggested that "leaders create and shape the events and institutions that define society" (p. 182). Negative stereotypes of followers find their roots in social Darwinism and capitalist competitiveness; winners are leaders, leaders are winners, and everyone else is a loser. This position ignored – and continues to ignore – the inherent value of the follower as an individual contributor, though, and assumes the follower's presence in support of a leader. Kelley defines followership as "active engagement in helping an organization or a cause succeed while exercising independent, critical judgment of goals, tasks, potential problems, and methods" (p. 181).

In Kelley's model of followership, a two-by-two matrix places independent, critical thinking at the top of the Y axis and dependent, uncritical thinking at the bottom. The X-axis addressed passive vs. active engagement in the workplace, and what kind of energy the follower contributed. In 1992 Kelley took a different approach from those who focused on followers solely relative to the leader, instead exploring the instance and characteristics of exemplary followers. This revolutionary approach took a non-leader-centric view and focused directly on followers, classifying them as Alienated, Exemplary (Star), Conformist ("Yes-person"), Passive ("Sheep"), or Pragmatists (Kelley, 2010) (see Figure 10.1).

Beyond merely labeling followers as one type or another, Kelley suggested that followers had multiple options in terms of behavioral paths in the workplace and in their leader-follower relationships. The behavioral paths included the Path of Loyalty, the Lifeway Path, the Dreamer's Path, the Apprentice's Path, the Disciple's Path, the Mentee's Path, and the Comrade's Path (see Figure 10.2). These paths are not mutually exclusive and the follower may

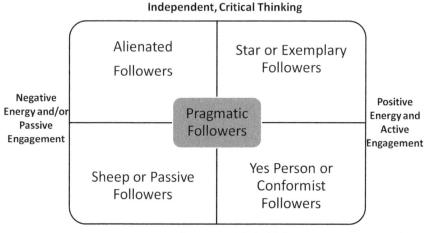

FIGURE 10.1   Kelley's model.

pursue more than one path, based on whether he or she prefers self-expression or self-transformation at the time, and whether the emphasis is more on relational bonding or achieving personal goals. Through these paths, individuals seek self-expression, demonstrating that the follower is comfortable with him or herself and motivated to contribute toward larger goals (the Path of Loyalty, the Lifeway Path). Or, he or she can seek transformation, when not satisfied with self, and seek to become different and better (the Apprentice's Path, the Disciple's Path, the Mentee's Path). The follower may seek to develop relationships, following the person of the leader rather than any specific goals (the Comrade's Path), or may be seeking to achieve personal goals, with an inward focus (the Dreamer's Path).

The Apprentice's Path represents the follower's aspirations of growing into a leader role, and includes work that requires "learning the ropes" and "paying dues." The Disciple's Path represents an emotionally committed, obedient position in which the follower seeks to identify with and bond with the leader in order to be part of something greater than himself. The Mentee's Path represents a clear one-to-one relationship in which the leader as mentor directs the talents and personal maturation of the follower as protégé. The Comrade's Path represents the follower manifesting a sense of community and social support, choosing to give his or her all for the sake of the group's success. The Path of Loyalty indicates an individual's personal affective commitment to the leader and choice to follow that leader, regardless. The Lifeway Path is the path in which the follower simply lives out a commitment, stating that there is no other way of being for him or her. The Dreamer's Path represents a choice to follow as long as the leader shares the follower's goals and ambitions.

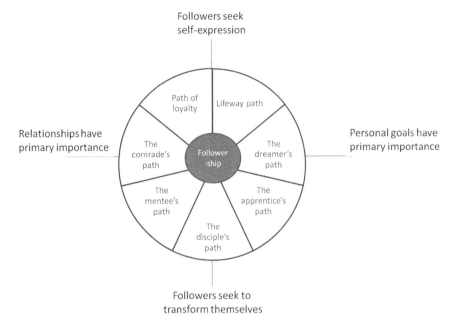

FIGURE 10.2   Kelley's follower paths.

Leaders often assume that people will *only* follow them if the leader offers great charisma or vision, but some followers' motivation originates from their own personal vision and, in recent years, many followers have a healthy wariness of charisma, preferring their leaders instead to facilitate the achievement of followers' personal goals. Dixon (2008) states that the pressure for companies to achieve greater quality, innovation, productivity, and flexibility has led to the erroneous search for the "all leader organization," an idea that perpetuates an error of attribution and traditional definition of subordinates as valuable only in relation to their leaders. Followership, Dixon states, is a proactive state, one that is dynamic and value-adding. Followers, like leaders, are "stewards in organizational endeavors" (p. 1386) whose development and performance are key to the leadership process.

The courageous follower

Kelley offered a trait-based follower typology, while Chaleff's model provides a dimensional behavior-based follower typology. Followership, according to Chaleff, represents the condition that permits leadership to exist, and that gives it strength, through several specific interdependencies: workers follow their own light, and leaders intensify that light; followers add value by helping the leader and organization pursue a common purpose within the context of their own personal values (Chaleff, 2009, p. 19). The key characteristics of courageous followers include cooperativeness, collaboration, the ability to serve rather than compete with the leader, caring enough to try to form bridges between leaders and peer followers, and a sense of balance, such that the well-balanced follower can help a leader navigate the pitfalls of his or her own ego (p. 20). Chaleff's work on courageous followers offered four similar followership styles: Implementer, Partner, Individualist, and Resource, based on a two-axis model measuring level of support for leadership and degree of followers' challenging behavior (Chaleff, 2009; Kellerman, 2008). Both Kelley and Chaleff acknowledge followers for their own value and as contributors to the organization's effectiveness. While most of the management literature promotes "a submissive subordinate concept" (Dixon, 2009, p. 36), using language that implies manipulation techniques from the contingency, equity, and transactional leadership theories, these follower-specific typologies avoid manipulation and address the follower's orientation as it stands.

Followers demonstrate courage across five different dimensions:

1. Ownership/assuming responsibility;
2. Service through supporting the leader in areas where their strengths complement those of the leader;
3. Confronting and challenging leadership;
4. Participating in transformation; and
5. Taking moral action even at personal risk.

Courageous followers choose to relinquish some of their autonomy, conceding authority to the leader while both implementing and challenging the leader's ideas (Chaleff, 2009, pp. 14–15). Followers have the power TO do certain things, in the leader-follower-context relationship, and they bring the power OF certain things to that relationship. Specifically, followers bring the power of purpose, or commitment to the common good; the power of their knowledge, skills, and abilities; the power of their personal history with the organization and group; the power of their own self-efficacy and belief in their intentions; and the power of their relationships and networks when used with integrity. Followers also have the power to: truthfully speak to leadership, set an influential standard/model, choose how to react in any situation, follow or not follow a given direction, communicate through a variety of channels, organize others of like mind, and finally, *withdraw support* if leadership actions violate personal values.

Disagreeing with various criticisms of the "follower" term, Chaleff insists that follower is "not synonymous with subordinate" (2009, p. 15), because a subordinate can be a supporter, an antagonist, or indifferent to the goals of the leader and organization. Followers, instead, share a common purpose with the leader and believe in what the organization is trying to do; they want the leader and the organization to succeed and will work energetically toward this goal.

To be sure, the leader and follower roles are relational. Dixon (2008, 2009) states that unfortunately, the majority of empirical studies focus on leadership and its effects at the lower operating levels of formal organizations, taking a predominantly dyadic approach in regard to level of analysis and leaving followers ignored in the process. But there does tend to be a core followership style independent of the leader. It is important to identify the style so that individuals can understand and make their own decisions about it. Chaleff (2008) offers a positive model of followership style combined with a review of followers' power. This approach can help organizational members understand and accept their ability to influence leaders, and improve organizational commitment.

Followership types and behaviors vary in different workplace environments; in certain high-intensity, high-ownership settings, some followership behaviors may be more appropriate than others and require higher engagement, as a partner rather than as a resource (Chaleff, 2008, 2009). In my study, participants provided their own interpretations of what their self-identified follower orientation meant and sounded like.

Partner

Participant K. explained what being a Partner-type follower meant, with regard to communication: "Well I think we talk to each other, everybody's friendly. I try to be more, a person that likes to share and put out, I guess, my opinion or my ideas and new things that I've learned." Collegiality, though, seemed limited in this individual's group context:

> It's difficult on our team because we have a team, a bunch of individuals. There's never a time when we get to work on a project together or a project team. It's just a bunch of individuals getting work thrown at them and you're expected to get it done as fast as you can.

Participant E. shared:

> It was either going to be Partner or it was going to be Individualistic. One of the two… It puts you at odds, consistently. That was one of the issues I had with going to my boss. Because by going to him and complaining about an[other] employee, puts… it puts me in for lack of a better word the narc position.

Participant D1 had a unique response, interpreting the matrix differently:

> Well I wasn't pointing to the Partner thing so much as the X-Y. Up here. Extreme in both… I would line out #2 [*cultivates relationships*] completely,

> I would asterisk #3 [emphasizing *holds self and others accountable*]. Oh yeah, check, asterisk [*confronts sensitive issues*]... I'll come back to number 1 [*purpose-driven, mission-oriented risk taker*]. Focuses on strength... no, fake egoism aside, I have actually no self-reflection at all.

This participant continued:

> I exist to solve problems, primarily. So I don't focus on strength and growth. I don't. The ... with one exception, that I think every adult human being should spend some level of time and effort on a continuous basis attempting to refine their own thought processes. It's what separates us from the animals, it's what needs to be done. If you don't know how to think, if you're mouth breathing your way through life, you might as well BE an animal.

Coming back to the first descriptor, *purpose-driven, mission-oriented risk taker*, D1 said:

> Most people don't actually understand good definitions of risk, so that's a highly problematic statement I would rather not... for example, do I take risks? Yes! Most people think I'm a risk averse person. No, not at all. I take calculated risks, because I go out of my way to know how to calculate the risk. Most people never approach risk taking that way. For me, when I decide to do it, what other people see as risk taking or risky behavior is not a risk. I have a high if not 100 percent chance of success for me if I do it. For me it is not a risk.

When asked to review the other three quadrants on the matrix, D1 did not at all identify with the Individualist follower type. But D1 later noted that with regard to the mission and integrity of the company:

> ...the company is not morally offensive to the point where I would feel any obligation to leave... That having been said, I'm not at all fond of their moral behavior, but that's different. I will NEVER have a sense of pride in that company. That company is at some level, despicable... their decision making does not come from a core set of moral values... The people running the company have no problem hurting the company in order to achieve to them a much higher goal of preserving their clique.

Participant D2 refused to choose between Partner and Implementer, but had a solid rationale (interviewer comments in italics):

> Yeah can we like squish those together? *Which of the items do you like under Implementer?* All of them. *Ok I'm going to circle that one. But you have some*

under Partner that you like too, right? All of them, too. *OK then, I'm going to make you choose between the two.* No, it's all-all. At work, yeah. Well, I'll put it this way. It's all-all with the group that I just left. It's not all-all with the group that I'm currently in. Partly because I don't know them well enough. *So with the home group, you're more Partner, but with the host group, maybe more Implementer?* I would agree with that.

Implementer

Participant M1 hesitated to choose one type:

Ach, you're killing me… OK 60% Implementer 40% Partner… I think probably on the Partner side, the 40%, because this is more confrontational or more challenging, I think when it's easier, if that makes sense… I always weigh and say ok even if it's true, what does it gain you other than saying it and getting it off your chest? So I think I'm less likely to do the challenging behavior if I perceive that there really isn't much to be gained on the back side.

Participant T. stated:

I like to believe that I support leadership. Like I said, up until March of this year, I really thought I did, because I did what was asked of me. I didn't complain, I didn't fight back. I just jumped in, did the best I could.

Participant A. said:

Everyone complains to third parties. Hm, I don't think I'm an individualist. I'm a modest guy at work, with the most skill. I don't know where that goes. I guess I'm a Resource. Like I'm more, out of all of them, I don't execute the minimum, that's about the only thing I don't do on that list. There's just like a couple things, like the helpful guy that's there to… is that what that's [pointing to Implementer] about? I think I'm in between Implementer and Resource. I guess I'm there to be committed with my boss. Like, he's really, he usually says like, I need this done. Or if he doesn't say anything, it's just … [you] work. [The boss says, or implies,] "I need it done." So you kind of go out of your way to get it done.

Participant S. indicated Implementer, near to Partner:

Somewhere in here… there are a lot of things on this list that I know I am that way, but… As a good leader you should recognize good followers and as a good follower I want to let you know, I didn't agree with that [regarding Partner behavior, confronting management]."

Resource

Participant M2 explained:

> Currently, I am a Resource. Except that I am… well I'm very committed, but only for those eight hours. And as far as complaining, well, I don't complain. And I heard it once said that a person that complains is not happy, or is not accepting of how God is working things out.

The interaction between leader practices, which set the tone for the workplace, and followership approach, leads to a potential reduction of the need for significant leadership intervention at all. Howell and Mendez (2008) state that the followership literature, overall, "rejects a subservient role for followers as inappropriate for organizations today… [But] some leaders still tacitly reward this behavior in followers" (p. 26). The literature suggests, though, that followership is more of an active role, joining with the leader to achieve jointly shared goals and organizational outcomes. Maroosis (2008) reinforces Follett's and Chaleff's perspective that leadership is a partnership in reciprocal following, with both leaders and followers oriented toward a common purpose or organizational goal. This perspective situates leadership and followership equally as a response to a call of some sort. Neither is self-generated, self-validated, or self-actuated. This centering of the whole relationship outside both parties requires an outward focus rather than a leader focus or a follower focus.

Maroosis (2008) situates followership as a moral practice requiring discipline, discrimination, and guidance from the leader to learn to use the same thinking and decision-making practices that the leader uses. By adhering to specific cardinal virtues, both followers and leaders develop critical behavioral practices that lead to effective followership and effective leadership. Effective followers manifest specific behaviors. They:

1. demonstrate job knowledge and competence at work tasks;
2. build collaborative and supportive relationships with coworkers and leader;
3. defend and support the leader in front of others;
4. exert influence on the leader in a confident, unemotional way to help leader avoid costly mistakes;
5. demonstrate proper comportment for the organization (through speech, dress, and etiquette);
6. show concern for performance as well as for a supportive, friendly atmosphere; and,
7. show willingness to participate in necessary organizational changes.

Followership becomes a mimetic situation in which the follower learns to think like the leader in the reciprocal, goal-focused relationship suggested by Follett, Chaleff, and Maroosis. The purpose of the relationship between leader and follower is that the followers need leaders to help them follow what the leaders are following, and to work together to focus on primary goals and eliminating distractions or secondary priorities.

Adair (2008) asks why people prefer to follow, and suggests that the decision is situated within the individual's self-perception. Specifically, personal values may lead the individual to feel that he or she will respect the decision or choice of another as the leader. Economic status may drive the individual to perceive that they make more money *doing* than leading.

Dixon and Westbrook (2003) suggest that the history of leader-follower relations is based on a social contract in which leaders were viewed as great, better than their followers (e.g. Master-Apprentice relationships). By the late twentieth century, the paradigm changed to one of savvy managers, who sought high productivity with low overhead costs, seeking new ways to manipulate workers to achieve that goal. The concept and study of followership acknowledges the impossibility of an all-leader organization (2003). The focus on leaders has long blurred the importance of the follower and the follower's relationships with colleagues and formal leaders. Dixon and Westbrook (2003) further state that absent any discussion or understanding about followership, organizational leaders revert to a transactional management style. When leaders and followers do engage in meaningful dialogue about the roles and requirements of each participant, then the organization's employee engagement increases. Its competitive positioning is strengthened by this human capital equity. Dixon and Westbrook's (2003) study found that follower orientation can be empirically defined and measured, using Chaleff's courageous follower model.

Weisbord (1987) expresses concern with "responding to needs for dignity, meaning, and community in work" (p. 233). Organizational leaders may not immediately perceive the critical importance of this focus, but renowned leadership author and Harvard Business School professor Barbara Kellerman has said in her book *Followership: How Followers are Creating Change and Changing Leaders*, as well as on panels and in personal conversations, that she believes we in this generation have entered a new era, one driven by and focused on the follower rather than the leader. Contemporary workplaces bear little resemblance to the "plants" and industrial factories of the nineteenth and twentieth centuries (Fox, 1994; Weisbord, 1987). A recent university guest speaker at the college where I teach asked a group of undergraduates why they think we work. The deeper level of the question had to do with why go to the trouble of getting a liberal arts education at the collegiate level only to go into the workforce and perform drudgery for 40 years? The speaker suggested that motivation to work stemmed from a desire for meaning as well as a need for money. My own working history, though, suggests that the work environment affects employee engagement far more than does money or even meaning.

Dixon and Westbrook (2003) further state that absent any discussion or understanding about followership and transformational leadership, organizational leaders revert to a transactional management style. When leaders and followers do engage in meaningful dialogue about the roles and requirements of each participant, then the organization's employee engagement increases. Its competitive positioning is strengthened by this human capital equity.

The implications for human resource management include directives to recruit for individuals supportive of the organization's mission and values as opposed to primarily recruiting for task skills; developing rewards and incentives that address followers' specific needs to increase retention; promoting penalty-free risk taking behavior by followers; and, improving managers' and leaders' perceptions of safety and self-esteem to increase their likelihood of listening when challenged and accepting constructive criticism. The 2003 study suggests that organizational members must understand followers and followership as vital to organizations, equivalent to leaders in importance and prominence. Managers learning to respect and expect courageous followership encourages personnel development, but to develop this respect and expectation requires training that is case-based, experiential, and effective at explaining and developing followership.

Engagement... and purpose

Rucker and King (1985) indicated that American managers were interested at that time in having employees participate in planning their own work activities. Factors influencing this renewed orientation toward employee engagement were increased educational levels, changing expectations in the workforce, and competitive pressures from abroad. Early research on participative decision-making (PDM) indicated that PDM leads to higher satisfaction, but not higher productivity, than do authoritative management styles. Even for job satisfaction, though, 40% of relevant studies find no support for the superiority of PDM over other leadership styles. Rucker and King (1985) concluded that the efficacy of PDM depended on contextual factors. The first factor addressed the relationship between leadership style and follower/subordinate response. Vroom's early research on PDM in 1959 hypothesized that higher follower needs for independence led to greater responsiveness to PDM, resulting in increased job satisfaction and productivity. However, replication of Vroom's work has not yielded similar results. The second conceptual factor that influences the effectiveness of PDM is path-goal theory. The nature of the task represents a contingent variable that alters the effect of personality on the relationship between participative leadership and subordinate responses. For complex tasks, all subordinates found PDM useful in clarifying task demands. For simple tasks, low authoritarian employees preferred PDM.

Harter (2012) states that "engaged workers feel as good" at work as they do during their downtime. These organizational members report frequently experiencing feelings of happiness, and incidences of laughing and smiling often at work. Over 90% of those surveyed reported that they perceived that they had been treated with respect, and over 75% had learned something new or done something interesting every day over the past week. In contrast, less than 10% of engaged employees reported experiencing anger on any of the previous week's workdays.

Gallup's employee engagement index is grounded in extensive poll data and research on specific workplace elements that have been empirically linked to measurable organizational outcomes including productivity, customer service, quality, retention, safety, and profit. In 2012, 30% of U.S. workers reported scores in the "engaged" category, comprised of people who are committed to and excited about the work they do, and who channel that positive energy into achieving organizational goals (Harter, 2012). Of the remaining workers surveyed, 52% reported that they were "Not Engaged," while 18% were "Actively Disengaged." The latter group report feelings of being emotionally disconnected from the organization and were least likely to contribute to organizational productivity. Among the Engaged workers, under 40% report experiencing stress in any given workday, while over 60% of Actively Disengaged workers report experiencing stress during the work week, most frequently on Mondays, Tuesdays, and Thursdays. Of those in the Not Engaged group, 50% report experiencing stress every day during the five-day work week. The statistics are similar for experiencing worry.

Harter (2012) points out that the correlations for work engagement and emotional health by day of week remain significant after controlling for household income, age, gender, and number of children in the household. Disengaged workers experience worse workdays and worse weekends; those individuals' work experiences carry over into their home life. Engaged employees maintain their positive mood throughout the whole week, are more productive, maintain better health, are immune to stress from commuting, and are more likely to be thriving in general. Harter (2012) and the Gallup organization have demonstrated the mediating role of stress in the relationship between low engagement and poor dietary choices, which lead to health issues and the conclusion that the wellbeing of actively disengaged workers is significantly worse than that of the engaged, but also even of the unemployed.

Reliably measuring leadership and its relationship between organizational commitment and productivity has interested social scientists for decades (Posner & Kouzes, 1993, p. 191). The value to human resource and organizational development practitioners, managers, and scholars alike of identifying factors that increase engagement has been demonstrated in the leadership and social science literature. These employees report lower turnover intentions and more frequent organizational citizenship behaviors (OCBs) than other employees (Dessler, 1999). Conversely, lower engagement has been correlated with high turnover, career entrenchment, lower frequency of OCBs, lower productivity, and health and safety issues on the job (Carson & Carson, 1997; O'Reilly & Chatman, 1986). Additional contributions of this research include expanding the organizational leadership literature by testing the impact of five specific leader practices (encompassing 30 behaviors) on organizational engagement, some of which align with transformational leadership and some of which can be considered transactional (Fields & Herold, 1997). These behavioral practices can be taught and reinforced, and have been influential in organizational initiatives in organizations around the world (Abu-Tineh, Khasawneh, & Al-Omari, 2008; Aimar & Stough, 2007; Posner, 2002; Zagorsek, Jaklic, & Stough, 2003). Followership types and behaviors vary in different workplace environments; in certain high-intensity, high-ownership settings, some followership behaviors may be more appropriate than others and require higher engagement, as a partner rather than as a resource (Chaleff, 2008, 2009). The interaction between leader practices, which set the tone for the workplace, and followership approach, leads to a potential reduction of the need for significant leadership intervention at all. It is instrumental to consider whether leader behaviors continue to have a significant impact on organizational engagement when substitutes for leadership such as high-performing work groups, experience, and level of expertise moderate the relationship between leader practices and organizational engagement.

Church (2011) links the science and practice of psychology in applied organizational environments, particularly human resource management uses, putting industrial and organizational psychology theory into practice. Organizational engagement has represented a source of interest in business and management practitioner literature for years, but has come to the forefront of theoretical research only since 2008. There is no unified theoretical approach to engagement, though, and practice is leading the way with measurement models. Still, no single clearly defined practical construct has emerged. And, the very consideration of organizational engagement may become a moot topic during a significant (global) economic downturn. Performance management has a critical role in maintaining an engaged workforce. This represents a challenge to researchers and practitioners seeking to define and promote best practices; many organizations hesitate to allow external engagement research, and internal engagement activities may be limited due to their significant impact on overhead budgets.

Church (2011) states that one of the potential negative outcomes of low employee engagement is high turnover. If management would focus on employees as customers and consumers of management services, rather than as an instrumental means to a more important end, there would be a marked effect on organizational engagement.

Harter, Schmidt, Killham, and Asplund (2006) explain that in the 1930s, the Gallup organization studied human needs and satisfactions and pioneered sampling processes to gauge popular opinion and factors of wellbeing. In the 1970s, Gallup's research found that less than 50% of American workers reported being highly satisfied with their work. Demonstrating the global relevance of this line of research, the numbers were even lower in Western Europe, Latin America, Africa, and the Far East. Job satisfaction was studied in over 10,000 articles and publications. Psychologist Donald Clifton, PhD., studied the causes of success in education and business, focusing on positive psychology and "what makes people flourish" (Harter et al., 2006, p. 4). Through hundreds of research studies on successful individuals and teams across industries and job types, especially learning and workplace environments, Clifton ran multiple studies on teachers and managers who had experienced significant career success. This led to several new discoveries, specifically: simply assessing the level of employee job satisfaction did nothing to "create sustainable change" (p. 5) in that level. Researchers and managers needed to operationalize that construct, job satisfaction, in a meaningful way that could be measured, reported, and influenced. In 1988, Clifton and the Gallup organization merged their two lines of research, combined their organizations, and began to offer a blend of "progressive management science with top survey and polling science" (p. 5). This led to an iterative process of refining, rephrasing, and analyzing questions to form the Gallup Q12® instrument to measure employee engagement. Harter et al. (2006) offer a meta-analysis of 166 research studies that investigated "the relationship between employee engagement and performance across 125 organizations and 23,910 business or work units" (p. 5).

Harter et al. (2006) report that in the 1950s, Clifton used science and the study of strengths to identify factors that allowed employees to contribute in positive ways to their workplace environments. From the 1950s to the 1970s Clifton continued to study teachers, students, counselors, managers, and employees via survey and interview. One source of question item data came from exit interviews, to determine causes of employee turnover. The most common reason employees left organizations was identified as "quality of the manager" (p. 6).

In the 1980s, the Gallup organization continued Clifton's research by studying high-performing work teams and high-performing individuals. They started with qualitative data from interviews and focus groups. Gallup researchers then generated hypotheses about distinguishing factors that lead to individual and team success. The quantitative research followed, with a specific focus on exit interviews and factor analysis of the survey data gathered in the qualitative phase through organizational development audits and other detailed questionnaire instruments, some of which included 100 to 200 items. The end result was the Gallup Q12©, an easily administered instrument that may provide significant insight into the truth about your organization's culture and climate.

GALLUP Q12® ITEMS

00 – Overall satisfaction
01 – I know what's expected of me at work
02 – I have the materials and equipment to do my work right
03 – At work, I have the opportunity to do what I do best every day
04 – In the last 7 days, I have received recognition or praise for a job well done
05 – My supervisor seems to care about me as a person
06 – At work there is someone who encourages my development
07 – At work, my opinions seem to count
08 – The mission of my company makes me feel my job is important
09 – I believe my associates are committed to quality work
10 – I have a best friend at work
11 – In the last six months, someone has talked with me about my career progress
12 – At work, I have the opportunity to learn and grow

Employee engagement is not just a buzzword. It has money attached to it.

Employee engagement has many definitions; it has even inspired a movement (Shantz, 2017). It is not the same thing as job satisfaction (Nimon, Shuck, & Zigarmi, 2016), even though the uninitiated may make that claim. It is an active, work-related psychological state operationalized by the intensity and direction of cognitive, emotional, and behavioral energy (Shuck, Owen, Manthos, Quirk, & Rhoades, 2016). It is the employee's level of commitment to the organization (organizational commitment), at both the emotional and intellectual/cognitive levels, characterized by that employee's willingness to expend energy, or discretionary effort, at work (Saks, 2006).

Honestly though, as a leader, manager, HR professional, are you tired of hearing about engagement? Ready to switch to "inclusion"? Fine, but please acknowledge the dollar value of deeper employee engagement. Research has shown that if you can improve your employee engagement by one standard deviation, then you will see a corresponding increase in your key metrics, like revenue per employee (Finnegan, 2012). Up to 2 percent! So a significant increase in your employee engagement could lead to significant increases in productivity and resultant revenues! What's not to like? It certainly sounds worth the work. Lower turnover, higher productivity, higher revenues… definitely worth the work.

People stay because they find it more worthwhile to stay than to go through the effort of changing. They stay because there are components of life that only this job, in this company, on this team can provide. This is something you can influence. People stay because they have become part of a relationship, on their team and with you their manager. Those relationships can either anchor them with you (like roots) or propel them out of the organization (like a lever).

Transformational leadership and engagement

At the root of effective leadership are specific leader practices that demonstrate credibility and promote transparent, authentic, transformational leadership (Hall, Johnson, Wysocki, & Kepner, 2002; Kouzes & Posner, 2007; Kouzes, Posner, & Biech, 2010; Mancheno-Smoak, Endres, Polak, & Athanasaw, 2009). Kouzes & Posner (2002, 2007) offer five key leader behaviors that inspire stronger organizational attachment and higher employee performance, based on Bass and Avolio's transformational leadership theory. They include Modeling the Way, Encouraging the Heart, Enabling Others to Act, Challenging the Process, and Inspiring a Shared Vision. The five key leader behaviors have been affirmatively linked to authentic, transformational leadership as developed by Bass and Avolio (1998). Transformational leadership leads to superior results because leaders deploy what Bass and Avolio call the "four I's" – idealized influence over colleagues and followers, inspirational motivation of others toward a mission or vision, intellectual stimulation of others to challenge and grow their ability and competence, and individual consideration of each member of the group (Bass & Avolio, 1998, p. 136). This set of behaviors is associated with high quality leadership, based on empirical testing of the theoretical constructs (Mancheno-Smoak, Endres, Polak, & Athanasaw, 2009, p. 10). Effective leaders motivate higher job satisfaction, employee commitment, better performance, and fewer turnover intentions (2009, p. 12). Each of the four I's (inspirational motivation, individualized consideration, intellectual stimulation, and idealized influence) has been linked empirically to the five leader behaviors.

The Four I's of Transformational Leadership

Inspirational Motivation
Individualized Consideration
Intellectual Stimulation
Idealized Influence

"What helps people, helps business."
– Leo Burnett, founder of Leo Burnett Worldwide
ad agency (Roberts, 2016)

A leader who deliberately works to apply a balance of transactional and trans-formational leadership behaviors can do this through Kouzes and Posner's five key leader behaviors. Fields and Herold (1997) showed that Model the Way and Challenge the Process are transactional, and Encourage the Heart, Inspire a Shared Vision, and Empower Others to Act are transformational. You should know that leaders who engage in the five key leader behaviors experience greater effectiveness in meeting job-related demands, more success when representing your business units to upper management/external constituents, a larger number of high-performing teams, greater loyalty and commitment, and significant personal credibility. The takeaway here is that leaders who Model the Way, the first of Kouzes and Posner's key leader behaviors, would be expected to clarify core business (and personal) values and to express personal beliefs in the workplace. These leaders should also motivate others and inspire deeper organizational engagement without encouraging their followers (employees) to become dependent on them.

Kouzes and Posner's five key leader behaviors

Model the Way (transactional)
Challenge the Process (transactional)
Encourage the Heart (transformational)
Inspire a Shared Vision (transformational)
Empower Others to Act (transformational)

Other research has been done on the impact of specific, trainable leader behaviors like transformational leadership on employee engagement and organizational commitment. Robert Freeborough and my friend Kathleen Patterson have done quantitative studies to expand the dialogue around employee engagement in the nonprofit environment. They considered the impact of transformational leader behaviors on employee engagement and organizational commitment with empirical research using response data from nearly 400 nonprofit employees. What they found was that a significant positive relationship does exist between higher levels of transformational leadership and higher levels of employee engagement on three subscales of engagement: vigor, dedication, and absorption. And, they found a positive correlation between intellectual stimulation (a transformational leader behavior) and the number of employees in the workplace (Freeborough & Patterson, 2015). This could be because a transformational leader draws more employees to him or her, through the promise of challenge, purpose, development, and encouragement. Their study also found that transformational leadership behaviors had less of an impact on older followers and those who were more educated, so proceed with caution as you encourage your managers to behave in transformational ways.

> "Your team is one of your most important investments… and if you are careful about hiring only the best people, it will pay dividends."
> – Sheila Johnson, cofounder of Black Entertainment Television (Roberts, 2016)

Specifically, how you communicate with your associates *matters*. As a leader or culture monitor, you set the tone, you create the culture, and you design the target level of employee engagement. As my study participants revealed, the consistency between what leaders *say* and what they *do*, as well as consistency in how leaders communicate with different associates on the same team, definitely has an impact on engagement.

Key takeaways

1. It's important to value followers as individual contributors.
2. Kelley offers a trait-based perspective on follower typology and detailed follower paths. When you know what a person values and what their path is, you can craft a more effective career trajectory and set more effective expectations.
3. Chaleff offers a slightly different, behavior-based perspective on follower typology, outlining the characteristics of courageous followers and describing the power they have.

4. Dixon and others remind us that the term "follower" should not imply subservience, but instead suggest active engagement and partnership.

5. Effective followers manifest several specific behaviors (seven are listed). HR and management should generate specific directives to encourage effective followership in the organization (four specific suggestions are provided).

6. Use transformational leader behaviors to support transactional exchanges in your organization to increase engagement. Whether you follow Bass and Avolio's 4I's of transformational leadership or Kouzes and Posner's 5 key leader behaviors, you'll see deeper commitment and engagement and an improvement in perceptions of justice as well.

PART V

Where to, from here?

Executive summary

Specific suggestions for HR and executive leaders are provided in this final section, based on the frustrations of participants who saw no "follow-through" or enforcement of the values statements and corporate policies in their organization.

> "We must intertwine business and ethics in a very fundamental way."
> – Robert Bruner, business professor (Roberts, 2016)

11
CONNECTING THEORY AND PRACTICE

"Goodwill is the only asset that competition cannot undersell or destroy."
– *Marshall Field, founder of Marshall Field department stores*

Human capital. Intellectual capital. Customer goodwill. Potential employee attraction. Employee retention and engagement. All of these are clear and relevant concepts in today's business world, and their connection to profitability and organizational longevity is clear. How can you protect them from all the ugliness I've described here? You can start with scanning your organizational and external environment. You can set a specific cultural tone inside your organization, and assess the net effect of the behavior of your leaders and managers on organizational commitment. You can examine the degree to which you are practicing and supporting participative decision-making, which is known to increase engagement. And you can deliberately value the associates, employees, *followers* in your organization just as they are, for what they bring and what they do, rather than only in relation to someone else.

Environmental scanning should be a process, just like using the Balanced Scorecard. The International Society for Performance Improvement (www.ispi.org) has a specific way of driving process and performance improvement through environmental scanning that's definitely worth a look. Basically, they understand that your organization is situated within a specific world context, including country and regional culture, societal expectations, and social responsibilities. Do your organizational mission, vision, and values reflect awareness of those? Do your associates all understand the mission, vision, and values? This is where we narrow down to looking closely at the workplace – your organizational structure, culture, climate, resources, stakeholders, competition. Next consider the work that your people are expected to do. What is the work flow, what are your processes for taking an input through your system and sending it out as a completed product? Do the procedures for work flow and the allocated responsibilities assigned to leaders and teams mesh with your stated values and priorities? Do you address the ergonomic and individual needs of the associate, visibly and tangibly? This brings us to considering the worker – what is the level of knowledge capital, how are you refreshing and improving upon your knowledge capital, do your employees know and understand that you value them and are investing in their personal *and* professional development? As the Gallup Q12© asks, do they know what you expect of them? And do they have what they need to meet (or surpass) those expectations?

Expectations has been one of the driving themes of my professional career – that is, my observation of difficult relationships and interactions in the workplace has often led me to believe that employees not knowing what is expected of them, due to stilted or stifled communications in the work relationship, is the root of most conflict and job dissatisfaction. When the desired performance goals regarding schedule, cost, quality, and safety are not made absolutely clear, and then the actual performance is not measured objectively, we cannot provide any gap or cause analysis to resolve discrepant results, because the associate doesn't know there is a discrepancy. Often the employee thinks he or she is performing up to or above par, expecting rewards or other performance incentives to validate that assumption, and becoming frustrated when they receive not only no rewards, but no significant, substantive performance feedback.

> "Interdependent people combine their own efforts with the efforts of others to achieve their greatest success."
>
> – *Stephen Covey, educator, author, and businessman*

The voice/exit option

> "People have been known to achieve more as a result of working with others than against them."
>
> – *D. Allan Fromme, psychologist, teacher,*
> *and writer (Roberts, 2016)*

Hirschhorn (1988) states that the Wagnerian bureaucratic process is a "common feature of modern life" (p. 163) and a prevalent social defense, but in attempts to overcome this social defense managers may create a "psychologically violent culture" (p. 167). Rituals of communication, such as documentation and formalized procedures, can become substitutes for true collaboration, leading to institutionalized passivity and compliance on the part of followers and controlling behavior by managers. Managers, leaders, begin to judge the followers, or subordinates, as good or bad, and enact a closed system. Followers may then experience the workplace as a hostile, oppressive, toxic environment. As a result, their levels of trust and organizational commitment are reduced, leading to negative organizational as well as personal outcomes. That is, they'll leave. This is the Exit Option: employees know that if they become dissatisfied enough, they can exit the workplace.

The most avoidant reaction possible is to leave the organization, exercising one's "exit" option, mentioned earlier in this book, which carries emotional and financial voluntary turnover costs to both the individual and the organization. This option is explained in Hoffman (2006, p. 2313), referencing Hirschman's 1970 voice-exit theory, which provided the basis for the assertiveness and avoidance concepts. Hirschman asserted that when people confront workplace problems, their two courses of action are to leave the organization (exit) or to stay and express their displeasure (voice) (p. 2313). Although both voice and exit behaviors send a similar message to the organization and to the individuals involved, voice is a much harder option, and Hoffman (p. 2313) asserted that those with a high degree of organizational loyalty or engagement would be more likely to stay and try to amend their situation. Their level of success on each attempt would bolster their level of problem-solving or conflict-resolution self-efficacy.

Productive workplaces "require continuous (ongoing) work both on ourselves and our structures" (Weisbord, 1987, p. 256). But Hirschhorn (1988) states that organizations can only function when their managers draw and maintain boundaries between divisions and units inside the organization. They must also draw boundaries between the organization and the environment outside. Boundaries create anxiety where "the risk of working and deciding is located and where aggression must be mobilized" (p. 38). Because of the anxiety caused by the boundaries, organizational members retreat from them. This retreat leads to psychological injury to co-workers, as with my story about "Nonprofit Nancy" earlier in this book. And no, it's not that employees are so fragile ("snowflakes" is the latest insult) these days. This has been going on since the Industrial Revolution, as all of the research cited here has shown. Only in the last couple of decades have we become more conscious and intentional about our workplace relationships. Apparently, especially in the United States, we have crafted our workplaces into war zones.

"Individual commitment to a group effort – that is what makes a team work, a company work, a society work, a civilization work."
— Vince Lombardi, legendary professional coach (Roberts, 2016)

Exit and stay interviews

> "There are few, if any, jobs in which ability alone is sufficient. Needed, also, are loyalty, sincerity, enthusiasm and team play."
> — *William B. Given Jr., author (Roberts, 2016)*

The most useless half-hour of the employment life cycle is the perfunctory exit interview. Yes, I said it. The key word, though, is perfunctory. If you are just doing a basic exit interview to go through the motions, you might as well not do it at all. In some companies the exit interview consists of an online survey of maybe five questions, using rating scales. You know, I recently had a survey given to me for a project that had taken several weeks, significant group and individual investment, and significant resources, and that had recently been completed in an organization in which I serve. The survey was administered by someone handing the instrument out after a meeting that was unrelated to the project, in the evening, when only a few of the members were even present to take the survey. In essence: the way in which you administer an instrument speaks volumes about whether you really want to hear from your participants and whether you respect what they have to say. In that instance, there was no time given, no confidentiality assured, and no invitation for true candid feedback for performance improvement. A rushed instrument suggests that you are saying, "I only want you to give me surface-level feedback, preferably high or neutral ratings, and then please go away." It's insulting. Don't bother.

On the other hand, if you are interested in administering substantive exit interviews that may lead to significant performance and process improvement, it would make sense to do the interview in person, face to face or over the telephone, both of which are more media-rich means of communicating than an online or paper survey. You could even do it via video chat, but it's the personal touch that matters. Not to convey a message of guilt or shame to the individual leaving the organization, but to convey one of gratitude for their contributions and curiosity about what recommendations they might have for your organization and the team they're leaving.

> "The greater the loyalty of a group toward the group, the greater is the motivation among the members to achieve the goals of the group, and the greater the probability that the group will achieve its goals."
> — *Rensis Likert [LICK-urt], social psychologist (Roberts, 2016)*

Specifically, an effective exit interview program can identify when your organization may be promoting for technical skill and neglecting managerial skills training. This will surface when your exiting employees identify that specific managers are doing a less than stellar job of offering recognition, supporting engagement initiatives, clearly communicating expectations, and clarifying the organization's mission, vision, and values. *Harvard Business Review* studies have shown that of the companies that do conduct exit interviews (many don't), very few actually "collect, analyze, and share the data and follow up with action". Why is that? Why is it so hard for us to invite employees to share their thoughts? Well… uh, of course. It's scary, because it feels like we are inviting the employee to evaluate – to criticize. So, oftentimes our exit interviews are just an exercise, because we collect scant, surface-level data, and wave farewell.

Then there's the employee's side of the exit interview: many voluntarily exiting employees will be "less than candid on their way out the door" because they want to preserve the relationships they have with the company and not be perceived as burning bridges. They may need references in the future, and thus withhold potentially valuable information that would reflect poorly on current management. Or they may have checked out already, emotionally, and just have very little to say.

The most effective way to get past these issues is to incorporate a combination of survey and interview interactions, and ideally to have the first interview during the first week after the employee has announced his or her resignation. That interview is best conducted by the associate's second-line manager – their boss' boss, and should take no longer than an hour. Then, schedule a second interview two weeks after the employee has transitioned out. This conversation should be handled by an outside consultant, who will capture the survey data and qualitative feedback as well, and package it so that management can use it to have more effective stay interviews with the employees who remain.

> "Consider hiring a consultant… An external consultant typically has several advantages over an internal interviewer, including expertise in exit interviewing and a complete lack of bias, so he or she is more likely to produce reliable data."
>
> *(Spain & Groysberg, 2016)*

As an external consultant doing this work myself, I try to help managers and executives sift through multiple information sources to identify specific HR-related concerns and issues. By listening to the worker talk about him or herself, the workplace, and the work itself, I can create a profile that will also give me some idea about the workplace leadership theories and practices in use, and their effectiveness. External consultants doing exit interviews can also get information for you about competitive factors that may have lured employees away, such as benefits and salary. But most importantly, I listen for possible suggestions for the organization that has hired me, so that I can make recommendations about how to retain their valued employees rather than focus on recruiting and hiring new ones.

Organizations do still promote high-performing individual contributors into management and leadership roles, sometimes without providing the professional development needed for those individuals to effectively lead others. Thus, when there is unwanted turnover via transfers or resignations in that manager's department, the exit interview data may indicate that the manager does not demonstrate leadership skills such as communicating the organization's vision or explaining the department's strategy, or that the manager is poor at showing appreciation and recognition, which encourage commitment (Spain & Groysberg, 2016).

Many organizations take great pride in their attempts to gauge employee engagement and satisfaction through surveys and interviews. Those with a learning orientation gather information as employees leave through exit interviews and exit surveys. The main thing that exit interviews show us is that the cliché really is true; people leave their managers as opposed to their job or their company. Too often though, we miss that message by failing to conduct exit interviews, or conducting them and then just filing the data. Possibly worst of all, as Spain and Groysberg noted, there are the companies in which exit interviews are conducted as common practice, but the data – whether analyzed or not – never get shared with the frontline managers who could incorporate it and make formative adjustments to their management styles and practices. These researchers identified two reasons for the failure of exit interviews to improve retention: one, the quality of the data collected is limited by the candor (or lack thereof) of the exiting employee's responses. And two, the Human Resources community is unclear on best practices for using exit interviews. Actually, they offer an opportunity not to talk meaningfully with employees before they leave. Managers may know that an associate is experiencing frustration and considering making a transition out, but rather than hold what may be a "crucial conversation" (see the excellent work by Patterson, Grenny, McMillan, & Switzler, 2012), the manager simply waits for the turnover to happen. The expensive, and perhaps emotionally traumatic, perhaps morale draining for the survivors, turnover of a "valued" employee.

Besides the loss of human capital, intellectual capital, and remaining employee engagement, the exit interview for that turnover may not yield the valuable information managers might hope for. Hope is no management tool, no leadership behavior. And managers who rely on it will not uncover the deeper issues related to how they do human resource management, nor understand their associates' role perceptions that, when faced with completely different expectations, may have led them to abandon the work relationship altogether. Other potential benefits of effective, candid exit interviews would be that the Human Resources group gains insight into the leadership style employed in the exiting employee's department, and that benchmark data from other companies, like salary and benefit offers, may emerge in the conversation. One personal experience of a poor exit interview follows the pattern that Spain and Groysberg found – HR had (and missed) the opportunity to solicit ideas to improve the organization and create an advocate in the exiting employee.

Stay interviews help you gauge, and increase, engagement

The opposite, then, of the exit interview, is what's known as a "stay" interview, in which a manager (or a consultant) holds a scheduled but informal chat with individual employees about why they stay. Along the lines of my study, but without the focus on antisocial workplace behaviors, this conversation allows me as a consultant to identify specifically what factors about the workplace the employee likes, appreciates, and enjoys about the job, of what accomplishments he or she is most proud, things like that. I ask about professional development, perceptions of career wellbeing (one of the five areas of wellbeing that the Gallup organization documents and tracks, and one which definitely limits and defines the amount of organizational engagement an associate will give you), and perceived opportunities for growth. I can then prepare a report that enables you as an executive or leader to understand, for your organization, *why people stay.* If you have internal managers do this interviewing, they can ask similar questions and then specifically ask questions like, "How can I help? What would you change, if you had a magic wand?" I encourage caution and diplomacy here, because again, this can be perceived by the manager as a somewhat threatening, even crucial, conversation. But it's worth the effort.

We must accept that exit surveys in and of themselves do not improve retention or engagement. In fact, they may be a waste of time. Finnegan (2012) pointed out that when employees are leaving their current position, they may not want to burn bridges by telling the candid truth about their reasons for leaving. In some cases, the exit interview is actually an online or paper survey, which may take more time and effort than a departing employee is willing to give. Additionally, once the Human Resources department has analyzed, summarized, and forwarded the exit survey data to the manager of the former employee's department, the manager may set aside the report as an "autopsy" – a parting shot, even. Managers will claim they prefer to focus on the employees still in the department, still in the organization, and not attend to the "sour grapes" of an employee (or three, or eight, or more) who chose to leave the team. There is no message to the former employee, except "farewell."

In contrast, the stay interview gives the employer real-time information from current associates, allowing Human Resources or the Organizational Development team to capture detailed data from those associates on exactly what matters to them. Current employees feel like valued team members when invited to share their candid opinions in a safe situation. The message to the associates, according to Finnegan, is "We want you to stay." The key is treating employees with respect and acknowledging their intelligence. In my experience, employees resent it when they do not believe HR, or management, will do anything with the responses if they participate candidly. People feel disrespected when management requests, urges, or requires them to participate but offers no plan for how and when the employee participants can expect to see the outcomes and the action steps that management will take.

In response to the Gallup Q12 survey for example, employees at one organization state that they get frustrated knowing that they will be expected to come up with the action plans to increase engagement scores on their teams. Knowing this, some individuals and teams will deliberately inflate their scores so that they can skip this step, which they perceive as extra, uncompensated, work. When a manager's team reports low engagement, several additional steps are required – the creation of action plans, additional activities during the associates' personal time like lunch and after work, and meetings required "to increase engagement" – not to improve the culture. Some employees resent this approach and attempt to head it off by artificially inflating the engagement scores they report when the survey comes out, but if Human Resources and management used stay interviews instead, they might get a more detailed picture.

Companies can administer stay interviews at low cost, or outsourced to a consultant. If they are properly crafted, associates may find them non-threatening, and perhaps inspiring. The Society for Human Resource Management website (www.shrm.org) even offers a set of questions for conducting effective stay interviews, so that the situation is non-threatening, comfortable, and inviting. Ensure that the associate clearly understands what you want (to chat with the associate about why they stay). Tell them why you are interviewing them (to listen and capture their actual thoughts and feelings). Be candid about the purpose of the data collection (to translate the data gathered into actionable steps to make, or continue to make, the company a great place to work). Summarize what they shared, and solicit specific process and performance improvement suggestions. Then let them get back to work, but publicize it when you enact changes based on their ideas.

A warning – stay interviews will best serve your organizational development efforts when times are good. In periods of low engagement and high turnover, a stay interview may well be too little, too late. If it is obvious that management has initiated this intervention in response to some critical event, employees may shade, mask, and conceal their true feelings and withhold potentially valuable ideas. Doing them when there is nothing wrong, though, invites calmer, more thoughtful suggestions. Invite selected individuals to meet with you (if you are the manager, Organizational Development specialist, or HR manager) individually, at a mutually agreed-upon time, preferably in a conference room. This is not a focus group meeting; the employee must feel comfortable and individually valued, convinced that her opinions will be respected. Taking the meeting out of your "turf" and making it convenient to the associate will help with this. Explain why you are meeting with them and ask about the aspects of the job that make them excited about working there. Ask about critical events – special moments that have made them feel like they really contributed. Ask open-ended (who, what, when, how, where, why) questions, not yes/no, and follow up with requests for more detail. What does he find most rewarding about the work? If she could change one thing about the team/department/company, what would it be?

Intentional mentoring programs

Another area of problematic communication in the workplace is the difference in gendered communication and professional roles. Without a doubt gender is still in an issue in the workplace, especially in professional and management positions, although here I am not referring to the typical issues of "work-life balance, maternity leave, unequal pay, and differential ambitions" (Russell & Lepler, 2017, p. 2). Instead, where you need to remember the gender differential is in terms of regular day-to-day mentoring and apprenticeship. Russell and Lepler define apprenticeship as the "working relationships of junior team members learning alongside experienced colleagues," and in many cases your female executives and managers may find that they just don't get significant mentoring in their roles. In some cases, in engagement and exit surveys, female employees rated that as their primary reason for leaving. In my consulting business I emphasize identifying and playing to individual and team strengths using the Clifton StrengthsFinder© instrument, and I have found with women in management and top leadership that this approach, along with an intentional mentoring program, increases their engagement and organizational commitment. The key with associates of whatever gender is to identify ways in which you can ensure that they feel seen, safe, and valued.

The definition of *mentor* as a verb is: to advise or train someone, particularly a younger colleague. The noun form – the person – is a guide, guru, counselor, confidant, or other experienced and trusted adviser. The word originates from Homer's *Odyssey*, in which the character Mentor was a companion of Odysseus, whom Odysseus commissioned to train his son Telemachus. A mentor serves a mentee, apprentice, or protégé. In the workplace, the term "mentor" represents any higher-level employee who can be depended upon to share personal insights and to provide guidance and support that can enhance the junior colleague's performance and lead to her career development. It is often an intense, long-term developmental relationship, and it is a legitimately instrumental relationship. That is, it is focused on sponsorship – one individual is sponsoring the other, guiding and directing him or her toward specific milestones and achievements. A mentor is distinguished from a guide, coach, or peer in that he or she provides an advisory relationship rather than a helping relationship. Often there is a formal, organizationally initiated effort to match mentors and protégés.

> "Remember teamwork begins by building trust. And the only way to do that is to overcome our need for invulnerability."
> – *Patrick Lencioni, author and management expert (Roberts, 2016)*

Mentoring has actually been a professional practice since 1931, when newly hired MBA graduates were assigned to mentors at the Jewel Tea Company.

In the 1980s, mentoring received significant attention due to economic and societal trends like the competitive work environment demanding highly qualified entry-level personnel to satisfy labor shortages, the political mandates for Affirmative Action programs to address leveling the professional playing field for women and minorities, a significant number of mergers and acquisitions that required cultural integration, and the need for better succession planning and management development (Eby & Lockwood, 2004; Stone, 2007).

According to the Fortune 500 website, in 1995 women and minorities represented 5% of senior-level jobs in corporate organizations. Today, women make up 5% of the CEOs in the U.S. and 17% of corporate board membership for the Fortune 500. These numbers are still very low, so there is a renewed focus on intentional mentoring and apprenticeship for professional development. Companies that have implemented successful intentional mentoring programs include Honeywell, Apple, Johnson & Johnson, IBM, Allstate, Procter & Gamble, General Motors, FedEx, and S. C. Johnson. Additionally, Texaco, Xerox, Polaroid, Dow Chemical, Ceridian, and Ameritech all have mentoring programs as part of their diversity and inclusion retention initiatives. Hewlett-Packard used mentoring as a retraining program to move employees rather than lay them off. All of these companies identified the clear value of a formal mentoring program with regard to seeing their employees, helping them to feel safe in their jobs and professional development journey, and valuing their contributions to the organization.

But a formal mentoring program must have specific organizational goals. First, with regard to recruitment, it's a useful tool to attract and recruit quality employees, particularly for new first-line managers. Second, a mentoring program is valuable for effective succession planning, helping to identify, develop, and move high performers into emerging leader jobs. Third, a mentoring program can support your Affirmative Action Plan (AAP) by helping you to strategically move women and minorities into senior roles and increase the diversity of your middle and senior management ranks. Fourth, an effective mentoring program supports retention goals (so your employees *stay*) by decreasing turnover, increasing organizational commitment, and increasing employee's perceived self-efficacy. Fifth and finally, an intentional mentoring program supports organizational change initiatives by easing cultural transitions, fostering innovation and creativity, and helping to transfer the values and culture of the parent organization in a merger or acquisition.

Participation in a formal mentoring program also satisfies specific individual needs, obviously. In terms of personal professional development, a mentoring relationship can ease onboarding and acclimation for new managers. A mentoring program can facilitate development for individuals who lack access to the traditional, informal mentoring relationships like women and minorities. And, a mentoring relationship can provide support and challenge to individuals who are clearly high potential/emerging potential.

The roles of the mentor in this relationship are varied and nonrestrictive, as long as the goal is for the mentor to provide productive input that leads to increased quality and quantity of output and deeper commitment. The mentor may at different times be sponsoring, teaching, coaching, protecting, counseling, or role-modeling. Thus, it is important to consciously and intentionally identify participants who are authentic, transparent about their motivations, and willing to share their interests and expertise. As a leader or HR professional you can identify these people through client feedback, peer feedback, voluntary engagement, and, of course, management observation. But once potential mentors and protégés have been identified, how do you match them?

There are a few ways to do this, according to the SHRM website, but the most appropriate would be through authority ranking, where relationships are primarily based on differences in experience, age, status, or rank, such as in formal mentor-protégé relationships.

I've learned through experience and from the research that there are five very clear phases of the mentoring relationship that all parties should know about and for which they should be prepared. This is the value of a formal program: the organization provides education and support for these transitions so that they don't shock either party and damage the effectiveness of the initiative. Those phases include Goal Setting (defining expectations), Initiation (kicking off the relationship), Cultivation (maintaining the relationship), Separation (the protégé begins to become more independent), and Redefinition (the relationship must be renegotiated).

The program itself should be structured according to organizational priorities. The key components of a formal mentoring program, though, are that you must link your program to your business strategy, and ensure that it is consistent with other HR practices. As the executive or champion for the program, you must ensure visible support by top management. And now here is where it becomes *work* and I often have potential clients shy away from engaging in developing a formal mentoring program: you need to do some comprehensive planning regarding the development, implementation, and monitoring of your program. Ensure that there is a supportive organizational culture, so that the program fits in the company's comfort zone. There should be voluntary participation, but required training for mentors and protégés that fosters awareness of mentoring and its role in career development. Finally, there should be visible structural changes that support the initiative (like changing reward systems, performance appraisal systems, etc.).

There are definitely specific advantages to launching a facilitated mentoring program. These include the level of individual attention to the protégé, compared to other career development initiatives, the minimal involvement required after startup of the program, and the significant reduction of the rate at which women and minorities will leave the organization if they are significantly engaged in the mentoring program. There are also challenges to standing up an effective mentoring program, like having mismatched pairs. Or, the resentment that may be felt by nonparticipants. Both mentors and protégés may experience anxiety, or set unrealistic expectations. And there may be supervisors who feel their authority is undermined. Scheduling, geographic distance, neglect of the relationship, and feelings of personal inadequacy are all additional challenges that may arise. But to manage those risks, identify the purpose and goals of the program and develop it with those goals clearly in mind. Articulate the intended outcomes of the program explicitly, and hold group meetings with participants to glean their expectations and build commitment. Train mentors and protégés separately to clarify roles and objectives in the program, and do follow-up activities to cement the relationship. Finally, do evaluations of the program at the midpoint and at a designated endpoint. With careful planning, voluntary participation, a formal orientation. and ongoing evaluation, your mentoring program will help ensure that employees choose to stay, and that they feel seen, safe, and valued.

Recommended reading

Fritz, J. M. H. (2013). *Professional Civility: Communicative Virtue at Work*. New York: Peter Lang.

Lencioni, P. (2012). The Advantage: Why Organizational Health Trumps Everything Else In Business. San Francisco: Jossey-Bass.

Lencioni, P. (2016). *The Ideal Team Player*. San Francisco: Jossey-Bass.

> Let's make this #Interactive – Here's a challenge: pick a book, get it, and connect with the author on LinkedIn and/or follow them on Twitter. Let them know you read their book, and ask them a question about it. #Dialogue #WPS #WhyPeopleStay

BIBLIOGRAPHY

Abu-Tineh, A. M., Khasawneh, S. A., & Al-Omari, A. (2008). Kouzes and Posner's transformational leadership model in practice: The case of Jordanian schools. *Leadership and Organization Development Journal*, 29(8),648–660.

Adair, R. (2008). Developing great leaders, one follower at a time. In R. E. Riggio, I. Chaleff, & J. Lipman-Blumen (Eds.), The art of followership: How great followers create great leaders and organizations (pp. 155–176). San Francisco: Jossey-Bass.

Agho, A. O. (2009). Perspectives of senior-level executives on effective followership and leadership. *Journal of Leadership and Organizational Studies*, 16(2), 159–166.

Aimar, C., & Stough, S. (2007). Leadership: Does culture matter? Comparative practices between Argentina and United States of America. *Academy of Educational Leadership Journal*, 11(3), 9–43.

Andersson, L. M., & Pearson, C. M. (1999). Tit for tat? The spiraling effect of incivility in the workplace. *Academy of Management Review*, 24(3), 452–471.

Appelbaum, S. H., & Roy-Girard, D. (2007). Toxins in the workplace: Affect [sic] on organizations and employees. *Corporate Governance*, 7(1), 17–28.

Aquino, K., Grover, S. L., Bradfield, M., & Allen, D. G. (1999). The effects of negative affectivity, hierarchical status, and self-determination on workplace victimization. *Academy of Management Journal*, 42(3), 260–272.

Ardichvili, A., & Kuchinke, K. P. (2009). International perspectives on the meanings of work and working: Current research and theory. *Advances in Developing Human Resources*, 11(2), 155–167.

Ashforth, B. (1994, July). Petty tyranny in organizations. *Human Relations*, 47(7), 755–779.

Bandura, A. (2002). Selective moral disengagement in the exercise of moral agency. *Journal of Moral Education*, 31(2), 101–119.

Baron, R. A., & Neuman, J. H. (1996). Workplace violence and workplace aggression: Evidence on their relative frequency and potential causes. *Aggressive Behavior*, 22(3), 161–173.

Baron, R. A., & Neuman, J. H. (1998). Workplace aggression: The iceberg beneath the tip of workplace violence: Evidence on its forms, frequency and targets. *Public Administration Quarterly*, 21(4), 446–464.

Bass, B. M., & Riggio, R. E. (2010). The transformational model of leadership. In G. R. Hickman (Ed.), *Leading Organizations: Perspectives for a New Era* (2nd ed., pp. 76–86). Washington, DC: Sage.

Blanchard, S. (2010). *Managing People's Energy: The Power of Alignment*. s.l., s.n.

Blau, G., & Holladay, E. B. (2006). Testing the discriminant validity of a four-dimensional occupational commitment measure. *Journal of Occupational and Organisational Psychology*, 79, 691–704.

Bocchino, C. C., Hartman, B. W., & Foley, P. F. (2003). The relationship between person-organization congruence, perceived violations of the psychological contract, and occupational stress symptoms. *Consulting Psychology Journal: Practice and Research*, 55(4), 203–214.

Buckingham, M., & Clifton, D. (2001). *Now, Discover Your Strengths*. New York: Gallup.

Burton, R. M., & Obel, B. (2005). *Strategic Organizational Diagnosis and Design: The Dynamics of Fit*. (3rd ed.). New York: Springer.

Carson, K. D., & Carson, P. P. (1997). Career entrenchment: A quiet march toward occupational death? *Academy of Management Executive*, 11(1), 62–75.

Chaleff, I. (2008). Creating new ways of following. In R. E. Riggio, I. Chaleff, & J. Lipman-Blumen (Eds.), *The Art of Followership: How Great Followers Create Great Leaders and Organizations* (pp. 67–87). San Francisco: Jossey-Bass.

Chaleff, I. (2009). *The Courageous Follower: Standing Up To & For Our Leaders*. (3rd ed.). San Francisco: Berrett-Koehler.

Chalofsky, N. (2003). An emerging construct for meaningful work. *Human Resource Development International*, 6(1), 69–83.

Chalofsky, N. E. (2010). *Meaningful Workplaces: Reframing How and Where We Work*. San Francisco: Jossey Bass.

Chalofsky, N., & Krishna, V. (2009). Meaningfulness, commitment and engagement: The intersection of a deeper level of intrinsic motivation. *Advances in Developing Human Resources*, 11(2), 189–203.

Chapman, J. (2006). Anxiety and defective decision making: An elaboration of the groupthink model. *Management Decision*, 44(10), 1391–1404.

Chiaburu, D., & Marinova, S. V. (2006). Employee role enlargement: Interactions of trust and organizational fairness. *Leadership and Organization Development Journal*, 27(3), 168–182.

Church, A. H. (2011). Bridging the gap between the science and practice of psychology in organizations: State of the practice reflections. *Journal of Business and Psychology*, 26(2), 125–128.

Collins, J., & Hansen, M. T. (2011). *Great by Choice*. New York: HarperCollins.

Cortina, L. M., Magley, V. J., Magley, J. H., & Langhout, R. D. (2001). Incivility in the workplace: Incidence and impact. *Journal of Occupational Health Psychology*, 6(1), 64–80.

Crampton, S. M., Hodge, J. W., & Mishra, J. M. (1998). The informal communication network: Factors influencing grapevine activity. *Public Personnel Management*, 27(4), 569–584.

Creswell, J. W. (1998). *Qualitative Inquiry and Research Design: Choosing among Five Traditions*. London: Sage.

Daniel, T. A. (2009). *Stop Bullying at Work: Strategies and Tools for HR and Legal Professionals*. Alexandria, VA: Society for Human Resource Management.

Darr, C. R. (2005, Summer). Civility as rhetorical enactment: The John Ashcroft "Debates" and Burke's theory of form. *The Southern Communication Journal*, 70(4), 316–328.

Davis, K. (1953). Management communication and the grapevine. *Harvard Business Review*, 31, 43–49.

Dayan, M., & Di Benedetto, A. (2008). Procedural and interactional justice perceptions and teamwork quality. *Journal of Business & Industrial Marketing*, 23(8), 566–576.

Dessler, G. (1999). How to earn your employees' commitment. *Academy of Management Executive*, 13(2), 58–67.

Dixon, G. (2008). Followers: The rest of the leadership process. *Proceedings of the 2008 Industrial Engineering Research Conference*, pp. 1385–1388.

Dixon, G. (2008). Getting together. In R. E. Riggio, I. Chaleff, & J. Lipman-Blumen (Eds.), *The Art of Followership: How Great Followers Create Great Leaders and Organizations* (pp. 155–176). San Francisco: Jossey-Bass.

Dixon, G. (2009, March). Can we lead and follow? *Engineering Management Journal*, 21(1), 34–41.

Dixon, G., & Westbrook, J. (2003) Followers revealed. *Engineering Management Journal*, 15(1), 19–25.

Dunham, R. B., Grube, J. A., & Castañeda, M. B. (1994). Organizational commitment: The utility of an integrative definition. *Journal of Applied Psychology*, 79(3), 370–380.

Dunlop, P. D., & Lee, K. (2004). Workplace deviance, organizational citizenship behaviors, and business unit performance: The bad apples do spoil the whole barrel. *Journal of Organizational Behavior*, 25, 67–80.

Eby, L. T., & Lockwood, A. (2005) Protege's and mentor's reactions to participating in formal mentoring programs: A qualitative investigation. *Journal of Vocational Behavior*, 67, 441–458.

Edwards, J. R., & Cable, D. M. (2009). The value of congruence. *Journal of Applied Psychology*, 94(3), 654–677.

Elangovan, A. R., & Shapiro, D. L. (1998). Betrayal of trust in organizations. *Academy of Management Review*, 23(3), 547–566.

Ferguson, S. D., & Ferguson, S. (1987). *Organizational Communication* (2nd ed.). New Brunswick: Transaction.

Fields, D. L., & Herold, D. M. (1997). Using the Leadership Practices Inventory to measure transformational and transactional leadership. *Educational and Psychological Measurement*, 57, 569–579.

Finnegan, R. P. (2012). *The Power of Stay Interviews for Engagement and Retention.* Alexandria, VA: SHRM.

Forret, M., & Love, M. S. (2008). Employee justice perceptions and coworker relationships. *Leadership & Organizational Development Journal*, 29(3), 248–260.

Fox, M. (1994). *The Reinvention of Work: A New Vision of Livelihood for Our Time.* San Francisco: Harper Collins.

Freeborough, R., & Patterson, K. (2015) Exploring the effect of transformational leadership on nonprofit leader engagement. *Servant Leadership: Theory and Practice*, 2(1), 49–70.

Fritz, J. M. H. (2012). A review of concepts relevant to problematic relationships in the workplace. In B. L. Omdahl, & J. M. H. Fritz (Eds.), *Problematic Relationships in the Workplace* (pp. 3–17). New York: Peter Lang.

Fritz, J. M. H. (2013). *Professional Civility: Communicative Virtue at Work.* New York: Peter Lang.

Fritz, J. M., Arnett, R. C., & Conkel, M. (1999). Organizational ethical standards and organizational commitment. *Journal of Business Ethics*, 20, 289–299.

Fritz, J. M. H., & Omdahl, B. L. (2009). Reduced job satisfaction, diminished commitment, and workplace cynicism as outcomes of negative work relationships. In J. M. H. Fritz, & B. L. Omdahl (Eds.), *Problematic Relationships in the Workplace* (pp. 131–152). New York: Peter Lang.

Gini, A. (2010). Moral leadership and business ethics. In G. R. Hickman (Ed.), *Leading Organizations: Perspectives for a New Era* (2nd ed., pp. 345–355). Washington, DC: Sage.

Giorgi, A. (Ed.). (1985). *Phenomenology and Psychological Research*. Pittsburgh: Duquesne University Press.

Goleman, D. (1998). What makes a leader? Best of Harvard Business Review. *Harvard Business Review*, 82–91.

Goleman, D. (1998). *Working with Emotional Intelligence*. New York: Bantam.

Gong, Y., Law, K. S., Chang, S. & Xin, K. R., 2009. Human resources management and firm performance: The differential role of managerial affective and continuance commitment. *Journal of Applied Psychology*, 94(1), 263–275.

Grant, A. M., Dutton, J. E., & Rosso, B. D. (2008). Giving commitment: Employee support programs and the prosocial sensemaking process. *Academy of Management Journal*, 51(5), 898–918.

Greenbaum, H. H. (1972, October). Management's role in organizational communication analysis. *Journal of Business Communication*, 10(1), 39–52.

Groenewald, T. (2004). A phenomenological research design illustrated. *International Journal of Qualitative Methods*, 3(1), Article 4.

Guzley, R. M. (1992, May). Organizational climate and communication climate: Predictors of commitment to the organization. *Management Communication Quarterly*, 5, 379–402.

Hall, J., Johnson, S., Wysocki, A., Kepner, K., Farnsworth, D., & Clark, J. L. (2002). *Transformational Leadership: The Transformation of Managers and Associates*. University of Florida IFAS Extension web site. [Online]. Available at: http://edis.ifas.ufl.edu/hr020 [Accessed 7 May 2018].

Harter, J. (2012). *Mondays Not So "Blue" for Engaged Employees*. [Online].

Harter, J. E., Schmidt, F. L., Killham, E. A., & Asplund, J. W. (2006). *Q12 Meta-Analysis*. Omaha, NE: Gallup Inc.

Harvey, P., Stoner, J., Hochwarter, W., & Kacmar, C. (2007). Coping with abusive supervision: The neutralizing effects of ingratiation and positive affect on negative employee outcomes. *Leadership Quarterly*, 18, 264–280.

Hicks, D. A. (2003). *Religion and the Workplace: Pluralism, Spirituality, Leadership*. New York: Cambridge University Press.

Hirschhorn, L. (1988). *The Workplace Within: Psychodynamics of Organizational Life*. Cambridge, MA: MIT Press.

Hodson, R., Roscigno, V. J., & Lopez, S. H. (2006). Chaos and the abuse of power: Workplace bullying in organizational and interactional contexts. *Work and Occupations*, 33(4), 382–416.

Hoffman, E. A. (2006). Exit and voice: Organizational loyalty and dispute resolution strategies. *Social Forces*, 84(4), 2313–2330.

Howell, J. P., & Mendez, M. J. (2008). Three perspectives on followership. In R. E. Riggio, I. Chaleff, & J. Lipman-Blumen (Eds.), *The Art of Followership* (pp. 25–39). San Francisco: Jossey-Bass.

Hutton, S. A. (2006). Workplace incivility: State of the science. *Journal of Nursing Administration*, 36(1), 22–28.

Johnson, P. R., & Indvik, J. (2001a). Slings and arrows of rudeness: Incivility in the workplace. *The Journal of Management Development*, 20(8), 706–713.

Johnson, P. R., & Indvik, J. (2001b, Winter). Rudeness at work: Impulse over restraint. *Public Personnel Management*, 30(4), 457–465.

Jong, D. I., & Avolio, B. J. (2000). Opening the black box: An experimental investigation of the mediating effects of trust and value congruence on transformational and transactional leadership. *Journal of Organizational Behavior*, 21(8), 949–964.

Kane, K., & Montgomery, K. (1998, Fall/Winter). A framework for understanding dysempowerment in organizations. *Human Resource Management*, 37(3–4), 263–275.

Kaplan, R. S., & Norton, D. P. (2007). *Using the Balanced Scorecard as a Strategic Management System*. [Online] Available at: https://hbr.org/2007/07/using-the-balanced-scorecard-as-a-strategic-management-system [Accessed February 2017].

Karathanos, P., & Auriemmo, A. (1999, March–April). Care and feeding of the organizational grapevine. *Industrial Management*, 41, 26–30.

Kelley, R. E. (1998). Leadership secrets from exemplary followers. In G. R. Hickman (Ed.), *Leading Organizations: Perspectives for a New Era* (pp. 193–201). Thousand Oaks, CA: Sage.

Kelley, R. E. (2008). Rethinking followership. In R. E. Riggio, I. Chaleff, & J. Lipman-Blumen (Eds.), *The Art of Followership* (2nd ed., pp. 5–16). San Francisco: Jossey-Bass.

Kets de Vries, M. F. R. (2006). The spirit of despotism: Understanding the tyrant within. *Human Relations*, 59(2), 195–220.

Kirkman, B. L., & Shapiro, D. L. (2001). The impact of cultural values on job satisfaction and organizational commitment in self-managing work teams: The mediating role of employee resistance. *Academy of Management Journal*, 44(3), 557–569.

Kouzes, J. M., & Posner, B. Z. (2007). *The Leadership Challenge* (4th ed.). San Francisco, CA: Jossey-Bass.

Kouzes, J. M., Posner, B. Z., & Biech, E. (2010). *The Leadership Challenge Activities Book*. San Francisco, CA: Pfeiffer.

Kusy, M. E., & Holloway, E. L. (2009). *Toxic Workplace! Managing Toxic Personalities and Their Systems of Power*. San Francisco: Jossey-Bass.

Lester, S. (1999). An introduction to phenomenological research. [Online]. Available at: from www.sld.demon.co.uk/resmethv.pdf [Accessed September 2012].

Lipman-Blumen, J. (2005, Spring). Toxic leadership: When grand illusions masquerade as noble visions. *Leader to Leader*, 36, 29–36.

Lipman-Blumen, J. (2010). Toxic leaders: They're plentiful. In G. R. Hickman (Ed.), *Leading Organizations: Perspectives for A New Era* (2nd ed., pp. 377–390). Washington, DC: Sage.

Mallory, L. (2016). *How to Write a Business Case: 4 Steps to a Perfect Business Case Template*. [Online] Available at: www.workfront.com/blog/write-business-case/ [Accessed 21 June 2016].

Mancheno-Smoak, L., Endres, G., Polak, R., & Athanasaw, Y. (2009). The individual cultural values and job satisfaction of the transformational leader. *Organization Development Journal*, 27(3), 9–21.

Maroosis, J. (2008). Leadership: A partnership in reciprocal following. In R. Riggio, I. Chaleff, & J. Lipman-Blumen (Eds.), *The Art of Followership: How Great Followers Create Great Leaders and Organizations* (pp. 17–24). San Francisco: Wiley.

McShane, S. L., & von Glinow, M. A., 2009. *Organizational Behavior: Essentials*. 2nd ed. New York: McGraw-Hill.

Meyer, J. P., & Allen, N. J. (1991). A three-component conceptualization of organizational commitment. *Human Resource Management Review*, 1(1), 61–89.

Meyer, J. P., & Herscovitch, L. (2001). Commitment in the workplace: Toward a general model. *Human Resource Management Review*, 11, 299–326.

Meyer, J. P., Allen, N. J., & Gellatly, I. R. (1990). Affective and continuance commitment to the organization: Evaluation of measures and analysis of concurrent and time-lagged relations. *Journal of Applied Psychology*, 75(6), 710–720.

Meyer, J. P., Becker, T. E., & Vandenberghe, C. (2004). Employee commitment and motivation: A conceptual analysis and integrative model. *Journal of Applied Psychology*, 89(6), 991–1007.

Mintzberg, H. (1990, March–April). The manager's job: Folklore and fact. *Harvard Business Review*, 53(4), 49–61.

Morgan, G. (1998). *Images of Organization: The Executive Edition*. Thousand Oaks, CA: Sage.

Mosley, D. C., Boyar, S. L., Carson, C. M., & Pearson, A. W. (2008). A production self-efficacy scale: An exploratory study. *Journal of Managerial Issues*, 20(2), 272–286.

Mourdoukoutas, P. (2014, November). How toxic leaders prompt the most talented employees to jump ship. [Online]. Available at Forbes Online: http://onforb.es/1xYfhQX [Accessed 7 May 2018].

Moustakas, C. E. (1994). *Phenomenological Research Methods*. Thousand Oaks, CA: Sage.

Mowday, R. T., Steers, R. M., & Porter, L. W. (1979). The measurement of organizational commitment. *Journal of Vocational Behavior*, 14(2), 224–247.

Nimon, K., Shuck, B., & Zigarmi, D. (2016). Construct overlap between employee engagement and job satisfaction: A function of semantic equivalence? *Journal of Happiness Studies*, 17(3), 1149–1171.

O'Leary-Kelly, A. M., Duffy, M. K., & Griffin, R. W. (2000). Construct of confusion in the study of antisocial work behavior. *Research in Personnel and Human Resource Management*, 18, 275–303.

O'Reilly, I. C., & Chatman, J. (1986). Organizational commitment and psychological attachment: The effects of compliance, identification, and internalization on prosocial behavior. *Journal of Applied Psychology*, 71(3), 492–499.

Obeng, K., & Ugboro, I. (2003). Organizational commitment among public transit employees: An assessment study. *Transportation Quarterly*, 57(2), 83–98.

Patterson, K., Grenny, J., McMillan, R., & Switzler, A. (2012). *Crucial Conversations: Tools for Talking When Stakes are High*. New York: McGraw-Hill.

Pearson, C. M., Andersson, L. M., & Porath, C. L. (2000). Assessing and attacking workplace incivility. *Organizational Dynamics*, 29(2), 123–137.

Penney, L. M., & Spector, P. E. (2005, November). Job stress, incivility, and counterproductive work behavior (CWB): The moderating role of negative affectivity. *Journal of Organizational Behavior*, 26(7), 777–796.

Posner, B. Z., & Kouzes, J. M. (1993). Psychometric properties of the leadership practices inventory – updated. *Educational and Psychological Measurement*, 53(1), 191–199.

Potter, E. H., Rosenbach, W. E., & Pittman, T. S. (2001). Followers for the times: Engaging employees in a winning partnership. In W. E. Rosenbach, & R. L. Taylor (Eds.), *Contemporary Issues in Leadership* (5th ed., pp. 163–181). Boulder, CO: Westview Press.

Price, T. L. (2010). Understanding ethical failures in leadership. In G. R. Hickman (Ed.), *Leading Organizations: Perspectives for a New Era* (2nd ed., pp. 402–405). Thousand Oaks, CA: Sage.

Pugh, D. S., & Hickson, D. J. (2007). *Writers on Organizations*. London: Sage.

Rana, S., Ardichvili, A., & Tkachenko, O. (2014). A theoretical model of the antecedents and outcomes of employee engagement: Dubin's method. *Journal of Workplace Learning*, 26(3–4), 249–266.

Roberts, J. L. (Ed.) (2016). *The Big Book of Business Quotations*. New York: Skyhorse Publishing.

Robinson, S. L., & O'Leary-Kelly, A. M. (1988). Monkey see, monkey do: The influence of work groups on the antisocial behavior of employees. *Academy of Management Journal*, 41(6), 658–672.

Robinson, S. L., & Rousseau, D. M. (1994). Violating the psychological contract: Not the exception but the norm. *Journal of Organizational Behavior*, 15(3), 245–259.

Rost, J. (2008). Followership: An outmoded concept. In R. E. Riggio, I. Chaleff, & J. Lipman-Blumen (Eds.), *The Art of Followership: How Great Followers Create Great Leaders and Organizations* (pp. 53–66). San Francisco: Jossey-Bass.

Rucker, M. H., & King, D. C. (1985). Reactions to leadership style as a function of locus of control and ascendancy of subordinates. *Social Behavior and Personality*, 13(1), 91–107.

Russell, M. S., & Lepler, L. M. (2017). How we closed the gap between men's and women's retention rates. *Harvard Business Review*, May, 1–6.

Saks, A. M. (2006). Antecedents and consequences of employee engagement. *Journal of Managerial Psychology*, 21(7), 600–619.

Schein, E. H. (1990, February). Organizational culture. *American Psychologist*, 45, 109–119.

Schein, E. H. (2005a). Intergroup problems in organizations. In W. L. French, C. H. Bell, & R. A. Zawacki (Eds.), *Organizational Development and Transformation: Managing Effective Change* (6th ed., pp. 119–124). Boston: McGraw-Hill.

Schein, E. H. (2005b). Organizational culture. In: W. L. French, C. H. Bell, & R. A. Zawacki (Eds.), *Organizational Development and Transformation: Managing Effective Change* (pp. 125–139). Boston: McGraw-Hill.

Schneider, B. (1987). The people make the place. *Personnel Psychology*, 40, 437–453.

Schwartz, S. H. (1992). Universals in the content and structure of values: Theoretical advances and empirical tests in 20 countries. *Advances in Experimental Social Psychology*, 25, 1–65. doi:https://doi.org/10.1016/S0065-2601(08)60281-6

Shantz, A. (2017). Coming full circle: Putting engagement into practice. *Organizational Dynamics*, 46(2), 65–66.

Shondrick, S., & Lord, R. G. (2010). Implicit leadership and followership theories: Dynamic structures for leadership perceptions, memory, leader-follower processes. *International Review of Industrial and Organizational Psychology*, 25, 1–33.

Shore, L. M., & Wayne, S. J. (1993). Commitment and employee behavior: Comparison of affective commitment and continuance commitment with perceived organizational support. *Journal of Applied Psychology*, 78(5), 774–780.

Shuck, B., Owen, J., Manthos, M., Quirk, K., & Rhoades, G. (2016). Co-workers with benefits: The influence of commitment uncertainty and status on employee engagement in romantic workplace relationships. *Journal of Management Development*, 35(3), 382–393.

Simons, T. (2002, January–February). Behavioral integrity: The perceived alignment between managers' words and deeds as a research focus. *Organizational Science*, 13(1), 18–35.

Sinclair, R. R., Tucker, J. S., Cullen, J. C., & Wright, C., 2005. Performance differences among four organizational commitment profiles. *Journal of Applied Psychology*, 90(6), 1280–1287.

Smircich, L., & Morgan, G. (1982). Leadership: The management of meaning. *Journal of Applied Behavioral Science*, 18(3), 257–273.

Sofield, L., & Salmond, S. W. (2003). Workplace violence: A focus on verbal abuse and intent to leave the organization. *Orthopaedic Nursing*, 22(4), 274–283.

Spain, E., & Groysberg, B. (2016). Making exit interviews count. *Harvard Business Review*, April, 1–9.

Steel, R. P., & Ovalle, N. K. (1984). A review and meta-analysis of research on the relationship between behavioral intentions and employee turnover. *Journal of Applied Psychology*, 69(4), 673–686.

Stone, A. G., & Dingman, W. (2007). Servant leadership's role in the succession planning process: A case study. *International Journal of Leadership Studies*, 2(3), 133–147.

Sutton, R. I. (2007). Building the civilized workplace. *McKinsey Quarterly*, 2, 30–39.

Taing, M. U., Granger, B. P., Groff, K. W., Jackson, E. M., & Johnson, R. E. (2011). The multidimensional nature of continuance commitment: Commitment owing to economic exchanges vs. lack of employment alternatives. *Journal of Business Psychology*, 26, 269–284.

Tepper, B. J. (2000, April). Consequences of abusive supervision. *Academy of Management Journal*, 43(2), 178–190.

Terkel, S. (1974). *Working: People Talk about What They Do All Day and How They Feel about What They Do.* New York: The New Press.

Tierney, P., & Tepper, B. J. (2007). Destructive leadership. *The Leadership Quarterly*, 18, 171–173.

Uhl-Bien, M., & Carsten, M. K. (2010). Being ethical when the boss is not. In G. R. Hickman (Ed.), *Leading Organizations: Perspectives for a New Era* (2nd ed., pp. 365–376). Washington DC: Sage.

Van Tiem, D. M., Moseley, J. L., & Dessinger, J. C. (2012). *Fundamentals of Performance Improvement.* San Francisco: Pfeiffer.

Vroom, V. H. (2007). On the synergy between research and teaching. *Journal of Management Education*, 31(3), 365–375.

Warren, D. E. (2003). Constructive and destructive deviance in organizations. *Academy of Management Review*, 28(4), 622–632.

Weick, K. E. (1979). *The Social Psychology of Organizing* (2nd ed.). New York: McGraw Hill.

Weisbord, M. R. (1987). *Productive Workplaces: Organizing and Managing for Dignity, Meaning, and Community.* San Francisco: Jossey-Bass.

Wooten, K. C., & White, L. P. (1999). Linking OD's philosophy with justice theory: Postmodern implications. *Journal of Organizational Change Management*, 12(1), 7–20.

Yang, J., Mossholder, K. W., & Peng, T. K. (2009). Supervisory procedural justice effects: The mediating roles of cognitive and affective trust. *The Leadership Quarterly*, 20, 143–154.

Yukl, G. (2006). *Leadership in Organizations* (7th ed.). Upper Saddle River, NJ: Prentice Hall.

Zagorsek, H., Jaklic, M., & Stough, S. J. (2004). Comparing leadership practices between the United States, Nigeria, and Slovenia: Does culture matter? *Cross Cultural Management*, 11(2), 16–34.

Zaleznik, A. (1970). Power and politics in organizational life. *Harvard Business Review*, May–June, 47–60.

Zaleznik, A. (1992). Managers and leaders: Are they different? *Harvard Business Review*, March–April, 126–136.

Zigarmi, D. et al. (2009). From engagement to work passion. *Perspectives*, 1 3.

Zimbardo, P. (2007). *The Lucifer Effect: Understanding How Good People Turn Evil.* New York: Random House.

Zoghbi-Manrique de Lara, P., & Verano-Tacoronte, D. (2007). Investigating the effects of procedural justice on workplace deviance. *International Journal of Manpower*, 28(8), 715–729.

INDEX

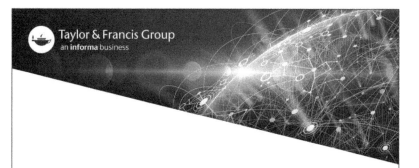